The International Monetary System

Springer
Berlin
Heidelberg
New York
Barcelona
Budapest
Hong Kong
London
Milan
Paris
Tokyo

Hans Genberg (Ed.)

The International Monetary System

Its Institutions and its Future

With 2 Figures

Professor, Hans Genberg
International Center for Monetary and
Banking Studies (ICMB)
Avenue de la Paix 11A
case postale 36
CH-1211 Geneva, Switzerland

ISBN 3-540-59130-3 Springer-Verlag Berlin Heidelberg
New York Tokyo

43/2202-5 4 3 2 1 0 – Printed on acid-free paper

Contents

Introduction

HANS GENBERG

An international monetary system should provide a stable and predictable environment for international trade and investment. At the very least, it should not by itself be a source of disturbances in the world economy, and it should be designed so that policy errors or unforeseen shocks are not unduly transmitted between countries.

In this perspective, worldwide integration of goods and financial markets present a particular challenge. Such integration increases the cross-border effects of economic policies at the same time as interlocking payments and financial systems transmit financial disturbances rapidly throughout the world. As the degree of integration and interdependence changes over time, is not a foregone conclusion that international monetary institutions and mechanisms always remain well adapted to the state of the world economy. Occasional review of the performance of the system as well as proposals for improvements are therefore necessary. The contributions to this volume have been brought together with this in mind.[1]

A number of specific factors make it particularly opportune to be concerned with the international monetary system at this time. The foundations of the European Monetary System have been shaken by the turbulence in the foreign exchange markets during the past two years. In addition, and presumably not unrelated, intra-european cooperation in macroeconomic policy making does not seem adequate. Countries in Central and Eastern Europe and beyond are knocking on the door of the international system. To accommodate them, institutions may need to be adapted or reformed. Finally, in view of the 50th anniversary of the creation of the International Monetary Fund and the World Bank, it seems timely to explore whether these institutions are well adapted to current circumstances, or whether potentially interesting alternative structures could be envisaged.

With these general considerations as background, the remainder of this introduction is divided into five sections, each of which has a counterpart in the volume itself. The questions addressed by the contributors deal with

---

[1] The papers were originally presented at a conference organized and sponsored by the **International Center for Monetary and Banking Studies** and held in Geneva on September 2-4, 1993. They were subsequently revised in light of comments received at the conference. The same procedure was followed for the contributions of the official discussants.

most of the pressing issues relating to the international monetary system. An indication of the wide variety of topics analyzed is given by the following list.

- Is worldwide financial intermediation effective? Are private capital market institutions sufficient to generate an efficient allocation of capital in the world, or are international institutions necessary? If so, on what principles should these institutions operate?

- Is the process of monetary reform in Eastern Europe and Central Asia likely to lead to stable monetary regimes in the countries concerned? What are likely effects of these reforms on the international monetary system as a whole? What is, and can be, the role of international institutions in this process?

- What kind and degree of internal and external constraints on national monetary and macro-economic policies are needed for an international monetary system to function properly? How, and by what institutional mechanism, can such constraints be imposed?

- What is the likely evolution of currency areas in the world system? Should we expect to witness the emergence of enlarged currency blocks in Europe and the North America? Where do Asian countries and the Yen fit in? How will a greater european currency block (i.e. one that would include much of what used to be the Comecon countries) be managed, and how will it influence the role of the US dollar as a international currency?

- In view of the increasing overlap between the functions of the IMF and the World Bank, is there a case to be made for combining the two institutions or should one on the contrary encourage competition between them in terms of policy advice and conditional lending?

Prospects for the International Monetary System

In the first chapter of the volume, Jacques Polak reflects on the process of reform of the international monetary system during the past half-century. He argues that reform discussions in general, but during the Bretton-Woods period in particular, have proceeded too much on the premise that the system "belongs" to governments, and that it can be managed as such. But failures of successive international monetary regimes can be explained, he argues, by the fact that the "official" monetary system was overtaken by changes in international monetary relations more widely. Any reform attempts must therefore take into account the everchanging nature of international financial markets and mechanisms.

Polak also maintains that as a matter of fact, "economic" considerations always dominate "monetary" ones, and that political relations have primacy over the economic. Thus, progress towards European Monetary Union is likely not to be substantial until a greater degree of political integration is achieved. Similar considerations imply that international monetary reform involving the establishment of a common world currency is unlikely to materialize.

In Chapter two Robert Mundell builds a case for attempting to forge a new international monetary system. His argument is based on an analysis of the historical evolution of international monetary orders and the perceived weaknesses of the current arrangements. Mundell argues that there is a natural tendency for countries to cluster into groups linked by fixed exchange rates. The metallic standards based on gold or silver were such arrangements which, in addition to being characterized by fixed exchange rates, also provided an anchor for the evolution of price levels in the participating countries. More recently, the Bretton-Woods and the European Monetary Systems are examples of attempts to limit exchange-rate fluctuations. Mundell argues that both of these systems broke down because of the dominant role that the pivot currencies - the dollar and the DM respectively - came to play in each case. Faced with situations in which they had to choose between policies that served purely domestic interests and those that served the monetary area as a whole, both the United States and Germany followed the former strategy, with the result that other countries were obliged to opt out of the system.

Mundell uses the lessons from history and his assessment of the defects of current monetary arrangements to argue for the establishment of an international monetary constitution, the main feature of which would be the creation, by the International Monetary Fund or a new international monetary authority, of an international currency with a stable purchasing power in terms of a basket of goods. Recognizing that blueprints for international monetary reform must be compatible with the "laws of monetary evolution" which themselves are determined by political power relationships, Mundell argues that the current post-cold-war transition period could be perspicuous for a serious monetary reform as power relationships are not yet entrenched enough to block cooperative solutions. He therefore concludes that the International Monetary Fund should be encouraged to take the lead in developing plans for an improved international monetary system.

In their comments on Mundell's paper, Eugene Rotberg and Lars Thunholm view the issue of monetary reform from the perspective of the private sector. Rotberg focuses his comments on recent developments in the private financial markets and their implications for the stability of the international system and for public policy. He identifies a number of factors that have led to the growth in financial markets over the past several decades. Demand for financial services in the form of risk-hedging instruments have expanded due to the observed increase in the volatility of exchange rates and interest rates. The potential supply of these instruments has grown as a result of improvements in communications technologies and financial engineering. Finally, the institutional environment - characterized by reductions in supervisory and regulatory controls, in part due to international competition in laxity - has encouraged expansion of the financial services industry.

Rotberg argues that these developments have increased the competitive pressures on financial institutions - and therefore the necessity to assume greater risks - in a situation where both the institutions themselves and the regulatory agencies are ill equipped to evaluate the implications of financial innovations for the stability of the financial system. This constitutes a challenge for national and international regulatory agencies which must strike a balance between measures that encourage competition on the financial markets and those that are designed to prevent imprudent behaviour.

Thunholm directs some of his comments to the issue of speculation in the foreign exchange markets. Mundell had argued that some transactions in foreign exchange markets are socially unproductive in that they only exists because of instability in exchange rates which could be eliminated by the adoption of a single world currency. Thunholm doubts that it is possible to distinguish in practice between productive and unproductive transactions. He argues that volatility of exchange rates is the reflection of instability and the lack of international coordination of macroeconomic policies. In this context, "speculation" in the foreign exchange markets can serve a useful function by exposing inconsistencies between countries more rapidly than they would have been otherwise.

In order to limit instability of exchange rates, some reform of international monetary relationships are needed. Thunholm does not view such reform as a technical problem. Proposals can be designed, but their adoption depends on the willingness of national political authorities to forego a significant amount of macroeconomic policy autonomy in favour of greater international coordination of policies. He does not think, however, that such coordination can be attained through consultations in contexts such as G-7 or G-10 meetings. Instead what is needed is a strong international institution which is given sufficient "authority to exert effective pressure for cooperative decisions when policy conflicts arise."

Eastern Europe and the International Monetary System

The abandonment of central planning in Central and Eastern European Countries (CEEC) and in the Former Soviet Union (FSU), and the process of transformation of these economies into full-fledged market economies involves, *inter alia*, the establishment of monetary, payments, and financial relationships within these countries, on the one hand, and between them and the rest of the world, on the other. Richard Portes sets out and analyses the major issues posed by the integration of the CEEC and FSU into the international monetary system. For a number of reasons such integration is seen to be important for the eastern countries themselves: it may increase the credibility of domestic economic policies, the rules and conventions imposed by integration into the international system can be a defense against pressures to halt or reverse the transformation process, the international monetary system may be identified with democratic political institutions and may hence aid the process of political reform. But the integration of these countries into the international monetary (and trading) system also has important implications for western countries. More openness of CEEC towards the West implies greater openness of western countries towards the East. This will perhaps have the greatest influence in the area of trade in goods, but the financial services sector will also be influenced.

Convertibility, intra-regional payments arrangements, and exchange-rate policies constitute major areas of reform that must be tackled within the CEEC and FSU. Portes argues that rapid introduction of current-account convertibility (but not capital-account convertibility) is important for the transformation process because it helps establish a rational internal relative price structure, it encourages domestic competition, and it removes bureaucratic allocation of foreign exchange. He also argues that hard-currency convertibility is preferable to, and eliminates the need for, the establishment of intra-regional payments unions, which in the case of the FSU, he argues, "could turn into a major economic and geopolitical error".

Portes finds Western support of the transformation of CEEC and FSU misguided in two major respects. First he argues that not enough has been accomplished in terms of debt relief. Countries which have made serious policy reforms should, he claims, have been rewarded with much more, and earlier, debt forgiveness than has been forthcoming, with the consequence that the domestic fiscal austerity has hampered economic recovery in the countries concerned. A second criticism of Western support concerns technical assistance (and lending support of the resulting stabilization programs). Portes argues that too much emphasis has been put on the macroeconomic aspects of this assistance and not enough on structural microeconomic issues. He also takes the international institutions and countries involved in the process to task for not coordinating their activities better rather than engaging in "simple turf battles" among themselves.

While agreeing with much of Portes' analysis, Henryk Kierzkowski brings up two issues which, in his view, did not receive sufficient attention. First, by its focus on only three countries - the Czech Republic, Hungary, and Poland - the difficulties of integrating the formerly centrally planned economies may have been underestimated. Not only is the economic structure of many of the republics of the FSU substantially different from that of their western partners, but the sheer number of potential new entrants into the international monetary system is such that it may not be possible to accommodate them without affecting the nature of the system itself.

Secondly Kierzkowski argues that a longer-term perspective might have usefully been added to Portes' focus on short- and medium-term issues. Such a focus would have permitted a more detailed discussion of the structural adaptation in western economies necessary to accommodate changes in international trade patterns brought about by the transformation in Eastern and Central Europe.

Jan Vit of the Czech National Bank describes the experiences of the Czech Republic (and the former Czechoslovakia) with its attempts to integrate its economy into the international monetary system. He stresses that the introduction of convertibility and maintaining an appropriate level of the exchange rate are crucial elements in this process. In this context he also argues that an initial maxi-devaluation was a very important ingredient in the Czechoslovak transformation process, since it permitted a subsequent long period of nominal exchange rate stability.

Policy Coordination

It is well known that spill-over of the effects of macroeconomic policies in one country onto the economy of another may result in inefficient outcomes when countries do not coordinate their actions. Daniel Cohen's contribution to this volume adds a new twist to this argument by analyzing the implications of specific asymmetries between intra-european spill-over effects and Europe-United States spill-overs. Based on empirical evidence he postulates that the effects of intra-european exchange-rate changes are felt primarily on export and import volumes and hence on aggregate demand in the European economies. In contrast, exchange-rate changes between the European currencies and the US dollar mostly influence production costs (for instance through the consequences on local-currency prices of oil imports due to swings in the dollar) and therefore aggregate supply relationships in Europe. Cohen shows that these asymmetries can explain part of the differences in policy response in Europe and the United States to the oil shock of the late 1970s. His analytical framework also allows him to deduce that actual policies - especially the loose fiscal policy adopted in Germany - followed in Europe in response to the disequilibria created by the German unification were inefficient from the point of view of employment stabilization. An appropriate response would have involved a looser fiscal policy in France and a greater divergence in intra-european monetary policies. This, of course, would have been inconsistent with the maintenance of fixed exchange rates within the EMS, and one might therefore question whether the idea of a monetary union in Europe should not be abandoned. Cohen argues that the case in favour of such a union is still valid, however, because he does not regard asymmetric shocks to be likely in the future. Instead he sees extra-european disturbances - fluctuations in the dollar, the yen, or in world interest rates - becoming more and more important sources of fluctuations for the European countries. Since these shocks affect the European countries symmetrically, exchange-rate stabilization implied by monetary unification is exactly the right response to follow.

In his comments, Mr. Shijuro Ogata, formerly of the Bank of Japan, makes a distinction between what he calls "passive" cooperation - which is activated in response to economic disturbances - and "positive" cooperation - which is more far-reaching and involves the establishment of institutional mechanisms, such as the Bretton-Woods institutions and the European Monetary System. Judging by recent international developments, he sees a decline in international cooperation, especially the positive kind. He ascribes this to weak political leadership that allows an inward-looking attitude of politicians as they are mainly concerned with re-election rather than with the international implications of their policies.

To improve cooperation between industrialized countries, Ogata proposes a reform of the G-7 summit meetings to make them more informal so that top leaders can engage in constructive discussions away from the spot-light. He also suggests that the role of the IMF and the World Bank in the G-7 meetings should be strengthened by making these institutions the *de facto* secretariat for their economic content.

Torsten Persson makes a distinction between international policy coordination which is carried out by discretion on the one hand and by rules on the other. Discretionary policy coordination is exemplified by summit accords such as those agreed on in Bonn, the Plaza and the Louvre, among others. Rules-based coordination has been attempted within the Bretton-Woods and the European Monetary Systems.

Persson argues that cooperation is easier within a rules-based system because, *inter alia*, it facilitates the creation of mechanisms that enforce cooperative agreements. He therefore suggests that future research and proposals concerning international monetary reform should be focused on institutional design both at the international level and at the national level.

Emerging Currency Areas

Jeffrey Frankel's contribution (co-authored with Shang-Jin Wei) to the conference dealt with the relationship between trading blocs and currency blocs. Frankel first used the so-called gravity model of trade to provide a benchmark for the "natural" intensity of trade between any pair of countries. He then presented evidence showing that countries with certain regional ties tend to have more intensive trade links than can be predicted by these "natural" forces. This could be interpreted as the consequence of belonging to a trading block. EC countries provide a particularly good example of this effect since they "trade an extra 55 percent more with each other beyond what can be explained by proximity, size and GNP/capita", but trading blocs can also be identified in the Western Hemisphere, East Asia, and the Pacific.

Evidence of the formation of currency blocs, identified as regions where exchange-rate fluctuations between members are relatively small, was presented next. Not surprisingly, the EC again could be classified as a currency block with Germany as a leader, and the Pacific countries were found frequently to link their currencies to the US dollar.

Frankel finally asked the question whether the reduction in exchange rate volatility associated with currency blocks could explain the increase in trade intensity between countries in a trading block. Although some evidence could be found for such an effect within the EC, the result indicated that it was quantitative quite small (less than 1 per cent) and that it was detectable only before 1980 and not after. Furthermore, the causal relationship between exchange rate volatility and trade intensity was called into question. Frankel suggested that the correlation between the two would be the result of central bank intervention policies designed to limit fluctuations in exchange rates with respect to main trading partners rather than the other way around. He thus concluded that "it does not appear that the stabilization of European exchange rates in the 1980s played a large role in the increase in intra-regional trade".

In his discussion of the paper by Frankel and Wei, Matthew Canzoneri brings up two reasons why he does not find their empirical analysis of the links between monetary integration and trade entirely convincing. First he questions the usefulness of the gravity model as an adequate representation of normal trade flows between countries. An important reason for the scepticism is the use and interpretation of the physical distance between countries as a good measure of transportation costs. To overcome some of the difficulties measuring transport costs, Canzoneri suggests that it would be preferable to focus the analysis on "natural" trading blocks (viz. EC, East Asia, US-Canada-Mexico) rather than involving also a Pacific block.

Next, Canzoneri expresses some reservations about the use of exchange-rate variability as a measure of monetary integration. Using the recent European experience as an example, he suggests that the process of monetary integration may not be associated with a monotonically declining degree of exchange-rate variability. Instead, due to occasional set-backs in the integration process, the variability may temporarily increase. Other, more direct, indicators of monetary integration would for this reason be preferable measures to use in the empirical analysis.

Canzoneri finally ties the Frankel and Wei paper to the more general issue whether one integrated market requires one money. He distinguishes between what he calls the American view - which denies this link - and a European view - which is more favourable - and suggests that it would be necessary to study in more depth the link between the dynamics of goods, factor, and financial market integration, on the one hand, and monetary integration, on the other, in order to determine which of the views is correct.

Morris Goldstein also expresses reservations concerning the gravity model used in the Frankel and Wei paper. Like Canzoneri he argues that physical distance is a poor measure of trade costs between countries, and suggests that other factors, such as information and familiarity, might be as important. For example, the presence of a large immigrant population is likely to increase the trade between their country of residence and their "home" country quite irrespective of the physical distance between them. Other important determinants of trade flows are also omitted from Frankel's model, in particular relative prices of traded goods and trade between multinational corporations.

While agreeing with Frankel and Wei's finding that exchange rate variability is not an important obstacle to international trade, Goldstein argues that empirical analysis based on cross-country data is not very convincing. He suggests that time-series methods found in the literature are more reliable.

Turning to broader issues of possible reform of exchange-rate arrangements between Europe, Japan, and the United States, Goldstein finds little evidence that a fixed exchange rate regime between these regions would be either likely to materialize or desirable.

Reform of the IMF and the World Bank?

In Chapter 6 entitled "The IMF and the World Bank at Fifty" Stanley Fischer describes the functions exercised by the International Monetary Fund and the World Bank, analyses their record in performing these functions, and considers possible areas in which reform of the institutions could be envisaged. Fischer's scorecard is generally positive. Be it in their lending activities, analysis and research, or technical assistance, he finds that the institutions have done a good job in delivering the services that have been assigned to them. This does not mean, however, that there is no room for improvements or reforms. Fischer suggests, for instance, that World Bank lending activities might be reduced and replaced an expanded guarantee activities. He also argues that the two institutions - particularly the Fund - should adopt a far more open policy with respect to information and dissemination of its policy analysis and recommendations.

Although all activities of the Fund and the Bank could in principle be carried out by the private sector, Fischer argues that public institutions do have an important role to play. He does not deny the possibility that some other institution could be designed and set up to carry out the functions more efficiently, but he suggests that the set-up costs would not justify the investment. He also argues that the two institutions should be maintained separate, even though some of their functions overlap. His reasons are that a merged institution would become too powerful in many countries and situations, and that the current arrangement provides a healthy competition between the two agencies as regards their policy analysis and advice.

Max Schieler and Jürgen von Hagen discuss Fischer's paper. Schieler does not subscribe to Fischer's contention that the *status quo* is desirable. He believes that reform of the Bretton Woods institutions is needed, justified, and feasible, and proposes parcelling out certain of the Fund's operations to other institutions and a merger of the Fund's and the World Bank's development functions. Specifically, he suggests that in the field of macroeconomic analysis and policy coordination the OECD should take over the current work done by the IMF, that in the area of monitoring the international capital and foreign exchange markets the Bank for International Settlements should be the principal institution, that lending to industrialized and advanced developing countries should be left to the private capital markets, and finally that the dealings with the poorest developing countries should be delegated to a merged IMF-World Bank institution. He also rejects Fischer's assertion that such a merger would make the resulting institution too large and inefficient by pointing out, on the one hand that downsizing of the institutions would be possible because some of the functions would be transferred to other institutions, and, on the other hand, that mergers in the private sector have created much larger institutions without obvious less of efficiency.

Jürgen von Hagen focuses on whether the private sector could carry out the functions of the Fund in a more efficient manner. He demonstrates that some of the functions exercised by the Fund can be justified on the grounds that they provide a public good, but he argues that the monopoly position occupied by the Fund in certain areas create inefficiencies. He therefore suggests that reforms of the institutions should involve more efficient pricing of IMF services provided to countries and a greater reliance by the Fund of outside consulting services in the areas of policy analysis and advice and technical assistance.

1 Repairing the International Monetary System - An Unfinished Task?

JACQUES J. POLAK

The disintegration of the European Monetary System that we have witnessed over the last 12 months proves once more that those of us who toil at the international monetary system would do well to adopt Sisyphus as our patron saint. Even the classical gold standard, sometimes described as the most efficient international monetary system that the world has ever seen - seen retrospectively, that is, and through rose-coloured glasses - did not endure for more than about a third of a century. It died with the outbreak of World War I. Something rather different under the same name was put together in 1925: that lasted for all of the next three years before it became a caricature of itself as the "Gold Bloc". The US, UK and France then pushed the monetary stone a short distance back up the mountain when they entered into the Tripartite Agreement. With its 24-hour exchange rate guarantee, that was at best a ghost of a monetary system. The negotiators at Bretton Woods, operating further away from constraining realities, managed (so to say) to reach the top of Mount Washington in agreeing on the Articles of the International Monetary Fund. The Fund contained all the required ingredients of John Williamson's (1983) definition of an international monetary system: an exchange rate regime - par values; a reserve regime - understood to be gold and dollars; and at least an implied system of adjustment obligations - consisting of the need to qualify for Fund credit for the deficit countries and the scarce currency provisions for what was expected to be the solitary surplus country in the system. That particular achievement started to run downhill from the middle of the 1960's, reaching bottom in 1973. There, in spite of the valiant efforts of the C-20, it rested for the next twelve years, until the Plaza days of 1985. But meanwhile the narrower task of constructing an EMS was undertaken in Europe. It met with commendable success until Jacques Delors, believing to possess not only the strong arms of Sisyphus but also the wings of Icarus, flew too close to the sun in his attempt to reach the EMU.

Before we go on and talk about repair of the international monetary system, let me first pose the question: What <u>is</u> the international monetary system ? My book case bulges with books carrying that title. It seems to be the default title for any recent book on international economics, including the re-issue of the 12 most admired of the Princeton Essays in International Finance. What is striking in many of these books is the often minimal effort made to define the international monetary system (Polak (1991)). Where an effort is made, the focus is almost always entirely on governments.[1] I shall come to my preferred, much wider, definition a little later. Here I want to signal the widespread proprietary bias about the "system" as belonging to governments and to suggest that this bias may account for some of the disappointment in the actual working of the system.

This bias is not limited to economics professors writing textbooks. It also surfaces when officials start to design the institutional aspects of the system. A clear example of this is seen in their approach toward international reserves in the 1960's. That approach envisaged the ideal of separate private sector and official sector asset circuits, with only the latter being recognized as part of the international monetary system. The private sector was expected to make do with balances in domestic currency, with perhaps a modest allowance of working balances in foreign exchange. All the gold and the bulk of foreign exchange was to be held by the authorities (exchange funds or central banks), to be fed into or skimmed off the private sector as that sector had a deficit or surplus in its international transactions. That still left some unavoidable spill-overs of gold and dollars between the private and official circuits. But when the need for a new reserve asset arose in the 1960's, we went out of our way to make absolutely sure that the newly designed SDRs could only be held in the official sector. Imagine SDRs being held privately, sloshing back and forth between the official and the private sector: how could we then hope to control the stock on international liquidity - by which we meant of course <u>officially held</u> international liquidity? And lest you have forgotten - and you may well have forgotten - control of this stock of international liquidity was seen at the time as <u>the</u> internationally available instrument by means of which governments, acting jointly in the IMF, were to maximize some ambitious multi-country welfare function that involved at least all of the following: the level of employment, inflation vs. deflation, exchange rate stability and the degree of freedom of international transactions.

If we look in the wreckage of international systems of the past for clues on how to construct a better system for the future, I would suggest at least three lessons.

1. We should adopt from the start a wide definition of the system - one that is not limited to governments. That definition cannot be very precise, but it would encompass the total ambience within which private and official agents in individual countries conduct their activities in the economic and financial fields. That ambience would include the international organizations - the IMF, BIS, OECD, GATT, EC and others. But, even more important, it would also include the multinational corporations, the worldwide information system that underlies private decision-making, the banks and the

currency traders, the international bond markets, and many others.

2. If there is one single reason for the repeated failure of successive (world-wide or regional) monetary regimes, it is that they were overtaken by changes occurring in the nature of the international system in the broader sense. Over the past 50 years this system, in the broad sense of the word, has undergone extremely rapid development in the private sector, in particular the extension of capital mobility from the national to the international scale - with which the official sector has found it difficult to keep pace. The banks, for example, have evolved from predominantly national deposit takers and lenders, to world-wide intermediaries of the flows of savings and investments. In individual countries the effect of this was to turn capital controls from semi-efficient insulators of national interest-rate levels to irrelevant irritants or indeed competitive handicaps to a country's banks. At the level of international liquidity, changes in the working of the private sector had two major - and wholly unplanned - effects on the functioning of the official monetary system. The new transnational availability of bank credits, first, freed the industrial countries from the conditionality of the IMF and thus unbalanced that organization into one that extended credit to - and policed - the developing countries only; and, second, it reduced greatly - some would say it eliminated - the need for an SDR scheme that had been constructed with so much effort in the 1960's.

3. Countries themselves have changed, and some of these changes have had a profound impact on the system. The system whose largest member launched the Marshall Plan was a very different one from that whose still largest member passed the collection plate for the Gulf War. An EMS structured around a Germany with a budget close to balance is one thing; an EMS around a Germany with a public sector borrowing requirement of 7.4 percent of GNP (in 1993) is something totally different. More generally, governments have become more subject to strong domestic forces that limit their ability to act in an international setting, and thus to give and take in the processes of international cooperation and coordination. Moreover, disenchanted with the results of years of finetuning, they have also become less willing to engage in the flexible operation of one of their main policy instruments, fiscal policy. I make these observations not to dismiss policy coordination as a negligible component of the international (or the regional) decision-making process, but to put it in what I hope is a realistic perspective.

I want to elaborate on the question of coordination because understanding it is essential to a clear picture of the present system. Unfortunately, much of the current theory on policy coordination - mathematically elegant though it is - is of little relevance to the real world.

Yes, in a formal sense it must be true that among N countries, each with its individually optimized policy package, it should be possible to devise a single coordinated policy package that gives every country a better outcome. In that sense it is selfevident that a cooperative solution will always be better than a non-cooperative one; otherwise, the negotiators would not have opted for it. What is wrong with this schematic description of international policy-making is that governments do not meet, say half yearly in the G-7 or the Interim Committee of the Fund, with their nationally optimized policy packages, which they then submit to a further process of joint optimization. Nor do they reach the same result, on the basis of each knowing the welfare functions of all other governments, by a process of joint decision making. There are two reasons why, even theoretically, things will not happen this way. First, governments do not have the luxury of moving their policy packages along smooth multi-dimensional welfare surfaces. As the passage of the Clinton economic package through the U.S. Congress made clear, the best they can hope for are one (or a few) corner solutions that may prove nationally acceptable, and second, even though there must, in principle, exist a cooperative solution that is "better" than the combination of the N individual solutions, the distribution among the N countries of the collective potential improvement is itself a zero-sum game to which the participants might well fail to find an agreed answer (Cooper (1985)).

To some extent the difficulties inherent in *ad hoc* coordination can be overcome, and the chances of better outcomes enhanced, by agreement in advance on certain rules. Examples are the proscription of competitive currency depreciation or a ban on export subsidies. I do not share the negative view of Ralph Bryant (1980) that such rules cannot be "both politically feasible and analytically sound", because rules agreed in advance do not take into account all information available at the time of application. If countries can, undisturbed by the tension of an actual case, agree to a limited number of rules with a strong appeal in logic, the chances are good that these rules will provide pretty good answers to most of the actual cases that will present themselves. By contrast, failure to agree on a rule (or the abolition of a rule once agreed upon without replacing it by a new rule) is likely to make it very difficult for countries to find a satisfactory solution to a particular case.

Rules vs. coordination is probably a false issue in any event. I would submit that in international trade and finance, the choice does not lie between a regime dominated by rules with a modest reliance on coordination in their application, and a regime with few if any rules where conflict situations are resolved by cooperative *ad hoc* decision-making. Rather, among countries and in periods where a cooperative spirit prevails, it will prove possible to agree on rules <u>and</u> to rely as necessary on joint decision-making. Among other countries or at other times, both methods of conflict resolution may prove unavailable and the system will suffer accordingly.

And - a very important point frequently overlooked - whatever the climate, the chances for a favourable outcome will be enhanced if the periodic discussions among country representatives take place within a framework that encourages objectivity and continuity. Staff work provided by an international organization is important in this connection, and so is a long-time chairman. In its heyday, Working Party 3 of the OECD was a good example of effective coordination among the G-10 countries.

The evolution of the G5/G7 since the Plaza agreement in 1985 provides interesting evidence how "policy coordination" develops if conditions are on the whole not favourable to the resolution of conflict situations. The subject at the Plaza was, of course, not one of conflict. The other Four shared Secretary Baker's desire to head off protectionist action by the US Congress by counteracting the extreme overvaluation of the dollar. But soon thereafter, countries' views on the appropriate policies began to diverge, and "peer pressure" was unlikely to improve the atmosphere for the pursuit of the delicate cooperative solutions that would be necessary for joint decision-making on macroeconomic policies. "Peer pressure", by the way, is the favourite U.S. term to describe the *modus operandi* of the G-7, a euphemism for arm twisting by public exposure.

It would appear that the G-7 have realized the limitations that apply to endeavors in the field of coordination and have, in fact, moved toward concentrating their activities in areas in which they do have a comparative advantage over the established international organizations. According to one of the main practitioners (Tietmeyer (1988)) policy cooperation among the major industrial countries has developed "into...much more than mere coordination of macroeconomic policies in the fiscal and monetary fields." He mentions cooperation "on all important economic issues such as trade, development and debt, energy and structural policy, and coordination through international organizations such as the Fund, GATT and the OECD." (That was the list five years ago; since then, of course, Russia has been added at the top of this list). In other words, the G-7 know better than to try, twice a year, to reset collectively their policy instruments with the aim of maximizing their countries' welfare functions. Instead they have, sensibly, concentrated on a number of clearly recognizable domestic and international public goods that they all support and which, with a lot of joint hard work on their part, can be expected to be promoted over the medium term.[2] Structural measures are also prominent on the list, among other reasons because countries can hope to give each other mutual support in resisting national vested interests (Shafer (1991)). Indeed, another long-time participant (Gyohten (1988)) describes them as "more fundamental" than exchange rates and macroeconomic policy.

But note what is not on the agenda of the G-7: improvement of the international monetary system. Indeed when the chairman of the G-10 proposed a few years ago that his group (which has been marginalized by the G-7) undertake a study of the system, the Americans blocked it.

Is that right? Fifty years after the glory of Bretton Woods, should Sisyphus just sit there among its ruins? Can we square it with our consciences to continue living under what some many observers have called a non-system (although I would guess that expression is gradually going out of fashion)? The answer to these questions is, I am afraid, mostly: Yes.

The events in Europe over the last year have demonstrated again that, to survive, any monetary system has to respect not only one, but two primacies: the primacy of the economic over the monetary, and the primacy of the political over the economic. On the first point, the developments of 1992/1993 have again proven the economists right over the monetarists: a fixed exchange rate has only that much power to keep economic policies in line. Beyond that point, the rate snaps. But the second point is perhaps even more important: while a single political entity may be able to pursue an economic policy that is beneficial to the country as a whole but costly to a particular region (perhaps by assisting that region with extensive transfer payments), separate countries with separate national decision-making processes will not, for the purpose of maintaining a monetary standard, be prepared to undergo economic policies that are seen as nationally detrimental. Acting rationally, they will therefore not enter into a monetary arrangement that might entail such consequences. This does not imply that I am predicting the demise of the ERM, nor that I am necessarily pessimistic about its return to narrow margins. But it does imply grave doubts about the attainability of EMU without the prior achievement of a much greater degree of political integration than appears anywhere on the horizon.

At the world level, it is probably correct to say that the informed majority has accepted floating among the major currencies as inevitable, with varying degrees of confidence in the benefits of managing the floats, for example by judicious, preferably concerted, intervention. But an important minority, including for example from time to time President Mitterand and senior Japanese policy makers, as well as droves of babes in Bretton Woods, would argue - in total disregard of the primacy of the political - that with enough will it should be possible to replicate something like the ERM on a world scale. The events of last year will perhaps put some damper on these and other romantic approaches to the subject.

Ten years ago, at a 40-year celebration held at Bretton Woods, Richard Cooper proposed monetary union among the industrial countries in order to save the system from the high cost of exchange rate uncertainty. To this end he suggested merger of national monetary policies into a collective monetary authority, but without abolishing fiscal autonomy. Cautiously, he put the target date for his vision 25 years ahead, in 2010. Now that we are nearly halfway there, this vision looks even less realistic than it did when first presented. Not only is it questionable in the abstract whether the world is an optimum currency area. Even if that seemed a plausible proposition, there would be no rational way to get from here to there, unless one also found a way to turn the world into something much closer to a single political area. But, come to think of it, would that not be a much more valuable achievement than mere monetary union!

NOTES

1. Thus for example Dick Cooper's throwaway definition in 10 words between dashes: "The international monetary system - the rules and conventions that govern financial relations between countries - ..." (Cooper (1985)).

2. At the same time their frequent meetings prepare them for the occasions where joint action in support of the system is called for, as for example in October 1987.

REFERENCES

Bryant, Ralph C., Money and Monetary Policy In Interdependent Nations, The Brooking Institution, Washington, D.C., 1980.

Cooper, Richard N., "Economic Interdependence and Coordination of Economic Policies", in: R. Jones and P. Kenen, eds, Handbook of International Economics, vol 2, North Holland, Amsterdam 1985.

_____, "Is There a Need for Reform ?", in: Federal Reserve Bank of Boston, The International Monetary System: Forty Years After Bretton Woods, Boston 1984.

Dobson, Wendy, "Should G-7 Cooperation be Buried?", International Economic Insights, Institute for International Economics, May-June 1993.

Gyohten, Toyoo, "Comments" in: W. Guth (Moderator), Economic Policy Coordination, IMF, Washington, D.C., 1988.

Polak, Jacques, "International Policy Coordination and the Functioning of the International Monetary System - A Search for Realism", in: H.J. Blommestein (ed.), The Reality of International Economic Policy Coordination, North Holland, Amsterdam, 1991.

Shafer, Jeffrey, "Structural Reform in the Process of International Policy Coordination", in: H.J. Blommestein (ed.), The Reality of International Economic Policy Coordination, North Holland, Amsterdam, 1991.

Solomon, Robert, The International Monetary System, 1945-81, Harper and Row, New York, 1982.

Tietmeyer, Hans, "Comments" in: W. Guth (Moderator), Economic Policy Coordination, IMF, Washington, D.C., 1988.

Williamson, John, The Open Economy and the World Economy, Basic Books, New York, 1983.

2 Prospects for the International Monetary System and its Institutions

ROBERT MUNDELL

The subject matter of this conference is ambitious in the sense that it deals with the *future* of the international monetary system and its institutions. It would be almost equally ambitious if it dealt with its *past*, about which a great deal more is known than of its future. Yet it is from the past that we can draw lessons and learn about the future. History is condensed into hypotheses, theories and laws that provide us with a roadmap of the future.

My task in this paper is to use theoretical regularities in the past to guess at the evolution of the international monetary system paying attention to both its private and public monetary spheres. A basic conclusion of the paper is that there is an externality in the world economy that remains to be captured by reform of the international monetary system.

1 Phases of the International Monetary System

The early history of the international monetary system was simplified by the use of the precious metals for coinage. Every independent country might have chosen to mint different coins out of copper, silver or gold (or lead, iron, nickel or tin) but there were common denominators based on the values of the metallic content of the coins and the relative values of the precious metals. The history of metallic coinage can be divided into periods when money was accepted *ad pensum*, and periods when it was accepted *ad talum*, in which one or more overvalued coins gained currency. Overvalued coinages could be maintained only by a strong central government, and the long-lasting coinage systems of the great empires were usually of this type; the monopoly of the coinage prerogative and fiscal seigniorage were enforced strictly by the doctrine of regalian rights and draconian penalties for counterfeiting.

The introduction of free coinage in the 17th century ushered in a new period when governments gave away the fiscal seigniorage to the financial intermediaries and, except for subsidiary coinage, silver and gold currencies were exchanged *ad pensum*; England set the pattern in the 1660's for what would become the bimetallic and gold standards of the 19th century. After 1717, Britain set in motion the sequence of forces that would land that country on the gold standard and which other countries would join after the

1870's.

French bimetallism in the 19th century, up until 1870, imparted a monetary unity to countries on the gold or silver standards. When that order broke down with the suspension of specie payments by the Bank of France,[1] the fluctuation of the bimetallic interchange ratio resulted in variability of exchange rates between gold and silver standard countries. During the 1870's, France, Germany and many other countries shifted to the gold standard, creating an excess demand for gold and deflationary pressure in gold-standard countries. Meanwhile, silver demonetization created an excess supply of silver and inflationary pressure in the countries that remained on the silver standard. The battle of the standards was finally settled once for all by the massive discoveries of gold in South Africa, and by 1900 all the major countries, with the exception of China, adhered to gold.

The all-too-brief era of gold was cut short by World War I when the European belligerents engaged in inflationary finance and depreciation. The United States (along with Japan) had remained on gold during the war, but all the other countries (with the exception of Japan) suspended - *de facto* or *de jure* - convertibility. Massive gold imports into the United States were monetized and the U.S. price level doubled, halving the real value of gold.

The post-war deflation of 1920-1 brought about a partial correction, but the dollar price level was still 35 per cent above the pre-war level and gold was correspondingly undervalued. At the existing price level there was enough gold liquidity for a gold-convertible dollar standard, but not enough for a pre-1914-style international gold standard. Nevertheless the other major countries - Germany in 1924, Britain in 1925 and France in 1927 - now led the way toward a restored the international gold standard, creating the fateful disequilibrium that would culminate in the great depression. The ensuing scramble for gold led to tight money, bank failures, deflation and the depression of the 1930's.[2]

The breakdown of the gold exchange standard strengthened the relative position of the dollar in the international monetary system. Devaluation in 1934 had made the dollar again the strongest currency (as it had been in the early 1920's) and, following the devaluation of the franc in 1936, it became increasingly the international currency, assuming, after the Tripartite Agreement, the role of key or pivot currency. The system that emerged after 1934 was closer to that which had prevailed in the decade between 1914 and 1924 than it was to the international gold standards before or after that decade.

Because most other countries had abandoned gold as backing for national money, and because none of the currencies were freely convertible into gold, there was now, temporarily, an excess supply of gold, leading to the gold scares of 1936 and 1937, based partly on the unfounded belief that the United States would stop buying and accumulating it. The dollar had now, temporarily, become the anchor of the international monetary system and the first murmuring of a "dollar shortage" appeared. For the decade between 1937 and 1947, it was the dollar that was supporting gold rather than vice versa. Other countries meanwhile valued their currencies in relation to the dollar. It was this dollar-gold system that came into force after World War II.

The Bretton Woods Agreement did not create a new international monetary system; indeed, the agreement almost made it impossible for the on-going system to operate. According to the agreement, countries were required to maintain exchange rates of all members within one percent of parity. This clause would have required the United States either to close the New York market in foreign exchange or else to intervene to keep all currency prices fixed within the prescribed limits of the IMF Articles.[3] To avoid this obligation, the United States, almost as an afterthought, had the crucial sub-clause, Article IV-4(b) inserted in the Articles, enabling a member to fix the price of gold in lieu of maintaining its exchange rate obligation. This clause established the legal basis for the asymmetrical exchange rate system in which the United States was responsible for the dollar price of gold and the other countries were responsible for the dollar prices of their currencies.[4]

History now began to repeat itself. Just as World War I had resulted in a higher post-war price level that undervalued gold, so did World War II. Just as gold became scarce when other countries rejoined the gold standard after World War I, so it became scarce after World War II, when - especially after 1958 - European countries made their currencies externally convertible and exchanged dollars for undervalued gold from the United States. But the authorities had learned a lesson and were determined to prevent any scarcity of gold from creating a new deflation; accordingly they created a gold-guaranteed SDR, a form of liquid gold designed to supplement and replace gold when it became scarce.

It was a good idea but badly implemented. Because too few SDR's were created too late, and because national monetary authorities - including the United States - were unwilling to concede important power to an international authority, there was an officially-designed run on gold, leading to a closing of the gold window by the United States.[5] The United States advised the International Monetary Fund that it was no longer fulfilling its obligations under Article IV-4(b), after which other major countries stopped fixing their currencies to the dollar.

Flexible exchange rates, however, proved to be an unsatisfactory solution. Initially, the European countries had considered the possibility of a joint float against the dollar, but the time was not ripe for that idea.[6] Instead, the major countries met at the Smithsonian Institution in Washington in December 1991 to arrange for a restoration of fixed exchange rates.

The Smithsonian arrangements turned out to be abortive, largely because the disequilibrium had been misdiagnosed: the U.S. deficit was treated as a national problem rather than a system problem. The basic problem was an incorrect relationship between all currencies and gold, but it was treated as a problem between the dollar and other currencies. The agreement resulted in a devaluation of the dollar by a few percentage points and an appreciation of a few other currencies, with a tiny increase in the price of gold. Raising the official price to $38 an ounce merely whetted the appetite of gold speculators. The error[7] was not understood at the time, however, and so it was repeated when, in February 1973, the dollar was again devalued, raising the official price of gold this time to $42.22 an ounce.

2 Currency Areas

After the failure of the attempt to set up a durable fixed-exchange-rate system based on the inconvertible dollar, the international monetary authorities decided, in June 1973, to abandon fixed exchange rates altogether.[8] This was a policy that had acquired favor in monetarist circles which had, indeed, captured the U.S. Treasury.[9]

Advocates of flexible exchange rates had expected most countries to let their currencies "float." But the real world did not match the blueprint. Countries in different positions require different solutions. Small countries sooner or later found it necessary to group themselves into currency areas, often relating their currencies to one of their larger economic partners. The breakup of fixed exchange rates resulted in groups of currency areas rather than universally flexible exchange rates.[10]

The dollar area formed around those countries that found flexible exchange rates unsatisfactory and could take advantage of the dollar link to the New York capital market. Such an arrangement of dependence on the dollar, however, was politically incompatible with European aspirations: it would have formalized the defects of the unanchored dollar standard that had proved to be a failure between 1971 and 1973. From the early 1960's the European Economic Community had established an unofficial goal of European Monetary Unity, and the flexible exchange rate system, in combination with a depreciating dollar, provided both the impetus and the opportunity.

The formation of the European Monetary System (EMS) in 1979 was simultaneously (1) a rejection of flexible exchange rates; (2) a reaction against the dollar as an anchor currency; and (3) an expression of a commitment to a deepening of European integration. The EMS became a regional monetary order within the (now very loose) Bretton Woods Order.

The EMS has operated more like a DM area than a symmetrical arrangement of currencies; this was to be expected by past experience with other dominated currency areas. But a DM area suffers from the defects of any unanchored currency area. An unanchored currency area has the defect that the pivot country can follow a monetary policy made for home consumption rather than for the benefit of the area as a whole; countries that reject the monetary policy of the center country will opt out of the currency area. The global dollar area broke down in 1971 and 1973 because the monetary policy of the United States was too expansionary for the surplus countries; and the exchange rate mechanism (ERM) split apart in 1992 because the monetary policy of Germany was too deflationary for the rest of the ERM members of the EMS.[11]

The world still operates, in a sense, under the Bretton Woods Monetary Order. Although the system envisaged in the Bretton Woods Charter never (and could not have) materialized, and the *de facto* dollar standard that ensued broke down, the Articles of Agreement, as amended, remain in force. For the first time the order is now world-wide, incorporating China and Eastern Europe as well as Russia and the other countries that became independent after the collapse of the Soviet Union.

3 International Intermediation

Only a part of the international monetary system is made up by national currencies. Most of the world's money supply is supplied by financial intermediaries, those institutions that facilitate the exchange of commodities and assets in the financial markets.

Intermediation in the international financial markets has grown by leaps and bounds since the early post-war years. Part of this growth is beneficial and benign, the rest is harmful and malignant. One of the major problems in the study of international intermediation is to find a means of distinguishing between benign and malignant intermediation.

To try to find orders of magnitude it is necessary to have a basis of comparison. One candidate is the growth of foreign exchange reserves. In the five-year period from 1957 to 1962 foreign exchange reserves more than doubled from about $8 billion to $19.9 billion (see Table 2.1); by 1967, they had grown to $29.4 billion; by 1972, to $104.5 billion; by 1977, to $244.7 billion; by 1982, to $313.2 billion; by 1987, to $647.7 billion; by the end of 1992, to $918.3 billion. In the thirty-five years from the end of 1957 to the end of 1992 official foreign exchange reserves had increased 114.8 times!

There is no exact measure of international intermediation. A good proxy for it, however, is Deposit Money Banks' Foreign Assets (DMBFA). By the end of 1962, these assets had (since 1957) had doubled to $12.3 billion; by

1967 they had more than doubled to $38.8; by 1972, they had soared to $225 billion; by 1977, to $884.3 billion; by 1982, to $2,373.9 billion; by 1987 to $4,752.3 billion; and by the end of 1992 to $6,776.7 billion. In the thirty-five years between 1957 and 1992 the "Eurodollar" market had increased by a factor of one thousand!!

Table 2.1. Reserves and Eurodollars

Year	For Ex $ b.	DMBFA $ b.	IMPORTS $ b.	FE/DMBFA %	FE/IM %	DMBFA/IM %
1962	19.9	12.3	138.9	161.8	14.3	8.9
1967	29.4	38.8	211.1	75.8	13.9	18.4
1972	104.5	225.0*	400.2	46.4	26.1	56.2
1977	244.7	884.3	1083.6	27.7	22.6	81.6
1982	313.2	2,373.0	1816.7	13.2	17.2	130.7
1987	647.7	4,753.2	2422.1	13.6	26.7	196.2
1992	918.3	6,776.7	3700.0*	13.5	24.8	183.2

*estimate
Source: *International Financial Statistics*, various years.

The phenomenal growth of foreign exchange reserves can be accounted for by three factors: the growth of trade, the acceleration of inflation (of which it was also a cause) and the substitution of foreign exchange for gold reserves as the latter became immobilized as an international means of settlement. The same factors would work to increase private international intermediation, but it would have been hard to predict before the event that the growth of private assets would exceed the growth of foreign exchange reserves by a factor of more than ten!

The phenomenal growth of the international short-term capital market, represented by international banking, is the most important tendency in international financial matters. What can explain a tendency that few people would have predicted thirty or even twenty years ago?[12]

The problem cannot be understood outside the framework of the multiple-currency system. The international currencies - mainly the dollar but also the yen and the mark - are used as money outside the national jurisdictions. Dollar balances in London can be leveraged on balances in New York, turning in effect low-powered money in the United States into high-powered money in Europe; analogous expansions are possible for the yen and mark.[13]

What is the limit of the process? In its most extreme manifestation, ignoring other currencies than the dollar, the entire stock of U.S. demand deposits would become the reserves for "international dollars" created in banks outside the United States. The process would not in practice go this far because some would be held for private purposes in the United States. A limit will therefore be reached when the international dollar expansion reaches an equilibrium relationship with dollars held in the United States.

It is possible that, after thirty years of phenomenal expansion, an equilibrium relationship is being approached. For example, after falling from 161.8 per cent in 1962 to 27.7 per cent in 1977, the ratio of reserves to international deposits has achieved a remarkable stability, since 1982, around 13.5 per cent. Let us now consider the relation between international deposits and the U.S. stock of liquidity assets, as measured by M_3.

From Table 2.2 it can be seen that the phase of phenomenal growth of DMBFA relative to U.S. monetary aggregates is over. While still increasing, it is clear that there is a convergence process toward an equilibrium, perhaps in the case of M_3, with a ratio of 2:1. The days of the phenomenal growth of international banking relative to other monetary magnitudes are numbered.

Table 2.2. DMBFA and Measures of U.S. Money

Year	DMBFA $b	M_2 $b	M_3 $b	DMBFA/M_2 %	DMBFA/M_3 %
1962	12.3	365.8	374.1	3.4	3.2
1967	38.8	528.0	560.0	7.3	6.9
1972	225.0*	806.0	886.3	27.9	25.4
1977	884.3	1288.8	1476.8	68.6	59.9
1982	2379.0	1958.1	2450.3	121.5	96.8
1987	4753.2	2933.9	3701.8	162.0	128.4
1992	6776.7	3560.0*	4325.8	190.4	156.7

*estimate

Source: *International Financial Statistics*, various years.

It is now necessary to try to evaluate the social usefulness of the growth of international intermediation. To the extent that cross-border transactions satisfy *bona fide* intertemporal exchanges, they increase wealth and are therefore utility-increasing. To the extent, however, that cross-border transactions aggravate the instability of the international monetary system by the creation of self-justifying speculation, they reduce the usefulness of money and are welfare-reducing.

It is necessary, however, to make a distinction between the transactions that arise because of the failure of international authorities to create a stable and predictable monetary system and the attempts on the part of the private market to make the best of a bad situation. If the policy authorities exhibit ineptness or signal uncertainty about policy intentions, defensive speculation cannot be considered welfare reducing.

The stock of foreign assets in the international banks (measured by DMFBA) is now about $7 trillion or about 20 per cent of a Gross World Product that is about $35 trillion; it is about equal to the level (exports plus imports) of world trade. Daily turnover in the foreign exchange market, however, now amounts to more than a trillion dollars, perhaps much more. Total transactions at that rate probably exceed $400 trillion dollars a year. Are all these transactions socially necessary?

If the world had a single unified currency, there would be no foreign exchange transactions and a large part of the trans-border transactions would disappear; only socially-desirable intertemporal intermediation would remain. The difference between the actual volume of transactions and the volume under an ideal international monetary system would impose an unnecessary transactions cost upon the world economy, draining resources from work or leisure that reduces real income.[14] What would be the social saving from eliminating the unnecessary component of these transactions? I am not aware that such a measure has ever been calculated.

To fix ideas, let us make some drastic assumptions. Assume that the dead-weight welfare cost of every defensive transaction is one-half of one percent of the value of the transaction. Let us also assume that one-half of all transactions are defensive in the sense that they would not be undertaken if a world currency existed. Under these assumptions, the welfare cost of the current international monetary system, compared to an ideal system, would be 1/200 x 1/2 x $400 trillion = $1 trillion, or 1/35 = 2.86 per cent of a GWP equal to $35 trillion. Under these assumptions, the welfare cost of the current international monetary system is thus about equal to the GDP of a country the size of the U.K. or Italy.

I hasten to emphasize that I am not advocating any kind of prohibition of "defensive" transactions, restrictions on the growth of international commercial banking, or "Tobin taxes" to increase the transactions costs of activity in the financial markets. These defensive transactions are made necessary by the artificial uncertainty created by a rudderless international monetary system. Given the existing international monetary system, these transactions provide utility-increments to asset-holders because they reduce their uncertainty, however spurious and unnecessary that uncertainty may be.

It is the international monetary system, not the transactions themselves that are malignant. The defensive transactions are means of coping with the exchange rate uncertainties that dominate every economic decision. The direction of reform should be toward reducing the unnecessary uncertainty of the present international monetary system, not the means by which the financial markets try to make the best of a bad situation.

4 Defects of the International Monetary System

The most important function of the international monetary system is to provide a means by which the scarcity relationships expressed in one currency unit can be translated into other currency units without unnecessary distortions. An ideal system might be one in which national currencies were dispensed with in favor of a single world currency. To the extent that national currencies continue to exist, however, the next best solution would be one in which national currencies were irrevocably convertible into one another at fixed exchange rates and the international monetary system had the same characteristics as a world monetary system based upon a common world currency.[15] Part of the these gains were achieved historically by the adoption of bimetallic or gold and silver standards as the common base for money, so that exchange rates became names for different quantities of a common metal.

Back in the 1940's, when preparations were being inaugurated for the post-war monetary system, one of the instructions laid down by Secretary-of-the-Treasury Henry Morgenthau Jr. to Harry Dexter White was "to provide for a post-war international currency."[16] Provisions were made for an international currency in the two major plans for reform, but neither Keynes' *bancor* nor White's *unitas* appeared in the final agreement. The idea of an international currency fell afoul of *real politik*. An international currency was rejected and the Bretton Woods agreement became an empty shell. By default, gold and the dollar collaborated to fill the vacuum.

The post-war regime worked tolerably well for most countries in the era of the *1944 gold dollar* when dollars and gold were interchangeable; international monetary discipline was maintained and the rate of inflation held in check. But the omission at Bretton Woods became increasingly unsatisfactory when, in 1968 and 1971, the dollar and gold went their separate ways. The need for an international currency in the 1990's is much more apparent than in the 1950's when the dollar and gold were interconvertible into one another.

The SDR, established in 1968 with the first amendment to the Articles of Agreement of the IMF, made a promising start in the direction of a world currency. But the promise was never delivered. The SDR started off with a gold-weight guarantee and, had the authorities persevered, could have become a substitute for gold. But after the dollar became inconvertible, the gold guarantee of the SDR was stripped away, leaving it dangling without a base; only the smile remained of what had become a Cheshire cat.[17] In its second manifestation, the SDR became a basket of sixteen currencies which changed with the political circumstances of individual countries. The SDR was later transformed again into a basket of five currencies which it remains today.

In its present form, the SDR is an unsatisfactory world currency. It is a mere derivative of inflating currencies and does not therefore provide a stable standard of value. It depreciates in terms of commodities with the inflation rates according to the weights of the dollar (40 per cent), the mark (21 per cent), the yen (17 per cent), and the franc and the pound (11 per cent each) in the basket. If on the average countries inflate at the rate of 4 per cent, the SDR depreciates in terms of commodities by a corresponding amount.[18]

Another defect of the SDR as international legal tender is that it lacks universality. The money prerogative is a manifestation of a state's sovereignty, and the creation of an international money implies the concession of sovereignty to a supranational body. In return for that political concession, what does a country receive in exchange? At the present time the answer is nothing. A legitimate *quid pro quo* would be a stake in the act of creation and management of the international money. However as unimportant a country's economy may be as a share in the world economy, it deserves some input, however slight, as a component in the international money.[19] [20]

Another defect of the present international monetary system - not unrelated to the absence of an international money - is the exchange-rate mechanism. Judged by performance characteristics, the world economy has been more unstable under flexible exchange rates than it was under fixed exchange rates in the early post-war period. The Bretton-Woods arrangements had provided for a par value system of fixed (but occasionally adjustable) exchange rates. This system had the merit that it managed the recognized mutual interdependence of exchange rates without tolerating monetary bilateralism in which large countries play the policeman with respect to the exchange rates of small countries. In the absence of international supervision of the monetary interdependence, small countries can be made the victims of large country "bashing," the bully tactics of monetary bilateralism. One of the functions of an international monetary order is to maintain the spirit and practice of monetary multilateralism and in this result the present system has failed.[21]

Another defect of the current international monetary order is its lack of collective monetary discipline. A system of fixed exchange rates anchored to an asset like gold (or an international money) provides a form of collective monetary discipline. Even an unanchored system of fixed exchange rates - or rather exchange rates anchored to the currency of a large stable country - has beneficial effects for national monetary discipline.[22]

Consider the usefulness of the international monetary order today from the standpoint of the new countries of Eastern Europe and the former Soviet Union. A major problem in these countries is to establish a price system that corresponds to scarcity relationships. The best way to do this is to import the scarcity relationships of a stable foreign country and this can be achieved best by fixed exchange rates.

In my judgement, the new countries today are less well-served by the international system than was the case for countries in the post-war period. How unrealistic today to advise these new countries to let their currencies float and fix the rate of monetary expansion! If there existed now a system of fixed exchange rates to which the major countries adhered, as was the case in the post-war period, it would be a comparatively simple matter for the countries of Eastern Europe and the new countries of the former Soviet Union to frame their monetary and exchange rate goals in terms of the international standard.

I have long maintained that it would be desirable to reform the international monetary system along lines that would restore a voluntary par value system to give countries a new option. Such a system would improve on the choices now available to these new countries: the dollar area, the ecu bloc or flexible exchange rates. There should be some half-way house in between flexible rates and joining one of the large blocs for these countries. Improved arrangements within the international monetary order would be the best solution.

5 Implications of EMU

A successful movement toward European Monetary Union would mean that the ecu or europa area will be a rival to the dollar.[23] Initially, there would be a tendency for the new European Central Bank to dump dollars in the process of getting rid of excess reserves. This would amount to a net capital import by Europe and would impose on Europe a corresponding current account deficit unless it were offset by compensatory long-term capital exports. Depending on the pace at which Europe releases its dollar reserves, and on U.S. monetary policy, there would be a tendency for the dollar to depreciate against the ECU. It would, however, be easy to exaggerate the importance of this effect, not only because the dollar will be the most important international reserve of the European Central Bank but also because of the reluctance to allow still further (if only temporary) improvements in U.S. competitiveness.

Each of the two major blocs would strive to build up its own currency area.[24] Up to now the dollar area has never been explicitly defined or managed; like the sterling area, it grew up like topsy. But the competition created by EMU would probably lead to the formulation of a dollar area policy. At first glance, it would seem that there will be a tendency for East Europe, Africa and India to go with Europe; and for Latin America, Canada, the Middle East, and much of the Pacific basin to lean toward the dollar. The position of Japan will become important. Without ruling out the possibility of an independent yen area, Japan will find its natural links to its complements in North America, Korea, China, the rest of South East Asia and perhaps Russia, rather than Europe. The tendency of Japan to join the dollar area (or a joint dollar-yen area) will be reinforced by Europe's discrimination against the exports of Japan and the rest of South East Asia.

There are four reasons, however, why Russia at least, and some countries of Eastern Europe might find a European solution difficult. First, it is unlikely that the Community will allow the countries of Eastern Europe to join the Community as full members in the near future. Members of the former EFTA countries, like Switzerland, Austria and the Scandinavian countries, might be welcome, but some of them might not choose to join; the requirements of labor mobility and equalization payments will provide barriers for the richer countries. There is a chance that Poland, Czechoslovakia and Hungary will be admitted before the end of the decade, but the other countries will probably have to wait well into the next millennium. Western Germany's experience in digesting its eastern half will make Germany and its western partners wary of additional huge investments and transfers to the rest of Eastern Europe that would be necessary to make those countries viable partners of the European factor-price-equalization area.[25] In the absence of a new European framework for countries of Central and Eastern Europe, they might find association with the dollar bloc as useful as association with Europe.

The second reason is that the deflationary stance of the Community, aggravated by a depreciating dollar, would impose a challenge that might be too difficult for the countries of Eastern Europe to meet. They are far more likely to adopt the easier standard that would be set by modest U.S. rates of inflation.

The third reason is that the countries of the Pacific Basin, counting North America, Japan, S. Korea, China, Hong Kong, Taiwan and the rapidly-growing countries of the rest of East Asia, have a good chance of maintaining their role as the high-tech growth centers of the world economy. By its very nature, the Community will be inward-looking and closed, rather than open-ended and competitive. In a static world, the Fortress Europe recipe covering a sufficiently large trading area can be successful. But in a rapidly changing world where new technologies are born every minute, a closed-economy outlook is a recipe for decline.

The fourth reason is that, even though the Cold War has ended, authority and military power are still important. Along with the blessings ensuing from the end of the Cold War and the fall of Communism have come a new political instability, giving new dimensions to the term "balkanization." In the face of this new instability, the Community often seems to be paralysed in inaction at times where strong positions are necessary. Although the Maastricht Treaty made a provision for political union in Europe, EPU has not received anything like the attention of EMU. It would be a mistake to expect from Europe the unity of purpose and political will needed to exert independent power on the world stage in the near future. A complete political union for Europe, if it comes at all, may have to wait decades into the next century.

For these reasons, the Eastern European countries, and perhaps even some of the African countries, will find links with the dollar area preferable to the uncertain prospect of an intimate association with Europe.

There are, however, two alternative scenarios. One moves through a European initiative to widen the European Monetary System to include the countries of Eastern Europe. The Economic Community could open the EMS to the countries of Eastern Europe without jeopardizing its own pursuit (at present damaged) of European Monetary Union. A European Monetary Fund that embraced the entire continent would provide a framework within which the newly-free countries could build the institutions necessary for eventual full participation in the European experiment.

An alternative scenario moves through international monetary reform. If, on its road to EMU, Europe paid some attention to global international monetary arrangements, it might be possible to work toward a better monetary system for Europe, the United States and the rest of the world. To this end, a restructuring of the IMF toward a system of non-compulsive fixed exchange rate parities for willing countries would be compatible with the formation of a European currency. It would also provide a framework, alternative to the development of monetary blocs, for the countries of the rest of the world. Rather than developing a world of two huge monetary blocs, a restructured IMF would be consistent with a dollar, ecu and yen area within the framework of an international system.

6 An International Monetary Constitution

Grand blueprints cannot defy the laws of monetary evolution. It is, however, both possible and useful to encourage a continued evolution of the international monetary system in a direction that better serves the international community. Let me therefore suggest some general principles around which an improved international monetary order could be redefined.[26]

1. There should be an international standard of value in the form of a international composite currency in which every country participates.
2. The international composite currency should be produced by the International Monetary Fund or an international monetary authority or world central bank that replaces the Fund.
3. The international composite currency should have a stable value in terms of an agreed basket of commodities; it would be kept stable by an adjustment for inflation at frequent intervals.[27]
4. Every country should have the opportunity, and assistance from the monetary authority if necessary, to stabilize its currency in terms of the composite currency. Acting on behalf of a member, or of a currency area, the monetary authority would be empowered to guarantee any member's stated parity (or its rate of change), with due provisions for asset settlements where the Fund accumulates an excessive quantity of a member's currency.[28]
5. Units of the international composite currency should be created in tangible form and utilized as international reserves by member countries, acceptable everywhere in the transactions domain of the international monetary system.
6. Seigniorage from international monetary expansion would be distributed to countries according to an agreed formula through allocations, or else retained, upon general agreement of members, for international purposes.
7. The allocations of the composite currency to the participating countries would be determined by an agreed-upon formula subject to modification, as and if necessary, by a procedure determined by the international monetary authority.
8. The international composite currency, being a stable money, would bear no interest.
9. Members of the Fund would be obligated to accept a given quantity of the composite currency equal to a multiple of their quotas (as under current SDR arrangements).
10. The values of the currencies of IMF members, as expressed in terms of the international composite currency, would be published at

periodic intervals (daily or hourly as required) by the international monetary authority.

11. The international monetary authority would hold assets in currencies and such commodity assets, including gold, designated by its Board of Governors.
12. The value of currency assets in terms of the composite reserve currency (and thus in real terms) would be maintained by maintenance-of-value depreciation allowances (as in the original IMF Articles)[29] paid by each member in proportion to its depreciation in terms of the international composite currency.
13. Gold could continue to be used as a secondary reserve for central banks in a future international monetary system[30] but it may be possible to put gold to better use in the transition period to a new international monetary system.
14. Gold should be revalued officially so that it can again be used in official transactions. After an increase in its price, it could henceforth be stabilized in terms of the international composite currency. Gold and the international commodity unit would then both be stable in terms of commodities and would be interchangeable with one another. Over time, the price of gold and the composite reserve currency would rise in terms of national currencies with the rates of inflation and depreciation against the international composite currency.[31]
15. The introduction of the international composite currency would be greatly facilitated in its early stages by its confidence-building identification with gold.[32] Any drain of gold from central banks could be replaced, if necessary, by an appropriate increase in the outstanding stock of the composite reserve currency.[33] The problem of recurrent breakdown and potential instability of the gold exchange standard would therefore be avoided by steps already in place for its successor.[34]
16. A special initial allocation of composite-currency-reserve units should be made to compensate for inequities arising from any aggravation of reserve maldistribution due to the official appreciation of gold, paying special attention to the reserve requirements of developing countries.[35]

These are some of the characteristics that would be desirable in the international monetary system of the next century. What are the prospects that discussions of international monetary reform will be brought to the front burner?

7 The Political Possibilities Schedule

International monetary reform will as always be driven by political as well as economic factors. The history of the international monetary system has been tied up with the nature of leadership and domination in the international economy. The possibility of reform is a function of the power configuration of the international economy and especially the relation between dominant powers and their rivals.

The self-interest of a big power with a dominant key currency lies in resisting change; international monetary reform can only limit its ability to dominate. A corollary is that ambitious would-be rivals which vex under domination seek monetary reform to share the money power. The following propositions seem to be robust in different historical situations:

(A) The dominant country of a currency area has an effective veto over monetary alternatives.
(B) The dominant country of a currency area resists monetary reform.
(C) The dominant country of a currency area withdraws in transitional periods toward or away from dominance.
(D) The leadership rivals in the currency area seek monetary reform, usually in transition phases to accelerate the transition.
(E) The small countries acquiesce in the monetary leadership of the dominant power.
(F) International monetary systems do not change without warning; the rule is evolution and transition, not revolution. Changes therefore are predictable.
(G) Reserve currencies start off strong when they are scarce in world markets, but end up weak as they are expanded beyond the point of need.
(H) Dominant powers are unwilling to compromise on questions where national interest is in conflict with the general interest.
(I) Major independent powers want to hold some international reserves in gold rather than rely solely on foreign exchange reserves.

A few examples help to support these propositions:

(1) Proposals introduced by the international congresses devoted to international monetary reform in the nineteenth century were rejected by the leading power, Britain, which was perfectly happy with the dominant position of the pound. These congresses were sponsored mainly by France, a former leading power under bi-metallism, and the United States, an emerging leading power.

(2) The United States, an emerging dominant power after 1915, began to follow policies - noted in the Federal Reserve Report of 1923 - stressing monetary independence, geared to internal, rather than external balance.
(3) Britain opted out of the international monetary system in 1931 when it became clear that she had lost control of it.
(4) At the 1933 World Economic Conference, Britain and especially France pleaded for American cooperation in re-establishing the gold standard, but the United States, now a dominating power, cherished its own independence and rejected new international commitments, scuttling the conference.
(5) Britain, no longer the top country, proposed a world currency (bancor) in discussions about the post-war future, measures which it had consistently rejected when it was the top power.[36]
(6) The United States - now post-war superpower - rejected the idea for a world currency; the dollar would suffice.
(7) The United States selected the gold option in Article IV of the IMF articles, absolving it of the need to intervene in foreign exchange; this put the burden of intervention and balance-of-payments adjustment onto the other countries.
(8) The small countries gladly ratified the dollar-based Bretton Woods system and subscribed to its rules even though they had little role in negotiating the agreement.
(9) France, leader of the West African region in the first two post-war decades (and currently), and former world leader, challenged US dominance and proposed a return to a full gold standard.
(10) The United States vetoed the international gold standard proposed by France, as it had earlier rejected bancor, suggested by Britain.
(11) The United States accepted the SDR as a means of preserving the dollar-based system because, with a "gold-weight guarantee," it was a substitute for gold, not the dollar.
(12) The United States opted out of the gold exchange standard in August 1971 when it could no longer control the system.
(13) The United States agreed to the devaluation of the dollar at the Smithsonian meeting in 1971 because the dollar would not be convertible into gold even at its higher ($38) price; the system set up at the Smithsonian was an unanchored dollar standard.
(14) When, in 1973, the gold-weight guarantee was removed from the SDR, making it a potential alternative to the dollar, the United States treated it with benign neglect; it has never become an important force in the international monetary system.
(15) Germany, as the dominant power in the EMS rejected fixed rates relative to the dollar or yen because that would limit its own

monetary independence.

(16) On the other hand, France and Italy became the leading proponents of a European currency, as a preferred alternative to a Mark-denominated EMS.

(17) When West Germany became the regional superpower in the Europe of the 1970s, it resisted European monetary reform in the form of a European currency because that would limit its own sphere of action. For political reasons, however, the resistance was indirect, taking the side of the "economists" against the "monetarists" in the European debates of the 1970s and 1980's.

(18) There is ample proof of the predictability of changes in the international monetary system. The use of sterling as an overvalued supplement to gold in the late 1920's was anticipated by the use of sterling in British colonies and nations associated with Britain; Keynes' first book, *Indian Currency and Finance*, published in 1912, was an exposition of the gold exchange standard.[37] The rise of the dollar was also easily foreseen, long before the 1920's. Half a century earlier, in 1869, an elderly John Stuart Mill could foresee the dominance of the United States, long before the currency of the new giant displaced the pound sterling as top international money.

(19) Sterling was a strong reserve currency in the heyday of the gold standard, but weakened in the interwar period, and was dismantled as a reserve currency in the post-war period.

(20) The dollar was a strong reserve currency in the inter-war and early post-war periods, and continued to expand after the advent of flexible exchange rates; in the 1980's and 1990's, however, the dollar lost ground to the yen and especially the mark. Predictably for a leading country in a transition period, the United States, during the administration of President George Bush, de-emphasized international monetary arrangements.

(21) The United States gave over-riding priority to domestic stability during the post-war years and this even after the dollar-gold system had become threatened. Germany gave over-riding priority to domestic stability during the unification shock at the expense of its partners in the ERM.

(22) Central banks have revealed strong preferences for gold as part of foreign exchange reserves even when, under the Second Amendment to the Articles of Agreement in 1977, the international monetary authorities tried to phase gold out of the international monetary system. Even when the price of gold soared above $800 an ounce in early 1980, governments held onto gold[38] in the expectation either that it will maintain its purchasing power or that it will have a role in a reformed international monetary system.

The prospects for reform, therefore, will depend particularly on how the future is perceived by the United States, European countries and Japan. A redefined international monetary order would be possible only if it suited the interests of the major blocs, including not just Europe, North America and Japan, but also rising new powers in Asia and elsewhere. Such a coincidence of interests, however, is most likely at the beginning of periods of transition from one international power configuration to another, before confrontational positions have had time to develop.[39] Such a transition has now occurred with the end of the Cold War. From the standpoint of its political configuration, the world is less like the world of the last two decades than it is like the world of the inter-war period or even before World War I. The transition represents both an opportunity and a challenge.

It is inevitable that, in the 1990's, much of Europe's intellectual and negotiating energy will be taken up by the problems raised by the attempt to transform the European Monetary System into a monetary union. Paradoxically, however, EMU could accelerate international monetary reform if its own thrust to monetary cohesion challenged the position of the dollar and provoked the United States and Japan to work together to promote a new system for the convenience of countries not party to the EMU agreement. This might be either a rival G-2 monetary area, or a more far-reaching global reform in which the Community, reluctantly or otherwise, chose to participate.

An organization of the international monetary system around two or three large currency blocs should not be mistaken, however, for an international monetary order. Policies in each bloc would tend toward self-aggrandizement through discriminatory practices and preferences, often at the expense of the smaller countries. Bilateralism or trilateralism is no more desirable in the monetary sphere than it is in the trade sphere. Nor is it likely to satisfy the ambitions of the large developing countries which will emerge as important actors in the world system in the 21st century.

Monetary agreements have usually been a catalyst for cooperation on other matters where it is necessary to manage international interdependence, including political rapprochement. A new function of international monetary reform would be to head off confrontation between the United States and Europe. The mere attempt to define formally the parameters of a desirable international monetary order within the framework of a modified Bretton Woods Order would provide a useful forum for other forms of cooperation.

Europe should not forfeit its stake in the territory of international reform but, without sacrificing its goals of continental monetary unity, should itself collaborate to bring about a reformed system that would not only accommodate the interests of new currency areas like EMU, but also facilitate a desirable evolution of the international monetary order for countries outside such blocs. The path for Europe in the international monetary arena will lie in constructive cooperation rather than in confrontation or isolation.

As the currently dominant superpower, the United States is in a position to block international monetary reform. But economic power positions evolve over time. Dominance begets countervailing power and there will come a time when the United States is checked, or threatened, by opposing coalitions. For this reason it is in the U.S. long run interest to lead in the creation of a future international monetary framework of its own liking. The threat and counter-threat route of regionalism could be avoided by encouraging, through the International Monetary Fund, far-reaching reform in the direction of a stable international unit of account along the lines I have suggested.

NOTES

1. The United States, the other bimetallic power in the 19th century, had suspended convertibility during the Civil War and was to reject a restoration of bimetallism in 1873, when no provision was made for minting a silver dollar, and in 1879, when the United States joined the gold brigade.
2. The Swedish economist, Gustav Cassel, was alone among the economists of the inter-war period, who worried about the consequences of the world-wide gold shortage after the reestablishment of the gold standard in the 1920's. In 1928 he wrote that

   "the great problem before us is how to meet the growing scarcity of gold which threatens the world both from increased demand and from diminished supply. We must solve this problem by a systematic restriction of the monetary demand for gold. Only if we succeed in doing this can we hope to prevent a permanent fall of the general price level and a prolonged and world-wide depression which would inevitably be connected with such a fall in prices."

   It is hard to imagine a more prophetic voice. Yet Cassel apparently never considered the option, as an alternative to restriction of gold demand or deflation, of raising the price of gold. Clark Johnson, in a forthcoming doctoral dissertation at Yale University, has called my attention to the above quotation from Cassel.
3. It is clear that the founding architects of the Fund had not yet discovered the realities of an international monetary system with a dominant currency.
4. I have discussed this issue in Mundell (1993).
5. It is remarkable that the system should have come apart just after the introduction of the SDR. No doubt the recession of 1970-1, which lowered interest rates and weakened the dollar, was partly to blame, as was the mistaken U.S. policy mix with its excessively easy monetary policy in the year before the presidential elections. I believe, however, that the real explanation lies elsewhere.

   With the creation of the gold-weight-guaranteed SDR, international officials had in their hands a weapon for relieving the "shortage" of gold without raising its price. According to the schedule of SDR allocations adopted in 1968, the total gold liquidity of about \$35 billion would have been supplemented by almost \$9 billion of SDRs by the end of 1972, an increase of over 25 per cent. With the possibility of future additions as needed, an SDR system could have been developed, gradually replacing any losses of gold to the private market with SDRs.

A more basic reason for the closing of the gold window by the United States in 1971 was the curious mixture of monetarism and keynesianism in the U.S. cabinet and hostility to the idea of an international monetary system in the U.S. Treasury.

6. A major reason is that Britain and France had not yet acknowledged the DM to be the "anti-dollar".

7. Errors have a tendency to perpetuate themselves when the lessons are not learned from them. The core problem in the 1920's was the undervaluation of gold against all currencies, misdiagnosed as a problem of the sterling-dollar exchange rate; and the problem in the 1960's and early 1970's was the problem of the undervaluation of gold against all currencies, misdiagnosed as a problem of the dollar-mark or dollar-yen exchange rate.

This description, however, is a slight oversimplification insofar as the creation of the gold-guaranteed SDR's indicated that many of the officials at the time did understand the problem. It is hard to reconcile the great effort to solve the liquidity problem through a gold substitute in 1968 with the deliberate destruction of the system in 1971, until it is realized that the Nixon administration had very different priorities and experience in these issues than the Johnson administration.

8. Astonishingly, in their announcement of the fateful step, the Committee of Twenty noted their intention to abandon the idea of international monetary reform "until the inflation problem had been solved," as if the central goal of international monetary reform were not the collective achievement of a stable price level!

9. Notably in the person of Dr. George Shultz, Secretary of the Treasury and, as Dean of the Graduate School of Business at the University of Chicago, a former colleague of Milton Friedman. Credit or blame for the new arrangements must also rest with Giscard d'Estaing and Helmut Schmidt.

10. One side-effect of the movement to flexible exchange rates was the displacement of the International Monetary Fund and its committee of deputies from the center of international monetary decision-making. In its mission "to promote exchange stability" the Fund had several functions: (a) to pass judgement on exchange rate changes; (b) to lend currencies to countries with deficits, with or without conditions while adjustment policies are taking effects; (c) to determine the adequacy of and make recommendations for increasing the level of international liquidity; (d) to provide technical assistance (consulting services) to individual countries; and (e) to gather statistics and other information relevant to the working of the international monetary system. Under flexible exchange rates, the first three functions all but disappeared, while the increasing sophistication of the poorer member countries rendered the need for consulting services increasingly redundant. To the extent that economic policy coordination was needed at all, it was carried out in the G-7 club. It began to appear, therefore, that under flexible exchange rates the role of the Fund had dwindled to fact-gathering and number-crunching, itself an activity that was being increasingly supplied by the commercial forecasting companies.

Nevertheless, three factors acted to compensate for the reduced need for the IMF in its original role: (a) in the 1970's, the instability of commodity prices that had been set in motion by the breakdown of the international monetary system; (b) in the 1980's, the debt crisis, also a function of the breakdown of the system; and (c) in the 1990's, the collapse of the Soviet Union and the creation of a large number of independent countries with a considerable demand for free consulting services. These activities have helped to justify the Fund's existence and its vast increase in staff, now exceeding 2,250.

In an important sense, however, the Fund has served to promote itself as an institution more than it has served as a satisfactory monitor or "guardian" - as J. J. Polak puts it - of the international monetary system. While the fixed exchange system was in operation, the Fund defended it in its annual reports with a truly missionary zeal, denouncing and deriding the idea of flexible exchange rates; see the IMF Annual Reports for 1951 and 1962. But after the Second Amendment's endorsement of "managed flexible rates", the IMF staff has shown equal fervor in denouncing fixed exchange rates or currency areas. In short, the Fund proved itself to be - and it still is - a supporter of the *status quo* and an enemy of international monetary reform, suppressing dissent and controversy among its staff whenever it threatened to undermine the monolithic image of the corporate credo.

The Fund's role as a self-protective institution has usurped its role as an impartial monitor of the system. The major cost of this attitude is that the Fund has ceased to be a center of intellectual discussion about the working and evolution of the system itself. This is just as true in the 1980's and 1990's as it was in the 1950's and 1960's.

11. Germany had suffered the tremendous shock of unification which it financed by government debt rather than taxation. Simultaneously there was an expansionary fiscal policy and a tight monetary policy, resulting in currency appreciation. (An analogous policy mix, but with supply-side effects, was introduced in the United States in the first administration of President Ronald Reagan.) The incipient appreciation of the DM lifted all the other currencies that adhered to the ERM. At a time when Europe was entering a recession, the appreciation imposed intolerable deflationary pressure on the countries outside the inner DM area, leading Italy, Britain and Spain to opt out of the ERM or undergo a realignment within it.

Under a post-EMU Europe-wide monetary policy the resolution of the German shock would have been different. The rest of Europe could have provided a better cushion for the German disequilibrium. The actual outcome would depend on the policies followed by the European Central Bank. If the latter had followed a monetary policy that fixed the ecu to the dollar over the period of the disequilibrium, the German fiscal policy would have raised European interest rates and attracted capital to Europe from the United States and Japan, cushioning the unification shock by inter-temporal expenditure smoothing. Alternatively, a fixed rate of ecu-money expansion would have lifted interest rates and induced an ecu appreciation, but smaller than that which occurred in the summer of 1992.

The defect of a DM area is that German production, important though it is, represents less than 8 per cent of the world economy. What happens if equilibrium requires that German prices rise relative to prices in the rest of the world? Under the Bundesbank regime, the rest of Europe would have to deflate. Alternatively, if equilibrium requires that German prices fall, the rest of the world would have to inflate. The 8 per cent of the world economy represented by Germany constitutes too narrow an anchor for a Europe-wide currency. With a transactions area thrice that of Germany's, even the dollar proved to be unsatisfactory. An EMU area would be better for Europe than the DM area.

12. See, however, Mundell (1971a).

13. Thus if R represents dollars issued by the Federal Reserve, and D represents demand deposits assumed to be a multiple of R, the total domestic money supply would be $M = R + D$, where $R = aD$. If, however, part of D is held in a London bank, it can be used as a reserve for additional monetary expansion equal to $M'' = D''/b$ where b is the London reserve ratio and D" are demand deposits in London. The total amount of money created is therefore $M^* = M' + M'' = R + D' + D''/b$, where $R = aD = a(D' + D'')$ and therefore, $M^* = (1+a)D' + (a + 1/b)D''$.

14. To go in reverse direction, try to imagine the social cost of having several currencies fluctuating vis-a-vis one another in the United States; this social cost for the United States was avoided by the creation of a single currency back in 1792. A similar gain could be achieved, in principle, by the creation of a single currency for the world economy.
15. National currencies connected by fixed spot and forward exchange rates would have most of the properties of a common currency. There would still be information costs involved in translating one set of currency values into another.

    It is perhaps not necessary to mention that the concept of optimality involved in the statement that "a world currency is optimal" is different from the optima usually derived from completely general conventional individual utility functions; on the *highest* level of generality it is not possible to prove that a large country is better off with a common currency than with fifty or a million different currencies. The unit-of-account function of currencies requires the adoption of a *convention* by which members of a group choose the same unit of measurement. For example, most countries use one system of measurement (English or metric), one calendar, one time zone, one language and one set of laws to maximize the gains from centralization, and minimization of the costs of information. There is a sense in which singularity is optimal and the benefits of diversity can be achieved only at considerable costs.

    If, for example, rates of inflation entered as an independent argument in individual utility functions, and inflation preferences were different, it could not be proved that inflation-lowers would not be prepared to sacrifice the bonus of a common currency for a particular rate of inflation. For example, if residents of Massachusetts were inflation-lovers, and, of Illinois, deflation-lovers, the former might be willing to sacrifice the gains from a common currency for a higher rate of inflation, and the latter, for a lower rate of inflation. One implicit assumption underlying the argument that a single currency is optimum is that the social cost of a convention that standardizes the rate of inflation (in terms of a common basket of goods and services) is less than the benefits from a common unit of account. Throughout history, however, most countries have revealed their preferences for a common unit of account. The same holds, internationally, to the extent that different countries elected to adopt the same metal (usually silver or gold) as the base for their monetary unit and thus base fixed exchange rates on the metallic content of their currencies.

    Another implicit assumption relates to the cost of dispensing with national inflation taxes as a source of government revenue. Under flexible exchange rates large countries whose currencies are also used by foreign countries and international institutions can shift part of the burden of the inflation tax onto the rest of the world, along the lines of the optimum tariff in the theory of trade; see Mundell (1971b). The implicit assumption is again that just as every province, county and municipality in a nation-state sacrifices its monetary autonomy and the fiscal use of the inflation tax, so countries would sacrifice monetary autonomy and the inflation tax in an international system. Under both the bimetallic and gold standards, the use of inflation as a fiscal device was by and large ruled out. Under an international system, a participating country's share in the seigniorage rights (and the proceeds from any inflation tax) of the international authority would tend to be larger or smaller than under the national system depending inversely on its power position in the world economy.

    Another implicit assumption (not unrelated to the first two) is that the monetary policy of the central authority is optimal, or at least not worse than the monetary policies of the formerly-decentralized unit.
16. Horsefield (1969).

17. Maintaining the gold guarantee would have increased the "public-money" component of the system beyond the amount the major countries would tolerate.
18. Europe's ecu suffers from the same defects as the SDR; see for example, Riboud (1989). Riboud's proposal for an ecu of constant purchasing power could be generalized for a the world economy.
19. The analogy of the SDR for European Monetary Union would be the definition of the ecu in terms of two or three of the major currencies, leaving out the smaller countries. The political analogy would be delegating control of international politics to a small group of the largest powers, as with the G-7 club.
20. The SDR is further removed from the role of money by the fact that it has become an interest-bearing asset, a feature that encourages its role as an asset to store rather than a money to circulate.
21. Fortunately, the United States has confined its aggressive bilateralism to what it perceives as defensive actions. However, the health of the international monetary system should not have to depend on the benevolence of the superpower. There was nothing optimal about the currency area formed by Hitler when the Nazis controlled the European Continent.
22. Ever since the 1930's there has been a debate among economists over whether the threat of depleting international reserves (under fixed rates) or the threat of currency depreciation (under flexible rates) is more of a deterrent to inflationary monetary policies. From the evidence of the 1970's and 1980's it seems to me clear that the former is the better deterrent. This is partly because Keynesian economists frequently urge depreciation as a means of stimulating employment, while monetarist economists praise fluctuations in exchange rates as evidence of the working of a "free" market.
23. The move toward EMU would be facilitated by restricting it to a narrower core of countries ready for it (regardless of the somewhat gratuitous requirements of the Maastricht agreement). If Germany, Holland, France, Belgium and Luxembourg moved quickly toward EMU, forming the ecu on which the future currency would build, the other countries could enter as soon as their economic conditions permitted. To this natural economic bloc, other countries, including Denmark and Austria could quickly adhere, forming the basis for a substantial currency bloc which Italy and Britain and the other countries would soon find it in their interests to join.
24. For further discussions of these issues see Mundell (1993b).
25. For a discussion of the significance of factor price equalization areas see Mundell (1993c,d).
26. This section builds on and replaces my presentation in Mundell (1993e).
27. In the first phase of the introduction of the composite currency, the value of the commodities in the basket could be determined in terms of a major currency such as the dollar, and then defining the appreciation of the composite currency by the rate of the inflation of the basket in term of the dollar.
28. Such a provision is somewhat similar to the procedure in which the French Treasury guarantees the exchange rate of the CFA franc.
29. Under the original Articles a country was required to maintain the gold value of the Fund's holdings of a country's currency.
30. The political arguments that squelched a proposal to double the price of gold in terms of all currencies (a universal halving of all par values) in the 1950's and 1960's no longer have any relevance. Failing international action on a moderate increase in the price in the 1960's, the price actually rose by a factor of ten or more, benefitting governments in South Africa and the Soviet Union much more than the proposals of the advocates of an increase in price (like Sir Roy Harrod, Professor Rueff, etc.). With rare exceptions, central banks have chosen to hang onto gold even when gold prices

were far above levels expected to be sustainable. Rather than trying in vain to reduce the importance of gold, the international monetary authorities would be better advised to find a way to put it to useful work.

31. Under these arrangements gold would increase or decrease in importance as a reserve in the international monetary system depending on whether its real price fell or rose. If its real price rose over time--as most people who object to the use of gold in the international monetary system have believed--gold would eventually be phased out of the system. Because this would be a matter of decades rather than years, however, the interim period of transition would provide time for confidence to be built in the new international composite reserve currency.
32. This solution would be closer, as earlier implied, to the intent of the First Amendment of the Articles of Agreement of the IMF establishing the gold-guaranteed SDR. It would, however, be free of the defects of that arrangement in that the real value of the composite currency and gold would be maintained in the future.
33. This mechanism bears some similarity to the mechanism for stabilizing international reserves under proposals for a gold substitution fund made by the Committee of Ten Deputies of the IMF after the breakdown of the system in 1971.
34. In an earlier paper, Mundell (1968), I used the term *intor* to designate the future world currency, an update on Keynes' gold-convertible *bancor*.
35. Sir Roy Harrod made a similar proposal over two decades ago.
36. On this and the following point, it is illuminating to read the diaries of Lionel Robbins and James Meade; those two distinguished economists were members of the British delegation that in the fall of 1943 met with their counterparts in Washington to plan the post-war institutions. The following passage is one of many that make the point: "Keynes then in a brilliant speech expounded the case for making Unitas into a real transferable money, and dealt with all the main British points...He argued that all these and many other points could be allowed for with much more ease and neatness if Unitas was made a real money. Bernstein seemed willing to consider all these points seriously except the making of Unitas into a real money." See Howson and Moggridge (1990). The reference is to Dr. E. M. Bernstein, Assistant Director of Monetary Research in the U.S. Treasury between 1941 and 1946, and the first Director of Research of the IMF between 1946 and 1958.
37. Earlier, the breakdown of the international monetary system in the 1790's occurred after the Revolution and the assignat inflation in France, then the most powerful country in Europe. The restoration of bimetallism in France in 1803 was forced on Napoleon to restore the new Emperor's credit. The trend toward gold in the 19th century became evident soon after the Californian and Australian discoveries drove silver out of monetary circulation in France, the pivot bimetallic country.
38. In 1992 a few central banks, including Holland, Belgium and Canada, sold several hundred tons of gold, depressing the price below $330 per ounce, only to see it rebound temporarily to over $400 in 1993 in the absence of such sales, fed by speculation and rumors that a significant upward movement was in the offing.
39. The Bretton Woods agreement was made during such a transition. in the heat of a world war. It is doubtful that the United States and the major countries on the continent of Europe could have concluded such an agreement two decades later in the 1960's.

REFERENCES

Horsefield, J. Keith, (1969). The International Monetary Fund, 1945-1965. Washington, D.C.: The International Monetary Fund, Vol. I, p. 12.

Howson, Susan and Donald Moggridge, (eds.) 1990. The Wartime Diaries of Lionel Robbins and James Meade 1943-45. London: MacMillan, 1990, p. 114.

Mundell, Robert A., 1968. "A Plan for a World Currency," U.S. Congressional Hearings, Subcommittee (Reuss) on International Monetary Reform, Joint Economic Committee of the U.S. Congress, Washington, September 9.

___, 1971a. "World Inflation and the Eurodollar," Note Economiche, No. 2.

___, 1971b. "The Optimum Balance of Payments Deficit and the Theory of Empires," in P. Salin and E. Claassen (eds.), Stabilization Policies in Interdependent Economies. Amsterdam: North-Holland Press, 1971, 69-86.

___, 1993a. "Tales from the Bretton Woods," in M. Bordo and B. Eichengreen (eds.), Retrospective on the Bretton Woods System. Cambridge, MA: National Bureau of Economic Research.

___, 1993b. "EMU and the International Monetary System," Working Paper No. 13, Österreichische Nationalbank.

___, 1993c. "Economic Convergence and the Theory of Factor Price Equalization Areas," Rivista di Politica Economica.

___, 1993d. "Economic Convergence in the North American Free Trade Area," in F. Saddiqui (ed.) The North American Free Trade Area. Sherbrooke, Quebec: Bishop's University Press.

___, 1993e. "EMU and the Definition of a New International Monetary Order," in Lyon Monetary Talks. Lyon: ECU Institute, June.

Riboud, Jacques, (1989). Theoretical Foundation of a Constant External Money and Its Applications. Paris: Centre Jouffroy pour la Reflexion Monétaire.

Discussion

EUGENE ROTBERG

I have just finished reading Robert Mundell's excellent historical summary and recommendations for the International Monetary System. Indeed, I find that it is so thorough and balanced that there is little that I could add or refine through peripheral comment. It may be useful, however, in the context of his macroeconomic analysis, to share with you how the private financial sector responded to the events of the last 25 years. I cannot say, with any degree of sureness, which of the events and activities which I describe below were causes of the turmoil described in Bob's excellent piece and which were occasioned by the macroeconomic forces he set out in his paper. I suspect, to use that awful cliche, that it's a "chicken and egg" problem, and that it is both cause and effect, and that, in any event, it cannot be unscrambled, etc. The cliches are probably right. It is even difficult to know what would have been politically feasible to cope with the fallout from domestic and international deregulation of interest rates and exchange rates.

Nonetheless, it is useful, I hope, to set out "what happened" in the private financial sector. My notes here are divided into three parts: first, a reminiscence of the financial developments in industrialized countries over the last several decades; second, an analysis of the cumulative effect of the environment on financial institutions; and, third, an examination of the concerns of official institutions in making wise and fair policy in the context of the pressures on and activities of private financial intermediaries. This text is but a collection of notes. I ask you, therefore, to bear with me if my comments are overstated, repetitious, or elliptical. My thesis here is a straightforward one: competition amongst financial intermediaries, given information and accounting systems, created a highly risk-oriented and potentially destabilizing financial environment. But I am already getting ahead of myself. Let me start with a review of some of the significant developments over the last 25 years.

1 The Environment

- Floating exchange rates. At first the world was fixed. Then the Yen, for example, went from 360 to the dollar to 300 to 240 to 200 to 300 to 120 to 100 - with many changes of direction in between. That volatility, which occurred in many currencies, created the incentive to speculate on potential exchange rate movements - or if possible, to cause them. That, in turn, led to market risk and a proliferation of products for protection and speculation.

- Volatile interest rates. In the United Stated, long-term interests moved one percent in the period, 1955-1965. Since then, long-term rates have moved from 7 % to 15 %, down to 8 %, risen to 12 %, down to 6-1/2 %. Short-term dollar rates have similarly fluctuated between 3 % and 20% and everywhere in between. That kind of volatility also led to the potential for profit by speculating on interest rate movements. That, in turn, put financial intermediaries at risk -- particularly if they were mismatched, as many were, between the asset and liability side of their balance sheets. It also created an environment for proprietary risk taking and trading where gains might be garnered intra-day.

- Shifts in savings flows: build-ups in Japan, Germany, elsewhere in Europe and Asia, OPEC. Governments soon permitted the tapping of domestic savings by borrowers and investors outside their domestic borders, both in dollars and local currency - and by "foreign" intermediaries. That, in turn, added to the competitive pressures on domestic financial institutions.

- Deregulation of financial intermediaries let everyone in on everyone else's traditional line of business. In industrialized countries, insurance companies, banks, pension funds, securities firms all competed for savings worldwide and offered remarkably similar products. Financial monopolies were dismantled.

- Lowest-common-denominator regulatory and supervisory controls. If a financial intermediary could not offer particular services because of national controls, it moved its operation to a more accommodating environment. Or, if the site became too intrusive, financial institutions shifted to a different product, say, foreign exchange trading, where controls and regulation were less sophisticated or invasive.

- Products incorporating floating or short term interest rates provided a natural hedge against inflation. It also provided a vehicle for playing the yield curve, basis trades and taking on large longer-term positions if the cost to carry in the short-term markets were favourable.

- Communications let everyone know what all markets and participants were doing and seeing at the same time. That, in turn, narrowed spreads between buyers and sellers. However, the efficiency of the information increased volatility because high levels of volume become destabilizing when markets are aware of and respond to the same information. The narrowing spreads between buyers and sellers, a natural consequence of the number and capital of the players, inexorably damaged middle man profitability. The increased liquidity, however, did not reduce volatility given the immediacy of the information flow. It increased it.

- Dis-intermediation: money market funds vs. bank deposits; commercial paper vs. loans; short-dated governments vs. C.D.'s; securitized mortgages vs. bonds. That permitted each product to "cannibalize" the savings base.

- Clients developed market expertise and capacity to deal with each other. That removed the necessity for the use of any financial intermediary between the ultimate buyer and seller.

- An accommodating accounting system that permitted failure and risk to stay undisclosed because of the practice throughout the world of not marking assets to market - despite their depreciating value.

- Very high compensation and an asymmetrical one, at that. That permitted risks to be taken by managers and traders with the potential for high rewards for getting it right with little downside penalty for loss.

- Government insurance of the funding source for banking institutions. In the United States the FDIC and the FSLIC insured the banks and S&L's, while at the same time deregulating how the deposits could be used. That removed the creditor as a constraining influence over the deployment of assets as governments permitted a wide range of investments for banks and thrift institutions. In a sense, the liability side of the balance sheet was nationalized; the asset side privatized.

- Direct and substantial government intervention into foreign exchange and credit markets. That meant a non-market-driven force would directly intervene in the market, but as a non-profit-driven player. That provided a potential source of profit for the private financial intermediary. Moreover, combined with depositary insurance, it meant that banks could now speculate on the value of a currency -- in an adversarial position against their own government or Central Bank with the government locked into making political, not financial, decisions. Yet the banks' funding for such activity was financed and guaranteed by the official sector. Governments therefore, found that (a) they were in an adversary position to their banks; (b) they did not have the resources of the private sector in conducting FX activity; (c) they were making political, not market-based decisions; and (d) they founded and guaranteed their market adversaries. Not a happy situation for Central Banks.

- Securitization. As a practical matter, that meant if you could sell an asset after putting it on your books, you need not worry about credit quality. Someone else would pick up the pieces. Securitization and the prospects for immediate liquidity, I believe, over time, damaged the normal attention to prudential credit assessment.

- Highly disparate regulatory controls across countries.

- Finally, financial engineering. It gave great advantage to first users. But it was easily imitated by others. Even the most sophisticated products could be replicated because of broad skills, communications and information technology. Arbitrage opportunities were quickly identified and disappeared. But more important, the products were complex, leveraged, not readily understood by managers or regulators, and off balance sheet, which meant that they were and are "unrecorded" with unknown or uncertain risk and not readily subject to capital requirements.

Such was the environment.

2 The Result

That brings me to my second point - the result: substantial competition and pressures on profitability in a volatile environment - all in the context of rather uncertain managerial and government expertise. But, again, I am getting ahead of myself. Let me comment on the competitive pressures.

There developed tremendous worldwide competition amongst financial intermediaries for five things: (1) for savings, (2) for new, and hopefully not easily replicated, products, particularly if off balance sheet, (3) for a protected or monopolistic position, or, if that were not available, the first contact point between buyer and seller, or between borrower and investor, (4) for methods to create liquidity for the sale of assets once not marketable, and (5) for a non-regulated environment.

Basically, over the last two decades, financial intermediaries sought to replicate each other's "historic" profit centre, as if these profit centres were infinitely expanding ones. It was as if profitability for a few firms from a particular line of business could be replicated by 50 firms worldwide, consistently. That was not the case. For example, firms sought to establish a trading capacity, as agents, but quickly spreads narrowed -- too many players, too much information, too much volatility for reasonably certain returns. Many firms shifted to financial engineering, but that, too, could be replicated, and arbitrage opportunities quickly disappeared even for the sophisticated players. Positioning was dangerous given the volatility, and shifts in the slope of the yield curve made the cost of carry uncertain. We became over-banked, over-securitized with some players protected, others not, because of diverse regulatory requirements within a country as well as across countries. There were, and are, simply too many intermediaries seeking the same investors or borrowers as access opened up worldwide. At the same time, the preoccupation with liquidity - with securitization - almost by definition contributed to an underestimation of market risk and a disdain for attention to creditworthiness - all furthered by unrealistic accounting conventions.

The effect of the pressures on profitability and of dis-intermediation should not be underestimated. I believe it directly resulted in the relaxation of regulatory standards which permitted, in an effort to foster profitability, high-risk assets to be taken on the books of S&L's and insurance companies in the United States -- permitted because their traditional profitability had been eroded by the dis-intermediation and narrow spreads on their traditional lines of business. All this was facilitated by government insurance of the deposits and accommodating accounting conventions.

Let me go back to the complexity of the products and management responsibility. Derivative products put considerable strain on senior management and on customers and regulators to evaluate risk and profitability. This, in large part, was due to the fact that there were, literally, scores of complex, highly-leveraged products, painstakingly constructed, for which there was little empirical experience to define and circumscribe the underlying risk. Moreover, even to the extent it was known (and it sometimes was not), the risk profile of the new instruments was (and is) too often kept solely within the trading community and operators, and not readily shared with managers. There were also pressures simply to skirt the edge of legality, sell to the least sophisticated, seek a marginal advantage -- sometimes for a few moments in a highly competitive world.

The key, inevitably, was to find a product which permitted leverage, minimal capital, few regulatory controls, low expense to operate, and proprietary risk taking where the other side is a non-market player who could not act rationally for political reasons. Foreign exchange trading -- in all of its arcane forms. I believe when the other avenues of profit shut down, foreign exchange became the new game in town -- an unregulated and one-sided game where the Central Bank could not act as a rational market player, did not have the staying power, and, in any event, was and is ambivalent about damaging institutions whose deposits it guarantees and whose viability it needs to finance domestic deficits.

Another major effect of the competitive pressures on financial institutions was felt on the day-to-day operations of U.S. commercial banks. They were and are subject to an unhappy combination of incentives: (a) over-banking - worldwide; (b) the holding of illiquid assets which, once made, were difficult to divest, despite the advances in "securitization;" (c) an accounting treatment which did not mark assets to market and which, in turn, diminished, inexorably, attention to credit quality; (d) competition for funds from money market funds, as well as for clients to lend to (they had other alternatives such as the securities markets); (e) a narrowing of spreads between the total cost of funding and the return on loans. (Indeed, the extreme reversal of that condition is the only reason for current bank profitability in the U. S.); (f) diminished U. S. economic activity ; and (g) rising skills, resources and requirements outside the United States. U.S. banks, inexorably, were under pressures to find ways to increase their margins to achieve a return on their equity. Given federal insurance in the U.S., it was clear they would lend in new areas with the highest potential profit margins despite the traditional tests of prudence - unproven agricultural land, energy exploration with equity kickers, illiquid LDC loans, junk bonds, etc. And the latest intervention - to put them into the high risk but low profitability securities business - will simply, I predict, create further risk and pressures on both the securities firms and the banks, with an inevitable tendency to create decent returns on equity by more and more leveraged and off balance sheet activity. There are simply too many financial intermediaries and already too many in each other's lines of business.

All of this took place in institutions with weak management. The world has simply moved too fast, even for most senior managers. Let me read to you how a trader described in a popular publication how he uses derivative products:

> *On the risk management side the bank runs five separate books: a spread book, a volatility book, a basis book, a yield-curve book and a directional book. The spread book trades swap spreads using Treasuries to hedge medium-to-long-dated swaps and a combination of futures and Treasuries for the short term. The volatility book makes markets in caps, floors and swaptions as well as captions, floortions and spreadtions. The basis book deals with the spread between different floating rate indices, such as Prime and CP versus Libor. The last two books are structured to arbitrage changes in the steepness of the curve as well as overall movements in interest rates.*

I doubt that his CEO was equipped to supervise that operation. Nor, moreover, was, or is, the regulatory agencies throughout the world. Nor can they efficiently assess the implications of these activities for the execution of public policy (say, in executing monetary policy), for the maintenance of fair and orderly markets, for the establishment of capital requirements or the risk potential of the underlying activity.

For S&L's, a banking subset in the U.S., the result was almost predetermined. Specifically, the mess had as its antecedents (a) the lifting of the interest rates that S&L's could pay on deposits; (b) the general deregulation over how S&L' s might invest those deposits beyond residential home mortgages; (c) a determined relaxation of supervision over such investments; (d) government insurance; and (e) the maintenance of an infamous accounting convention -- "a rolling loan gathers no loss." It was, and is, a structure virtually guaranteed to result in an unwise deployment of insured deposits because there is no potential private creditor loser.

The unhappy reality is that an accounting system which does not mark loans or assets to their market value, until sold, inevitably encourages flawed decision-making -- both for banking institutions and for securities firms. A system which provides government insurance and deregulates the deployment of assets, permits financial institutions to avoid a "market" test and to expand into a wide range of new markets and products was bound to run into trouble -- particularly given the minimal equity capital commitment of the owners. It inevitably will put pressure on all financial intermediaries and inevitably will cause them to seek out highly leveraged products or activities. With each failure or shutting down of a profit centre, the next has even greater potential for damage. As I noted before, the name of the game, I believe, will be Foreign Exchange trading.

3 Conclusion

Permit me to summarize and pull some of this together.

As profitability has eroded in traditional lines of protected businesses for all of the reasons I have noted, the risk is that there has been a seriatim of problems: junk bonds; capitalization of interest; huge losses on complex derivative products; an S&L crisis in the U.S. As each problem dissipates with a lot of damage in its wake, firms seek another profit centre: a controlled repo market, the use of equity derivatives to accelerate a decline in the Japanese market, foreign exchange speculation to test whether a government can match the strength of the private sector. The financial intermediaries - the banks and securities firms - have now become very powerful and destabilizing players, seeking out the least regulated and leveraged sector. It certainly will make difficult governments' attempts to allocate resources and make economic policy. This, of course, some would argue, is an appropriate constraint. Let the private sector decide. But, I would repeat, those intermediaries are also acting - some of them (perhaps most) - with direct government explicit backing.

That now brings me to some final points which, because of time constraints, I can only briefly note here - what do governments and Central Banks, worldwide, worry about, in the context of the financial environment. What are the choices and dilemmas they face?

- How to encourage banks to be prudent about lending without constraining their lending. The United States is a good example. The banking excesses and the warnings from the authorities have "cooled" bank lending - perhaps too much given the state of the economy. Increased capital requirements designed to protect the taxpayer inexorably reduce credit extension. Once burned, twice shy.

- How to maintain both an adversarial and supportive relationship with financial institutions, particularly in the context of institutions who may be acting in ways inconsistent with national policy in, say, FX trading, given the unique relationships between banks and the government.

- How to control banks who set up subsidiary activities offshore where there are few supervisory or regulatory controls and where, as a practical matter, any losses will be borne by the parent and its insured depositors.

- How to assess and set capital requirements for derivative products -- across countries and different kinds of financial institutions, including non-banks.

- How to mark assets to market without destroying confidence in the banking system.

- How to control (or whether to control) the credit extending activities and the speculative activities of non-banks - particularly in areas which directly affect national monetary policy.

- How to create an environment for banking institutions which is conductive to profitability when there are so many financial intermediaries and products worldwide competing for the same customer base.

- How to regulate the activities of "foreign" banks where those banks often represent savings from other countries which are needed for domestic growth.

- Governments are concerned about the domino syndrome. Too many intermediaries, too many non-creditworthy borrowers, too much expertise outside of government, too many loopholes, too much leverage, too much off-balance sheet.

- How to adjust interest rates to be sector-specific; say, to apply only to FX speculation. The freedom to move currencies across countries means exchange rate stability will be difficult to establish. Moreover, transactions are done routinely which, in the U.S., would result in severe criminal penalties. It is not a market which would survive careful scrutiny, say, by the United States SEC, without resulting in numerous indictments.

These are not easy problems to handle. Their "resolution" would require an international consensus which does not now exist. It also would involve a resolution of competing and divergent principles of regulation and control both within and across countries. Private sector management clearly needs to be better informed, as do governments and Central Banks, about the intricacies of market products. And the basic relationship among governments, taxpayers and financial institutions needs to be continuously reviewed and rationalized. It is a challenging and forbidding agenda.

Discussion

LARS THUNHOLM

Let me start by quoting the recent annual report of the Bank of International Settlements, when it says - with some understatement - that "the period under review has witnessed the most significant events in the international monetary system since the breakdown of the Bretton Woods arrangements twenty years ago." The Bank refers, of course, to the turmoil in the foreign exchange markets during the latter half of 1992. I am afraid the bank will have to repeat this statement - with some stronger wording - when they come to write the report for 1993, in view of the no less spectacular turmoil that played havoc with the markets in the spring and summer of this year.

The violent foreign exchange crises we have experienced in Europe since last year has, I am afraid, profoundly shaken our confidence in the present system of international monetary relations. One currency after the other has been the object of strong speculative attacks, to which one after the other has succumbed, in spite of massive central bank interventions and decisive recourse to the interest rate weapon. Even the currency that was backed by some of the strongest fundamentals, the "franc fort", had to give up the fight. In the end, the ERM system of fixed exchange rates broke down.

The immediate cause of these calamities is, of course, what is loosely referred to as "speculation". The attacks emanated from the enormous pools of funds that are sloshing around the world's financial markets in amounts of astronomical figures, jumping in and out of different currencies, seeking a safe haven or protection against financial losses, or just out for making a speculative profit. The enormous size of the pool of international assets and claims and the growth of their volume over the years is well illustrated by the figures given in professor Mundell's paper. We can also follow the substantial variations in the kind of international intermediation reflected in these figures in the current statistics of the BIS. Take, for instance, the developments over the last years. Net international bank credit in the area reporting to the BIS increased by the amount of 400 to 460 billion dollars in the years 1989 and 1990, whereas the increase was only 80 billion in 1991, then rose to 200 billion dollars in 1992. In part, the variations are due to fluctuations in the general business situation that influence lending to non-bank borrowers, but mainly they reflect the flow of funds between banks caused by developments in the foreign exchange area.

The enormous volume of international financial assets, and the great variations in cross-border financial transactions constitute no doubt an element of precarious instability in the international monetary system. We are well aware of the origin of these funds. They have to do with the far-reaching internationalisation of banking business, the emergence and growth of the eurocurrency activities, the growth of multinational enterprise in the areas of industry, trade and shipping, the currency diversification of investment portfolios etc. And the cross-border transactions have been facilitated by the spectacular development of information technology. Nowadays, at the touch of a button funds can be transferred to every corner of the world.

As illustrated by the recent foreign-exchange crises, these cross-border funds and their mobility can cause overwhelming pressures on the monetary authorities, and set definite limits to the effects of central bank interventions in support of weak currencies, or to the use of the interest rate weapon. Central banks have learnt that there is no way to stop an avalanche. But it is not only the monetary authorities that suffer. The prevailing instability causes great problems for the business community, adding significantly to the many uncertainties and hazards of economic life. True, the techniques of protecting firms against currency risks have been greatly improved. But hedging is usually a costly affair, and adds a lot to the regular transaction cost involved in all foreign exchange transactions.

In some quarters the power of "speculators" has caused a reaction in the form of a call for controls over the movements of speculative funds or a taxing of foreign exchange transactions in order to stem the flows. Typically such calls come particularly from France, which has a strong "dirigiste" tradition. The French prime minister, stung in his national pride, went on record to state that the ERM crisis had not been caused by the franc's weakness but by the deliberate attempt of the 'market' to break the EMS. And he called for reforms to tame wild speculators. But we know that nothing will come out of such wishes, as the sheer impracticality of instituting or maintaining such controls in the world of today make them wellnigh impossible.

Professor Mundell makes the distinction between beneficial forms of international financial intermediation and malignant ones, and even makes a calculation, admittedly very hypothetical, of the welfare cost to the world economy of the so-called malignant operations. I am rather sceptical of such a distinction, let alone the attempt to assess any welfare costs related to it. Nowadays, the world is one financial market, international intermediation has been of great benefit to the world economy and to individual nations. What we call speculation has helped the market to function like a free market, whether we like it or not. The forces of the market brought the exchange rate mechanism down. Was that a malignant action? I think not. The system had become too rigid, unrealistic in the present recession, and I think it was a good thing that 'speculators" killed it.

To be realistic, we must admit that what is called speculation is a symptom of monetary instability, not the cause of it. If we want to reduce the disturbing effects of speculative funds, the way must be to try to improve the stability of the international monetary system. The lack of confidence that make these funds move around will exist as long as the credibility of the international monetary order is under doubt. We can understand that such is the case today. Since the breakdown of the Bretton Woods system in the early 1970's the world has not had a structured, regulated international monetary system based upon a set of rules that are accepted and respected by the major nations. As a consequence we have had to live with recurrent currency crises. The question to be answered is: will we be able to reestablish such a system, bringing order instead of chaos, promoting the desirable measure of stability to the world economy, affording a durable basis for free trade and a sufficient flow of international investments?

The problem before us is not a technical problems. As we all know, there is no lack of ingenuity among central bankers or economists in devising plans and blueprints for such a system. What has failed, and is still failing, is the political will among nations to accept all the implications of such plans, namely above all the necessity to coordinate and harmonize national macroeconomic policies in a way that could reinstall the confidence of the market and make possible a smooth functioning and stability of the international monetary system.

The principal political difficulty of designing a viable international monetary system has by somebody been called the "inconsistent quartet": a group of countries cannot simultaneously have free trade, full mobility of capital, fixed exchange rates, and autonomous national economic policies. To make a system viable one or the other of these goals have to give way.

The economic order at Bretton Woods tried to reconcile these inconsistencies in various ways, principally by allowing official controls of capital flows and by making exchange rates adjustable on certain, admittedly restrictive, conditions. And one tried to cope with the autonomy of national economic policies by linking the recourse to IMF assistance to a system of consultations on economic policies - conditionality or what could be termed "moral suasion".

As we know, the inconsistencies could not be bridged indefinitely, and in the end the Bretton Woods system virtually broke down. The rules had to be changed, and a period of freely floating exchange rated ensued. If we look at the situation today, we must admit that this problem of reconciling conflicting aims is no less formidable now. For one thing, as I have already said, an official control of capital flows is out of the question in the present world. And we have to find a foreign exchange regime that is more flexible than the Bretton Woods one.

The main problem, however, is how to guarantee an effective coordination of national economic policies. In these respects we have a great deal to learn from the development of European monetary cooperation, the EMS. In the regional context the " inconsistent quartet" is just as relevant as in an international system. When the integration has reached the goal, the monetary union, the inconsistencies are reconciled. There is a single common currency, irreversibly fixed exchange rates, and a supranational central bank with responsibility for a common monetary policy. There are still in Europe fervent supporters of this ambitious goal, but, as we know, more and more doubts whether the goal is attainable are creeping in. After the breakdown of the ERM the road to EMU seems to be much more difficult than originally envisaged and the attainment of the goal, in any case, pushed quite a bit beyond the original time-table. This is true even if a multi-speed approach is adopted, meaning that a core of stability-minded partners form a monetary union, which other partners can join in later stages. In spite of these difficulties, however, much has been attained so far in the EMS. A vast coherent currency area has been created with common objectives and a definite set of rules for the actions of the participants. All over the area a commitment to price stability has been adopted as the overriding objective of monetary policy and a successful coordination of national economic policies has helped to achieve this goal throughout the area. This has not been possible without successive realignments of exchange rates and now, lately, the allowance of a much wider band for the fluctuations of exchange rates.

What has been achieved in Europe cannot be transplanted to the international scene. But the existence of a coherent currency bloc in Europe could help a lot towards building up international cooperation in the monetary field. At least, it affords one corner-stone of stability in a turbulent world.

A weakness in any future international monetary system is that there is no dominant national currency that can serve as its reserve asset. As in the present situation there will continue to be three key currencies - the dollar, the yen and the mark - and efforts at stabilizing or regulating the system will have to do principally with the relations between these three currency areas. Of course, the dollar area is not a currency area in the same sense as the EMS. Many nations, particularly in the Western Hemisphere and South East Asia link their currencies to the dollar, and the dollar is used as a unit of account and actual means of payments in many nations with rampant inflation, like in Brazil and in Russia. But it is not a question of a coherent, managed currency area with a set of rules governing the behaviour of participants. Moreover, as a reserve currency, the dollar is inherently instable in view of the colossal foreign debt and the huge deficit in the current balance of payments of the US.

As for the yen, its strength and importance has increased over the years along with the spectacular rise of the Japanese economy, but the yen is far from being an international currency in the same sense as the dollar. There is as yet nothing that you could call a yen currency area.

In any case, we have to do with a tri-polar world, and any structured viable international monetary system must aim at stabilizing the relations between these three currencies. This in turn requires a sufficient measure of coordination of national economic policies.

That is no easy task. So far, the effort at a certain regulation has been made through consultations within the Group of Five, the Group of Seven and the Group of Ten. Such consultations may be helpful, and will most certainly continue. In view of recent experience, however, one may have the right to be sceptical about how much of a durable nature can be achieved that way. You cannot rule the system by committee. In my view, if we want to get anywhere, the efforts must be directed and managed by a strong international institution. We know that the utopian dream of Keynes and others of creating a world central bank will never come true. But we already have a useful international institution in the IMF, that could be remodelled to serve as a manager of the international monetary system, promoting the stability of exchange rates. It will have to base this task on more flexible rules than those of the old Bretton Woods system. And, above all, it has to be given more authority to exert effective pressure for cooperative decisions when policy conflicts arise.

I think that sooner or later we may arrive at some solution along such lines. It may be a long and bumpy road we have to travel before we can reach the goal, the stability that politicians as well as the business community desire. Meanwhile - if you will allow me to make a cynical remark - as a banker, I can take consolation from the fact that trading in foreign exchange and helping clients to hedge against the gyrations of unstable currencies provide one of the most important sources of income for banks active in international business.

3 Integrating the Central and East European Countries into the International Monetary System

RICHARD PORTES*

1 What can one say?

This topic at first seemed a straightforward assignment. It was not. First, the Central and East European countries (CEECs) have become progressively more differentiated since they discarded their old economic systems at the end of the 1980s. There were modifications of the standard centrally planned economy (CPE), but the range from Hungary to the old German Democratic Republic was fairly uniform, nowhere more so than in their international monetary affairs. Today these countries are in no respect more diverse than in their monetary and exchange rate regimes and their degree of integration into the international economy.

I can deal with that by taking the Central European three (Czech Republic, Hungary, Poland) as leading cases; the others may follow similar paths in due course. Russia is clearly significantly different, if only because of its size and geopolitical role, which (for example) puts it in a special relationship with the international institutions. Others, too, are so much less industrialized and so much less developed politically that it is hard to see them as Hungary-in-waiting. But there is no space for case studies or for detailed, country-specific qualifications to some of the broad generalizations that the topic requires.

Nor is the international monetary system (IMS) very well defined these days. The new regionalism, global financial integration, the disintegration of the EMS - we have come a considerable distance from Bretton Woods along a sharply winding path. So what are these countries getting themselves into?

Third, it is impossible to separate integration into the IMS from trade. In both the institutional framework and trade flows themselves, there can be no dichotomy between international money and the real economy. The relationships go deeper into the economy - for these countries, entering fully into the IMS will require extensive adaptation of domestic laws and institutions. And it is a very long way to even the loosest coordination of monetary policy with other countries if you have never before had to run any kind of market-economy monetary policy at all.

That is perhaps why few analysts or policy-makers in these countries have gone beyond 'what can the IMF (World Bank, EBRD, ...) do for us now?' to think about what kind of IMF they would like to see, and in what kind of IMS. It will become clear, however, that there is already an extensive literature on the more pressing problems of convertibility, exchange-rate policy, debt management, and the relationship between regional and global, bilateral and multilateral links. It is not easy to say anything new here, although there are still highly contentious issues.

Subject to all these qualifications, this paper addresses its title on the basis of the lessons from economic transformation in the CEECs so far and the medium-term prospects. By medium term I mean no change in the institutional capital stock: the current international monetary regime and the structure of international monetary institutions that supports it. I begin by considering why we should be concerned with integrating these countries into the IMS. Section 3 briefly discusses where they started from. Section 4 looks more closely at what integration means. In Section 5, I deal with convertibility and exchange-rate policies. Section 6 covers external debt, aid, and conditionality. Section 7 looks at the relationships between these countries and both regional and global institutional frameworks. Section 8 concludes.

2 Who cares?

2.1 They do

Given the current institutional capital stock, what items from it do the CEECs want to use or adapt? To what ends? Do they want to be integrated? Should they, and how deeply? Economic interdependence is not unavoidable, and integration is not automatic, at least beyond some limits. The standard CPE was an extreme example of insulation from external monetary influences. But there are still countries that have never had that kind of central planning but maintain inconvertible currencies, multiple exchange rates, and highly differentiated tariff structures. Nor is it obvious from the experience of the past few decades that rising trade participation and financial integration brings about more international cooperation or stronger international institutions.

Some of these countries are in such acute economic and political difficulties, too, that they might even worry about a 'Groucho problem': why should they want to join a club that would accept them as members? Indeed, some of the existing members are unhappy about how the club rules are being interpreted, but more of that below. The Groucho Club in London has a waiting list, and similarly, almost all the CEECs do want to enter fully into the IMS as soon as they can. This has clearly been a key objective of the process of economic transformation (Bruno, 1993), because it is perceived as both a means to the end of becoming a capitalist market economy and a consequence of getting there.

Provisionally, let us take integration to be membership in the IMF; currency convertibility, including a reasonable degree of openness to capital flows, if not full capital-account convertibility; and a well-defined exchange rate policy. What do these offer to the representative CEEC? First, some credibility for domestic economic policies. Making the currency convertible is a strong signal, if it can be sustained, and understandably popular too. Second, the rules and conventions imposed by the system, going as far as explicit conditionality on economic policies, can be a useful defense against domestic pressures to go back to the old ways. Third, the IMS (or a regional structure like the EMS) may be identified with Western political structures and institutions and so may serve as a political pole of attraction, the more so as it symbolizes turning away from economic links with other formerly planned economies (Portes, 1991b). Finally, on a more practical level, monetary respectability is likely to give better access to international capital markets and external financing, and to goods markets as well.

It is less evident that going immediately to an 'outward orientation' through radical trade liberalization is unambiguously beneficial. Greenaway (1993) argues convincingly that the extensive World Bank studies of liberalization episodes view them 'through rose-tinted glasses'. Rodrik (1993b) analyzes the potential conflict between stabilization and trade liberalization. The CEECs' experience so far confirms that there are certainly costs in opening the economy very rapidly: 'It was a mistake for Poland to move so fast to one of the world's freest trade regimes' (Summers, in Foreword to Blejer, et al., 1993). Many others come to similar conclusions, though most would criticize only the abrupt trade liberalization, not the quick move to convertibility (see Dornbusch, 1991; Flemming, 1992; Flemming and Rollo, 1992; McKinnon, 1991, 1993; Nuti and Portes, 1993; and Pisani-Ferry, 1993). There is considerable support for replacing the quantitative planning of trade by fairly uniform but non-trivial tariffs, then negotiating tariff reductions in due course. If the political circumstances require, reformers may find it wise to make future tariff reductions automatic, in the framework of a conditional agreement with the IFIs or the EC.

The interval of 'senile industry protection' (a second-best to wage subsidies) should be used to restructure: break up monopolies and set the firms on a path to privatization. Evidence from both Poland and China suggests that many of these firms (even with initial 'negative value added') can be saved efficiently - the question is how to do that at the least transitional cost in output. That several of the CEECs chose to open up much faster and without any prior restructuring demonstrates their keen desire to become full members of the club right away, at a demonstrably high cost.

2.2 We may

Bringing the CEECs into the IMS is probably desirable for the industrialized countries too, although the balance is not as clear, and the gains are not as great for us as for them. Their entry might eventually affect the system itself, negatively from some viewpoints. They are unlikely for some time to be sufficiently important financially to have any effect on systemic risk, nor big enough to affect the balance of power in the international institutions. But there is a danger that bringing them in early will be feasible only with exceptions that will weaken the rules themselves. Some would interpret in this way the IMF's yielding to G-7 pressure to lend to Russia outside the Fund's normal criteria.

There are clear advantages in getting these countries to follow the rules - in facilitating financial transactions, in dealing with debt, the harmonization of prudential regulations, and so forth. Their opening up to the West does imply more pressure for us to open to them. That is unlikely to pose problems for financial flows, but market access for their exports is quite another matter. Yet the more 'normal' they become in international monetary relations, the less justification there will be for any special (discriminatory) treatment in trade (this is no comfort to Japan, Korea and Taiwan!)

3 Initial conditions

3.1 Insulation of the standard CPE

The mechanisms that insulated the classical CPE from external monetary shocks and made money 'passive' in most domestic contexts are often misunderstood. Thus, for example, the model and discussion in Berg and Sachs (1992) ignores the fact that until 1 January 1990 in Poland, most domestic prices of industrial goods and imports were not linked to international prices through an exchange rate. The official rate was merely an accounting convention; the actual conversion rates were many and various, and there was still a price equalization account. To say that the official rate was 'overvalued' is therefore meaningless (see Oblath, 1993a, pp. 67-68; see also Oblath's criticism of Rodrik, 1993a, for his interpretations of the relations between domestic prices and those denominated in transferable roubles).

The system is described and analyzed in many sources (e.g., Neuberger, et al., 1981; Portes, 1983, 1987, 1993b). It severed not only the links between domestic and foreign prices, but also those between foreign exchange flows and monetary assets of households and firms. Convertibility was simply not possible in this system, at whatever exchange rate: the planners could not allow residents, much less non-residents, to purchase domestic goods freely, because that would disrupt the quantitative plans and would permit foreigners to exploit the differences between foreign and domestic relative prices, where the latter did not reflect relative costs. Inconvertibility was fundamental and essential, not merely a barrier to capital flight or defence of an overvalued exchange rate.

All this held for trade with market economies as well as with CMEA partners. The system was internally coherent - consistent with the domestic monetary and physical allocation mechanisms. Within the CMEA bloc, moreover, monetary and trade relations were themselves consistent. They were essentially bilateral, despite an apparently multilateral institutional structure. 'Transferable rubles' were never really transferable, much less convertible. But the allocation procedures generated trade flows that were fairly regular, year after year, and maintained long-term links between suppliers and users (Schrenk, 1992). The pattern of trade was doubtless inefficient, but there is continuing controversy over how far specialization was distorted, how much 'over-trading' there was in CMEA, and how much of each country's traditional exports to the bloc could have been viable in Western markets.

3.2 The transition - from insulation towards integration

I have discussed the overall reform process in Eastern Europe recently in (1993b) and the current state of play in the 'Visegrad countries' of Central Europe with Mario Nuti (1993). Hungary began to modify its system for trade with market economies as early as 1968 and introduced further significant changes in the 1980s, as did Poland. But transformation - as opposed to reform - did not begin until the end of the 1980s. CMEA itself was dissolved in 1991. The move from central planning towards a market economy has progressed fairly rapidly, and individual countries have introduced varying degrees of convertibility (e.g. see Fry and Nuti, 1992, and the survey of Borensztein and Masson, 1993).

Most of the literature on economic transformation in the CEECs is devoted to the 'Visegrad three' (CE3). They are now four, but Slovakia must be classed in the 'second wave' of the transformation process, along with Bulgaria and Romania. Those six have concluded association agreements ('Europe Agreements') with the European Community. The next category might include Slovenia, whose level of development is comparable to the CE3, and the Baltic states. These countries offer fascinating, varied experiences of introducing new, convertible currencies (Bofinger, 1993b). The other successor states of Yugoslavia and the Soviet Union form a third group of even more widely differing economies, with Russia and Ukraine evidently standing out from the rest in economic and political importance. In this far-flung group, one fairly common characteristic is monetary disorder and disarray, with a relatively low degree of integration into the IMS.

Common to all the CEECs has been the sudden disintegration of the previous trade links among them and the collapse in the volume of that trade (Rodrik, 1992, 1993a; Rosati, 1992, 1993). Both the resulting push to find markets and the pull of earning convertible currencies have brought remarkable expansion in their exports to the West, especially from the first and second wave countries and especially to the European Community. In 1988, the proportion of the exports of these six countries that went to the EC was 23%; in 1992, it was 43%. In this overall shift, there is relatively little variation among the individual CEECs and no discernible correlation across countries with the degree of convertibility of their currencies (a proxy for their progress in integrating with the IMS). There is still great potential for further growth (Hamilton and Winters, 1992), provided the Community does not step back from the process of gradually opening its markets to these countries (Rollo and Smith, 1993).

The exchange-rate and trade experiences of the CE3 exhibit some common features. In comparison to the other CEECs, their nominal exchange rates have been relatively stable. This has combined with persistent inflation to give gradual but steady appreciation of their real exchange rates. Trade has been liberalized rapidly, and trade performance (in terms of net exports) was quite good until 1993. Still, that is perhaps not astonishing in view of the deep fall in output and, despite the appreciation, the continuing substantial undervaluation of their exchange rates relative to PPP (Oblath, 1993a).

4 Integration into what 'IMS'?

When we were supposedly operating under the Bretton Woods rules, it might have seemed easy to specify the international monetary system into which a country could integrate. The realities always differed significantly from the 1944 texts, however, and indeed they changed considerably over the period to 1973 (see the discussions by McKinnon and Feldstein in Bordo and Eichengreen, 1993). Nevertheless, we can take the essential features to be pegged exchange rates (the par value system); current-account convertibility from the end of the 1950s, with capital controls permitted; and the international financial institutions (with the IMF having a lesser role vis-à-vis developed countries than had been envisaged). This framework was seen to be conducive to free trade and monetary stability. And it was: the trade of the developed countries that were fully integrated into the system grew rapidly, as did their output; the persistence of their aggregate and relative inflation rates was low, as was the monetary and exchange-rate accommodation to aggregate and relative price shocks (Bordo and Eichengreen, 1993, Chs. 1 and 14; Alogoskoufis, 1992).

The IMS appears quite different now from pre-1973. Most industrial countries have floating exchange rates, now including the European Community, although many LDCs still peg; capital controls have been dismantled, contributing to the rapid growth of capital mobility and financial integration; at the same time, there has been some re-regulation in financial markets (in particular, capital adequacy rules). While the IMF's role in dealing with developed countries is less important since 1976, its activities in overseeing debtor LDCs expanded dramatically in the 1980s; and as that business fell off at the end of the 1980s, it found a major new market in the CEECs. Despite these changes, however, it can be argued that by comparison to the interwar period, the IMS still fulfils the Bretton Woods objective of supporting open trade and the financing of payments imbalances (Dornbusch, in Bordo and Eichengreen, 1993).

These changes in the system are the consequence and the cause of other changes in the international economy that have not yet affected our analyses. We have in practice gone well beyond the sell-by date of the standard paradigm of macroeconomic interaction among open economies. The transmission mechanisms that we were learning how to model are being supplanted by the processes leading to deeper integration of these economies, and that itself is generating pressures to remodel the IMS. The IMS towards which the CEECs are aiming is a moving target whose essential, underlying features are not transparently clear, as in the determinants of exchange rates or the viability of exchange-rate systems.

5 Convertibility, payments arrangements, and exchange-rate policies

5.1 Why convertibility, and how fast?

At a conference almost three years ago, I could already say that 'it is likely that more has been written on convertibility than on all other problems of the transition except perhaps for privatization' (Portes, 1991a). That did not close the discussion (see, e.g., Bofinger, 1991; Williamson, 1991; Greene and Isard, 1991; Oblath, 1993b). The subsequent literature and experience of the CEECs have not, however, altered my assessment then. The achievement of current account convertibility for residents should be a high-priority objective and should come early in the sequencing of the transformation process, at least for the smaller economies with relatively high trade participation and some initial access to international reserves. The precise timing and relationship to initial conditions will vary across countries (see Deszéri, 1993b, for a survey of the introduction of convertibility in the CEECs.)

The radical opening of the economy that this permits is necessary to import a new price structure and to create some degree of competition in the face of highly concentrated industrial structures. It is more important in the formerly planned economies than elsewhere, because it can play such a key role in creating markets and helping them to function properly. It eliminates bureaucratic influence on the allocation of foreign exchange. And early convertibility, if it can be sustained, will enhance the credibility of policy-makers, as noted above.

The discussion so far has ignored opening up the capital account. And so should the CEECs, for well-known reasons (Portes, 1991a; Fry and Nuti, 1992). There are dangers in uncontrolled capital inflows as well as outflows, while capital account inconvertibility need not discourage foreign direct investment as long as current account convertibility guarantees the freedom to remit profits. Opening successfully to capital account transactions requires positive real interest rates, a realistic exchange rate, and some depth in domestic financial markets. Moreover, as Fry and Nuti observe, CEEC governments can ill afford to sacrifice the revenues they collect through enforcing reserve requirements on their banks; but this implies a negative effective protection for the banks and hence the need for capital account controls (as well as some restraints on the banks' foreign competitors).

A further argument for convertibility has gained importance since the demise of CMEA and the rejection of proposals for some kind of Central and East European payments union (CEEPU). Convertibility facilitates the continuation of intra-regional trade flows without either an administered payments mechanism or the constraints of bilateral bargaining. There is a close relationship between convertibility and the liberalization of trade both between the CEECs and the West and among the CEECs themselves.

5.2 Payments union proposals

There is here a contrast between the current economic transformation of the East and early postwar Western Europe, in which convertibility was delayed and the European Payments Union took its place in fostering the growth of trade (while pushing the IMF offstage). There has been considerable controversy since mid-1990 over the relevance of the postwar example and the desirability of a CEEPU (perhaps the first record of the opposing views is in the CEPR *Bulletin* of June 1990). My own initially positive reaction to the CEEPU proposals was reversed as I became convinced of the independent, overwhelming merits of a quick move to convertibility (Portes, 1991c, pp. 11, 13). In any event, whatever the balance of the economic arguments for Central Europe, there was insuperable political resistance to creating any kind of institutional framework that in any way resembled, however superficially, the CMEA from which these countries had just emerged. The different positions expressed in Flemming and Rollo (1992) clearly reflect these political considerations.

So the CEEPU was killed off fairly quickly, and this undoubtedly accelerated the integration of the CEECs into the IMS. The argument was then renewed in regard to the successor states of the former Soviet Union. Williamson (1992) advocated either a ruble area or a payments union with a capital fund (from the West) of 'several billion dollars' (p. 48). Gros (1993) has promoted the Interstate Bank (IB) project not merely as a multilateral settlements mechanism for the CIS, some form of which is clearly needed to cope with the prevailing chaotic payments technology, but also as the beginning of a payments union: 'The more need a country has for credits, the higher should be the proportion indexed on a hard currency. This would essentially be equivalent to transforming the IB into a payments union...[Its] task would initially be limited, but endowed with enormous potential...[for] the creation of a payments union based on multilateral balances, cleared partially in hard currencies' (pp. 133-134). This objective is supported by Dornbusch (in Bordo and Eichengreen, 1993, pp. 103-104).

This is already a diversion and could turn into a major economic and geopolitical error, accentuated by Russia's tendency to use any levers available to reconstruct its hegemony over the states of the former Soviet Union (witness the recent monetary agreement with Belarus). There are two basic economic problems: a payments union cannot function effectively and to advantage if there is a single, dominant structural creditor country; and it is more likely to delay than to promote the essential move to convertibility, which holds much more promise for maintaining multilateral trade in the circumstances of the CIS. Eichengreen (1993), while defending the postwar EPU, argues convincingly that the analogy with current conditions in the CIS is misplaced. In particular, he cites the absence of an economic precondition, macroeconomic stabilization, and of the political stability necessary to underpin what he sees as the 'commitment technology' with which the EPU supported economic integration and trade liberalization. In his comments on the paper, Fischer agrees in rejecting a PU for the CIS (and indeed disagrees with Eichengreen's positive evaluation of the EPU). So a multilateral settlements mechanism is the best one can expect - but even that cannot function properly until the chaotic internal transactions technology is rationalized (de Boissieu, et al., 1993). The long delays in interbank clearing under conditions of rapid inflation are highly disruptive to normal economic activity.

We are in fact likely to see a wide variety of currency and payments arrangements in the former Soviet Union. There will be currency unions (e.g., Russia-Belarus), new currencies with and without currency board frameworks, floating and pegging, especially to the ruble, if it can be made reasonably stable. Thus integrating some of the other states of the FSU into the IMS will depend on how well Russia does and how its own international integration proceeds.

5.3 Exchange-rate policies

There are two issues here: the choice of exchange-rate regime - float, peg, or something in between; and to the extent that the rate is managed, how should the target level be determined? Again, the arguments are set out in an extensive literature (e.g., the surveys of Aghevli et al., 1991, and Borensztein and Masson, 1993), and I shall simply add a few observations to a previous statement of my own views: '...A sufficient devaluation of the nominal exchange rate will eliminate excess demand for foreign exchange, but that may give a real exchange rate so low as to be unsustainable and indeed undesirable...Going to convertibility must be accompanied by a sensible exchange-rate policy: do not devalue excessively; peg initially; then go to a crawling peg or tablita' (Nuti and Portes, 1993, p. 14; see also Portes, 1991c, p. 12, and the similar conclusions of Dezséri, 1993a).

The danger of serious overshooting with an excessive initial devaluation arises because the initial distortions are so great that it is impossible to make any reliable calculation of an equilibrium rate, so policy-makers are tempted to choose the pre-liberalization 'free market' rate - the only observable standard. But this rate is always and everywhere deeply undervalued. And as Oblath (1993a) points out, there are reasons to believe that even the 'equilibrium' rate suggested by purely monetary considerations will be significantly undervalued: the fall in exports to CMEA partners will release resources for export elsewhere; the fall in output will reduce the demand for imports; the rationalization of distortions should raise the efficiency of trade; trade restrictions by Western countries on the CEECs are being relaxed; and the required expansion of the non-traded service sector should be led by an increase in the relative price of services, hence a real exchange rate appreciation (ceteris paribus).

The macroeconomic costs of serious overshooting are clear from the Polish and Czechoslovak cases: an excessive initial price shock, requiring in turn excessive monetary tightness to stop it from setting off rapid inflation at the outset; hence a strong negative demand shock, coupled with a negative supply shock to import-dependent firms; and in due course, because the initial real wage was unsustainably low and domestic firms still had significant market power, a catch-up cost-push inflationary process. Williamson (1992, p. 43) sums up: 'The macroeconomic effect of an acutely undervalued currency is highly stagflationary...this is not a hypothetical danger, but rather what some of us regard as the major mistake so far identified in the design of the transition.' Hrncir (1993) argues that in Czechoslovak conditions, excessive initial devaluation fostered a shift to lower-value-added production and consequently was inimical to competitiveness in the medium run.

The tradeoff between peg and crawl is that between a nominal anchor for monetary stability and a real exchange rate target for external balance. Initially, the needs of stabilization are paramount and accentuated by the role of a fixed nominal rate as an anchor for the price structure, which is undergoing radical change with liberalization. But subsequent real appreciation is inevitable and must eventually be counteracted, so it is best to announce ex ante that the peg will be relaxed when the authorities judge that the real exchange rate is in a range appropriate for the longer run.

Bofinger (1990, 1992, 1993a) and Mundell (1993) discuss the relation between exchange rate policy and monetary policy in the CEECs. Both stress the need for monetary discipline. The former was initially inclined towards a stringent fixed-rate policy and subsequently came to believe that it would first be necessary to establish the microeconomic conditions for an effective monetary policy. He argues convincingly that the currency board solution (Hanke and Schuler, 1991) is too rigid for CEEC financial systems, which would be unable to cope with its stringency (see Begg and Portes, 1993, for the reasons why). The experience of Estonia's currency board, where the new currency has proved a great success but output fell by 40% after it was installed in mid-1992 (and major banks have failed - see Hansson in Bofinger, 1993b), indicates that Bofinger may be right. Mundell suggests that the CEECs should anchor to the ERM - but that was before August 1993.

6 External finance and conditionality

One motive for integration into the IMS is access to external finance as a member in good standing of the system, rather than as an outsider. Early postwar experience with the EPU may not be relevant to the CEECs, but an unambiguous lesson from that period is the potential importance of external assistance and debt consolidation in economic transformation and recovery (Dornbusch, Layard and Nölling, 1993). Given the existing debt burdens, the bulk of aid should have been grants or the equivalent, rather than new loans. Regrettably, the severe budgetary constraints in the major Western countries made substantial grants appear unrealistic. Subject to this constraint of political feasibility, the most effective way of giving aid with a significant financial impact on the CEECs would have been large-scale debt relief (Dornbusch, 1991; Portes, 1991b). Governments can only extend direct debt relief on government-held debt, through the Paris Club, so countries like Bulgaria and Hungary whose debt is primarily to the private sector would have to be helped through IMF-led debt relief exercises along Brady Plan lines.

So far, however, neither the IMS nor the IMF has really been much help to the CEECs in dealing with their debts. The 'best' performance so far has been for Poland, but the substantial (50%) Paris Club debt reduction was not agreed until March 1991; it was conditional; and neither governments nor the Fund appear to have put much pressure on the banks to follow on comparable terms, as has normally been the case. Four years after Balcerowicz went to Washington with his first plan for stabilization and reform, there is still no debt relief agreement between Poland and the banks.

Russia had de facto debt relief - it simply did not pay. But that was not a satisfactory solution, and it was complicated by 'the G7's joint and severe blunder' (Armendariz de Aghion and Williamson, 1993) in dealing with the successor states' responsibilities for the former Soviet Union's debt. Finally a Paris Club agreement earlier this year recognized the inevitable, but the category of loans on which payment was deferred was defined with insufficient precision. The still confused legacy has doubtless contributed to the Russian authorities' rather cavalier attitude in dealing with their obligations, which led to delays in payments on an EC loan that have threatened the continuation of the Community's aid programme to Russia.

Bulgaria is heavily indebted to the banks, but its plight has been pretty widely ignored, and it is struggling to come to some accommodation with remarkably little apparent sympathy or help from Western governments. Hungary started the decade with one of the highest levels of debt in the world (Cohen, 1991) and has had great difficulty in coping with the domestic fiscal burden of debt service. Yet the government and central bank have consistently rejected all suggestions for seeking debt relief - the comparison with Mexico seems to be taken as an insult (see the papers by Oblath and Riecke and discussion by Portes in Székely and Newbery, 1993); and of course no initiative in that direction has come from the creditors.

One could go on, but that hardly seems necessary. This behaviour by the West (and the domestic authorities, in the Hungarian case) seems incredibly short-sighted, in view of both the prospects for the future and the lessons from the past. The 1980s made it clear that debt relief should be provided as soon as serious reforms are under way, not long after; and that in appropriate circumstances, the capital markets will indeed forget after forgiving, as they have done historically (Eichengreen and Portes, 1989).

In Hungary, the current political malaise must be partly a consequence of the extreme austerity required by fiscal pressures over the past four years; and meanwhile investment is severely depressed by high real interest rates and constraints on banu audit availability, also due in part to the domestic financial impact of debt service. This cannot be an appropriate payoff to the East European country with the longest, most active history of integrating into the IMS.

The Fund has of course been active throughout the region in designing macroeconomic stabilization programmes and lending to support them. The World Bank has also invested substantial organizational resources and gradually increasing financial resources in the CEECs. The EBRD is also there, with more presence than investment so far, although this is understandable, and the premature criticism of the EBRD on this count is unfair. Nor should we forget the EIB, the OECD, and of course the EC, whose PHARE programme was the pioneer of the major aid efforts to the CEECs. After this enumeration I can only repeat my criticism (e.g., 1992, 1993b) of the lack of coordination among all these bodies. The IMS is very far from being systematic, and part of the reason is simple turf battles, not only among the international organizations but also among the G7 countries that so powerfully influence them.

This criticism is heard elsewhere (Aglietta, 1992; Fischer, 1991; Ners, et al. 1992). It applies in particular to the conditionality attached to assistance from the various international organizations, which is multiple, overlapping, and thus confusing. Pisani-Ferry (1993) goes further to argue that the leading role of the Fund has resulted in excessive emphasis on macroeconomic conditions, in circumstances where lacking their microeconomic foundations, such conditions were unrealistic. The correctness and importance of this criticism are not vitiated by the general lack of protest from CEEC governments against the Fund's approach or conditions. The issue is not about appropriate macroeconomic policies but rather about priorities, the sustainability of those policies and their consequences in an unsuitable microeconomic context.

From the outset, it was clear that the key problem was the extent and depth of the microeconomic distortions and weaknesses of the former CPEs, while too much attention was devoted to macroeconomic disequilibrium and the 'monetary overhang' (Portes, 1990). Pisani-Ferry suggests that this was due partly to the *déformation professionnelle* of the IMF, partly to the previous focus of the Fund and other advisors on Latin America. I would add that with a few notable exceptions, the Fund's experts in stabilization and adjustment, as well as other Western advisors, had little or no prior experience of CPEs and their specific features.

It was right for the Fund to focus on short-run macroeconomic policies in the CEECs. It was wrong, however, to make all other aid conditional on agreement with the Fund over a 'stabilization programme' and thereby to put the Fund's priorities at the top of policy-makers' agendas. Although the Fund did not mechanically apply its previous orthodoxies to the CEECs, it understandably could not devote much effort to the microfoundations of the macro policies it was constructing. That was not its comparative advantage, nor its specific mission. Moreover, macroeconomic conditions are readily quantifiable; structural and institutional change is not. But it was the specificity of the CEECs that their microfoundations were so extremely weak and distorted - in fiscal and financial and industrial structures - that mere liberalization would not create the microeconomic, institutional basis for a market economy and the macroeconomic policies appropriate for a market economy. The incipient hyperinflation in Poland and the seeming analogies with Latin America brought the Washington policy community to put the Fund up front, and the resulting strategy was then generalized to other countries. This was not good for the CEECs, nor perhaps for the Fund.

Despite these criticisms of the aid effort, it is still reasonable to ask whether massive financial aid could have made a significant difference to the course of events. Evidence from Brazil and elsewhere in Latin America to Russia itself (privatization) demonstrates that it _is_ possible to make major microeconomic changes without macroeconomic stabilization. Nevertheless, more balance-of-payments support with macroeconomic instability is likely to be wasted. With microeconomic distortions and chaos, could external assistance have limited the precipitous fall in output and have created the conditions for the investment boom that was initially expected? It is more likely to have done so in Central Europe than further East. Even now, the Russian government probably could not use quickly and effectively a large injection of funds to finance a 'social safety net'. A large World Bank SAL for that purpose has been stalled because the Russian side has not put forward a coherent programme, and it is likely to take another year to become operational.

Throughout the region, however, a much greater financial commitment from the West would have brought much more attention to the structures through which its aid was being delivered, to coordination and recipient-donor relations (cf. the Marshall Plan), and perhaps to the policies that were being advocated and implemented.

7 The regional and global institutional framework

The 'new regionalism' is likely to continue, perhaps to gain further ground against global institutional structures in both monetary and trade issues (de Melo and Panagariya, 1993). In that context, the Central European countries are likely to be better off integrating jointly with the European Community than with each other alone. That should not, however, exclude regional cooperation in Central Europe, which could have considerable benefits not only in reconstituting trade flows that since 1990 have fallen well below what standard models would predict, but also in a range of other activities like trans-European networks (Nuti and Portes, 1993).

Indeed, Baldwin (1994) makes a powerful case for replacing the current 'hub-and-spoke' configuration of EC-CEEC relations by a 'concentric circles' model. In a first stage, the CEECs with Europe Agreements would extend to each other the same preferential market access they have given to the EC. A next step before EC membership would be a grouping with rules like the EC-EFTA European Economic Area, but excluding migration. If the sequence were clearly specified and the EC led the way, perhaps the associated CEECs would come to see the logic and benefits of this dynamic framework for regional integration.

Three further observations seem important here. First, association with and (*a fortiori*) accession to the EC will not be offered to Ukraine or countries further East. Second, as we saw above, a regional payments union is unlikely to be the mechanism for reviving the potentially beneficial trade that has been destroyed. Third, the EMS is unlikely to be restored soon to its former status as a zone of monetary stability (Portes, 1993a). Thus events have passed by the proposal of Aglietta et al. (1992) for a regionally organized exchange-rate system for the CEECs, which would have involved coordinated crawling pegs (to the ECU) supported by a stabilization fund financed by the Community.

Accession to the Community is nevertheless the right medium-term objective both for the countries that might qualify and for the EC itself, and in due course that will affect the relationships between these countries and the IMS. The Europe Agreements were in some respects disappointing (CEPR, 1992; Inotai, 1994, and Discussion by Portes), especially relative to the needs of the historic juncture in which they were negotiated (Portes, 1991b). The June 1993 European Council in Copenhagen did, however, give new impetus to integration between the associated countries and the EC, by accelerating somewhat the opening of markets and emphasizing political cooperation. Membership is still a long way off (Baldwin, et al., 1992). But that will be more tolerable if forward momentum is maintained.

The monetary arrangements between these countries and the Community in the interim are unlikely to have significant consequences. Even if one or more peg to the DM or the ECU, research suggests this will not much affect the pattern of their trade (Frankel and Wei, this volume), which will in any case be adjusting to integration with the EC.

While the Bretton Woods institutions have welcomed the CEECs and have put substantial resources into helping them, the priorities of the Fund and Bank have understandably reflected those of their dominant shareholders, the G7, vigorously led here by the United States. Since the 1990 Houston summit, pressure from the G7 (mainly at US instigation) has focused their attention primarily on the (former) Soviet Union, especially Russia. This is unfortunate, because the problems of the FSU countries are and will for some time be so intractable, in good part for political reasons. Had the Fund not put so much effort into macroeconomic stabilization in Russia, a goal that was clearly unattainable in 1992-93, it might have been more successful elsewhere in the region. And for the longer term, G7 pressure on the IMF to make concessions endangers the integrity of the Fund's conditionality itself. If the G7 countries want to give aid outside the Fund's normal framework, or to have other funds released independently of IMF conditionality, let them do so - and take the responsibility as well as any direct fiscal burden.

8 Conclusions

In this volume, Stanley Fischer presents his report card on the performance of the international financial institutions. Since they are young at heart and constantly renewing themselves, we may call them collectively little Johnny. On my reading of Fischer, Johnny is working hard, good in mathematics (analysis) and languages (experience throughout the world), but he should read his essays aloud more often (increase openness).

I was asked to evaluate the school trip, however, and what I hear is less encouraging. Johnny had for a long time wanted to go East. When he got there, he found that he'd learned the right skills in school - his mathematics was applicable - but he had trouble using his languages with the inhabitants, and the tools therefore weren't so useful in practice. His phase diagrams didn't give convergent paths; some of the hosts didn't like or understand sequences; the aggregation problem invalidated his empirical work; he wasn't too good at differentiating, and they weren't inclined to integrate, at least with each other. They just wanted him to take them back to the West right away. Some of the kids on the trip tried to convince the Easterners to keep on playing with their neighbours - using rules from a game popular in the West after the war - but that just created suspicion on the Eastern side and second-guessing among the visitors. Worst of all, Johnny didn't bring enough money, and his parents are unwilling or unable to send more; they just send messages telling him what to do, some of which contradict the school rules. Johnny isn't likely to go home soon, but no one is very happy.

The CEECs have tried hard and with some success to integrate into the IMS. But the IMS hasn't done very well for them, and the European Community could do better too. The bottom line - flat on the bottom - is still the huge, persisting fall in output in these countries. In some countries it is finally beginning to turn upwards, but from a very low base, with no sign yet of a recovery of investment and sustainable growth. They are very far from the postwar catch-up precedent that formed the basis for the projections many were making at the beginning of the transformation. The picture might not have seemed so encouraging in Germany in 1948, but the initial conditions had been a lot worse. Success in recovery and growth must go side by side with further integration of the CEECs into the international monetary system and the global economy.

NOTE

* The author is grateful for comments from the discussants and participants, and particularly for subsequent written comments from László Csaba, Kemal Dervis, Barry Eichengreen, Kálmán Mizsei, Joan Pearce, Jean Pisani-Ferry, Jim Rollo, Massimo Russo, John Williamson and L. Alan Winters. They will still not be satisfied, but any faults that others find are certainly not the responsibility of any of these very helpful colleagues.

REFERENCES

Aghevli, B., et al., 1991, Exchange-rate policy in developing countries: some analytical issues, IMF Occasional Paper No. 78.

Aglietta, M., et al., 1992, 'Repenser le soutien de la communauté internationale à l'Europe de l'Est', Observations et diagnostics économiques No. 42.

Alogoskoufis, G., 1992, 'Monetary accommodation, exchange rate regimes and inflation persistence', Economic Journal 102, 461-480.

Armendariz de Aghion, B., and J. Williamson, 1993, The G7's joint and several blunder, Princeton Essay in International Finance No. 189.

Baldwin, R., 1994, Pan-European trade arrangements beyond the year 2000, London, CEPR.

Baldwin, R., et al., 1992, Is bigger better? The economics of EC enlargement, Monitoring European Integration 3, London, CEPR.

Begg, D., and R. Portes, 1993, 'Enterprise debt and economic transformation: financial restructuring of the state sector in Central and Eastern Europe', in C. Mayer and X. Vives, eds., Capital markets and financial intermediation, Cambridge, CUP for CEPR, pp. 230-255.

Berg, A., and J. Sachs, 1992, 'Structural adjustment and international trade in Eastern Europe: the case of Poland', Economic Policy 14, 117-155.

Blejer, M., et al., eds., 1993, Eastern Europe in transition: from recession to growth?, World Bank Discussion Paper No. 196.

Bofinger, P., 1990, 'The role of monetary policy in the process of economic reform in Eastern Europe', CEPR Discussion Paper No. 457.

Bofinger, P., 1991, 'Options for the payments and exchange-rate system in Eastern Europe', pp. 243-261 of R. Portes, ed., The path of reform in Central and Eastern Europe, Special Issue No. 2 of European Economy.

Bofinger, P., 1992, 'The experience with monetary policy in an environment with strong microeconomic distortions', in P. Bofinger, ed., Economic consequences of the East, London, CEPR.

Bofinger, P., 1993a, 'Macroeconomic transformation in Eastern Europe: the role of monetary policy reconsidered', manuscript.

Bofinger, P., ed., 1993b, The economics of new currencies, London, CEPR.

de Boissieu, C., D. Cohen and G. de Pontbriand, 1993, 'Gérer la dette interentreprise', Economie internationale 54, 105-120.

Bordo, M., and B. Eichengreen, eds., 1993, A retrospective on the Bretton Woods system: lessons for international monetary reform, Chicago, University of Chicago Press.

Borensztein, E., and P. Masson, 1993, 'Exchange arrangements of previously centrally planned economies', in Financial sector reforms and exchange arrangements in Eastern Europe, IMF Occasional Paper No. 102.

Bruno, M., 1993, 'Stabilization and reform in Eastern Europe: preliminary evaluation', pp. 12-38 of M. Blejer, et al. (1993).

CEPR, 1992, The association process: making it work. Central Europe and the European Community, Occasional Paper No. 11.

Cohen, D., 1991, 'The solvency of Eastern Europe', pp. 263-303 of R. Portes, ed., The path of reform in Central and Eastern Europe, Special Issue No. 2 of European Economy.

de Melo, J., and A. Panagariya, eds., 1993, New dimensions in regional integration, Cambridge, CUP for CEPR.

Dezséri, K., 1993a, 'A proposed approach for introducing currency convertibility in Eastern Europe: a multi-phase exchange rate policy during the transition period', Working Paper No. 20, Institute for World Economics, Budapest.

Deszéri, K., 1993b, 'First practical steps in introducing convertibility in the Eastern European countries', Working Paper No. 22, Institute for World Economics, Budapest.

Dornbusch, R.,1991, Priorities of economic reform in Eastern Europe and the Soviet Union, CEPR Occasional Paper No. 5.

Dornbusch, R., R. Layard and W. Nölling, eds., 1993, Postwar economic reconstruction and lessons for the East today, Cambridge, MA, MIT Press.

Eichengreen, B., 1993, 'A payments mechanism for the former Soviet Union: Is the EPU a relevant precedent?', Economic Policy 17.

Eichengreen, B., and R. Portes, 1989, 'Dealing with debt: the 1930s and the 1980s', pp. 69-86 of I. Husain and I. Diwan, eds., Dealing with the debt crisis, Washington DC, World Bank.

Fischer, S., 1991, 'Economic reform in the USSR and the role of aid', Brookings Papers on Economic Activity 1991:2.

Flemming, J., 1992, 'Relative price shocks and unemployment: arguments for temporarily reduced payroll taxes or protection', paper for TAPES Conference, Munich.

Flemming, J., and J. Rollo, eds., 1992, Trade, payments and adjustment in Central and Eastern Europe, London, EBRD and RIIA.

Frankel, J., and S. Wei, 1993, 'Emerging currency blocs', this volume.

Fry, M., and M. Nuti, 1992, 'Monetary and exchange-rate policies during Eastern Europe's transition: some lessons from further East', Oxford Review of Economic Policy, 8:1, 27-43.

Greenaway, D., 1993, 'Liberalizing foreign trade through rose-tinted glasses', Economic Journal 103, 208-222.

Greene, J., and P. Isard, 1991, Currency convertibility and the transformation of centrally planned economies, IMF Occasional Paper No. 81.

Gros, D., 1993, 'Mettre un terme à la désintégration monétaire dans la CEI', Economie internationale 54, 121-135.

Hamilton, C., and L. A. Winters, 1992, 'Opening up international trade with Eastern Europe', Economic Policy 14, 77-104.

Hanke, S., and K. Schuler, 1991, 'Currency boards for Eastern Europe', Heritage Lectures No. 355, The Heritage Foundation.

Hrncir, M., 1993, 'The exchange rate regime and economic recovery', Review of Economies in Transition, No. 2, Bank of Finland.

Inotai, A., 1994, 'The European Communities and Central and Eastern Europe: a critical assessment of the association agreements in strategic perspective', forthcoming in Europe: What Next?, ed. R. Henning and G. Hufbauer, Washington, Institute for International Economics.

McKinnon, R., 1991, The order of economic liberalization, Baltimore, John Hopkins University Press.

McKinnon, R., 1993, 'Macroeconomic control in liberalizing socialist economies: Asian and European parallels', in A. Giovannini, ed., Finance and development: issues and experience, Cambridge, CUP for CEPR.

Mundell, R., 1993, 'EMU and the international monetary system', Working Paper No. 13, Österreichische Nationalbank.

Ners, K., et al., 1992, Moving beyond assistance, Report of IEWS Task Force on Western Assistance to Transition.

Neuberger, E., R. Portes, and L. Tyson, 1981, 'The impact of external disturbances on the Soviet Union and Eastern Europe: a survey', in East European economic assessment, Part 2, Joint Economic Committee, U. S. Congress, Washington, DC, pp. 128-147.

Nuti, D. M., and R. Portes, 1993, 'Central Europe: the way forward', pp. 1-20 of R. Portes, ed., Economic transformation of Central Europe, London, CEPR and Commission of the European Communities.

Oblath, G., 1993a, 'Real exchange rate changes and exchange rate policy under economic transformation in Hungary and Central-Eastern Europe', Review of Economies in Transition, No. 2, Bank of Finland.

Oblath, G., 1993b, 'Interpreting and implementing currency convertibility in Central and Eastern Europe: a Hungarian perspective', Review of Economies in Transition, No. 2, Bank of Finland.

Pisani-Ferry, Jean, 1993, 'L'assistance internationale et les problèmes de la transition', in M. Lavigne, ed., Mutations à l'Est: transition vers le marché et intégration Est-Ouest, Paris, Presses de la Sorbonne.

Portes, R., 1983, 'Central planning and monetarism: fellow travellers?', pp. 149-165 of P. Desai, ed., Marxism, planning and the Soviet economy, Cambridge, Mass., MIT Press.

Portes, R., 1987, 'The impact of external shocks on centrally planned economies: theoretical considerations', in L. Pasinetti and P. Lloyd, eds., Structural change and adjustment in the world economy, London, Macmillan.

Portes, R., 1990, 'Introduction' to Economic transformation in Hungary and Poland, No. 43 of European Economy, pp. 11-17.

Portes, R., 1991a, 'The transition to convertibility for Eastern Europe and the USSR', in Economics for a new Europe, eds. A. Atkinson and R. Brunetta, London, Macmillan, pp. 89-98.

Portes, R., 1991b, 'The European Community and Eastern Europe after 1992', in T. Padoa-Schioppa, ed., Europe after 1992: three essays, Princeton Essay in International Finance No. 182.

Portes, R., 1991c, 'Introduction' to The path of reform in Central and Eastern Europe, Special Issue No. 2 of European Economy, pp. 1-15.

Portes, R., 1992, 'The European Community's response to Eastern Europe', in P. Bofinger, ed., Economic consequences of the East

Portes, R., 1993a, 'EMS and EMU after the fall', The World Economy 16, pp. 1-15.

Portes, R., 1993b, 'From central planning to a market economy', in S. Islam and M. Mandelbaum, eds., Making markets, New York, Council on Foreign Relations, pp. 16-52.

Rodrik, D., 1992, 'Foreign trade in Eastern Europe's transition: early results', CEPR Discussion Paper No. 676.

Rodrik, D., 1993a, 'Making sense of the Soviet trade shock in Eastern Europe: a framework and some estimates', in Blejer, et al. (1993), pp. 64-85.

Rodrik, D., 1993b, 'Trade liberalization in disinflation', CEPR Discussion Paper No. 832.

Rollo, J., and A. Smith, 1993, 'The political economy of Eastern European trade with the European Community: why so sensitive?', Economic Policy 16, 139-166.

Rosati, D., 1992, 'Problems of post-CMEA trade and payments', pp. 75-108 in Flemming and Rollo (1992).

Rosati, D., 1993, 'The impact of the Soviet trade shock on output levels in Central and East European economies', paper for IIASA conference on 'Output Decline in Eastern Europe'.

Schrenk, M., 1992, 'The CMEA system of trade and payments', pp. 217-242 of A. Hillman and B. Milanovic, eds., The transition from socialism in Eastern Europe: domestic restructuring and foreign trade, Washington, DC, World Bank.

Székely, I., and D. Newbery, eds., 1993, Hungary: an economy in transition, Cambridge, CUP for CEPR.

Williamson, J., 1991, ed., Currency convertibility in Eastern Europe, Washington, DC, Institute for International Economics.

Williamson, J., 1992, Trade and payments in Soviet disintegration, Policy Analyses in International Economics No. 37, Washington DC, Institute for International Economics.

Discussion

HENRYK KIERZKOWSKI

Richard Portes has written, as usual, a very lively paper on one of the most important problems of contemporary international economic relations. There is much to praise in the paper, however, as a critic, I want to concentrate on its deficiencies and on points of disagreement.

I had expected Richard Portes, perhaps unfairly, to develop a grand plan for integration of the Central and East European countries into the international monetary system, but, unfortunately, he does not quite achieve this objective. It is of course true that the clarity and consistency of the present monetary system leaves much to desire. So it is not easy to talk about bringing a group of countries into the system which itself is under a considerable strain and may well change in the near future. One needs a fixed reference point. On the other hand, the fact that the evolution of the international monetary system coincides with economic transformation in the former planned economies offers a unique opportunity to introduce not minor but major improvements, if necessary.

I think that Richard Portes' efforts suffer from three self-imposed constraints. First, his paper deals mainly with three Central European countries - Czech Republic, Hungary and Poland. Second, it offers a short-term, or at best, medium term analysis in which "the current international monetary regime and the structure of monetary institutions that supports it" remain basically unchanged. Third, although the inseparability of integration into the IMS from trade is stressed quite frequently, Richard Portes chooses not to explore to the fullest extent the implications of this inseparability.

It is quite natural that observers of the economic transformation in Eastern and Central Europe concentrate on a limited number of countries. Czech Republic, Hungary and Poland have attracted perhaps disproportionate attention, but innovators and pioneers usually capture imagination more easily than followers. The three Central European countries have achieved remarkable successes in moving towards market economy. In principle, there should be no difficulty in integrating them into the international monetary system. One could argue that this process could be completed within the time-span set by Richard Portes and without any need for changes in the existing international institutions.

However, the set of countries in transition is much larger than the three fast reformers. It is much less clear that the international monetary system can "absorb" Russia, Ukraine and twenty or so other countries as easily as it could "absorb", in principle, Czech Republic, Hungary and Poland. And one must not forget in this context China which also aspires to join the international monetary and trade system. One may ask whether any club could remain unchanged after so many new members joined it.

An interesting example of the relationship between the scale of economic transition in Eastern Europe and the character of an international institution set up to foster it is offered by the European Bank for Reconstruction and Development. It will be recalled that its capital base of 10 billions ecus seemed, at the time, sufficient for the purpose at hand. Initially, the new bank was to emphasize development of the private sector in just seven countries of operation based on sound market criteria. Very quickly, however, the number of countries of operation increased to 25 and it has also become apparent that promoting the private sector in Armenia or Kazakhstan is much more difficult than in Poland or Hungary. There is a strong possibility that if the European Bank for Reconstruction and Development were to be created today, it would be a different institution; its capital base, priorities and management structure would have to reflect a much larger membership and much greater diversity.

I want to use another example to suggest that the existence of a large number of economies in transition may influence the nature of international arrangements which are feasible. The European Community responded to the liberalization process in Eastern Europe with the so-called Association Agreements negotiated initially with Czechoslovakia, Hungary and Poland. Later on, the Community embarked on similar negotiations with Bulgaria and Rumania. It is hard to imagine, however, that association can be extended to all the countries in transition. Of course, the question of full membership will present even greater problems.

Portes correctly identifies convertibility as a central issue in integrating the Central and East European countries into the international monetary system. No country can hope to introduce full convertibility very quickly; the experience of Western Europe shows that opening up the capital account may take many years if not decades. But there are no reasons to delay the introduction of current account convertibility. The insulation of the ex-planned economies from the world market needs to be broken decisively and at an early stage. This view is now commonly accepted and it represents a dramatic change from an early doctrine which placed convertibility at the final stage of the liberalization process. After many decades of distorted relative prices, the reforming economics need correct price signals. Also, a decisive linking of the domestic economy with the world market can help to contain market power of domestic monopolies. Interestingly enough, under the old system big enterprises would not freely exercise their monopoly power because the central planner had means of controlling their behaviour. Liberalization has increased their market strength so now a threat of foreign competition is needed to prevent monopolistic price fixing.

When a reforming country introduces convertibility, it faces a number of options with regard to the exchange rate system. The economic profession seems to favour a fixed exchange rate system although the recent experience of Slovenia and Baltic States shows that alternative systems may well be viable.

In assessing the merits of the fixed exchange rate system Richard Portes draws our attention to the danger of overshooting and argues that excessive initial devaluations which have been frequently observed result from the fact that it is "impossible to make any reliable calculation of an equilibrium rate". I think that something more fundamental is involved here. The difficulties associated with calculating the equilibrium exchange rate should sometimes produce overshooting and sometimes undershooting, yet we observe the former and not the latter.

The main source of overshooting stems, in my view, from the fact that foreign currencies and especially U.S. dollar had been highly demanded in countries such as Poland prior to the introduction of reforms and convertibility. With inflation running at 700% per annum, shortages of goods, monetary overhang, and negative domestic real interest rates, the dollar was by far the best asset to hold. Thus asset demand determined the equilibrium rate at a very low level at that stage. With liberalization, rapid disappearance of goods shortages, reduction of inflation and interest rate increases, the demand for foreign currencies has been reduced and hence the equilibrium rate has changed as well.

One lesson that can be drawn from reforming countries' experience with the fixed exchange rate system concerns a tendency to postpone subsequent devaluation for far too long in spite of rapid domestic inflation. The rigidity of the nominal exchange rate should not become a false test of liberalization.

It is less obvious that trade opening should be as rapid as introduction of convertibility. The existence of adjustment costs in terms of employment and output prompted many authors, including Richard Portes, to suggest gradual trade liberalization. Poland is sometimes criticized for lowering its trade barriers too quickly. It should be recognized, however, that the passage of time often erodes the policy makers' freedom to act. The emergence of pressure groups and political developments observed in many reforming countries could well prevent gradual liberalization from being fully carried out. A carrot in the form of an improved access to Western markets could be very helpful to contain increasing protectionist forces in Eastern and Central Europe. International trade is a two-way street. And here we come to the central point: to what extent is the West itself willing to open up and adjust.

We all recognize that enormous changes will be required in the East to establish competitive market system. Resources will have to be reallocated from inefficient sectors and towards industries with comparative advantage.

The scale of this adjustment, if successful, will be unprecedented. It is virtually impossible that no reallocation of resources in the West will be required in response to economic liberalization in the East. In economics a disturbance or a change which occurs in one market tends to spill over into other markets, calling for appropriate adjustment. Thus a successful economic transformation in Eastern and Central Europe will demand structural adjustment in the markets of developed countries. A new international division of labour cannot occur only through reforms in the ex-centrally planned economics. It remains to be seen whether the West will be willing to reduce the size or even close down some of its inefficient sectors to accommodate new producers and exporters from Eastern and Central Europe. The evidence so far is not very encouraging as can be seen by the resistance of the so-called sensitive sectors in response to export expansion from reforming countries.

I wish to re-emphasize the last point. Richard Portes is absolutely right when he argues that it is impossible to separate integration into the international monetary system from trade. In fact, I think that trade integration is even more important than monetary integration in the sense that the latter's benefits cannot be fully achieved without the former. The emerging market economies will represent, no doubt, a threat to developed countries, especially in the short run. One needs a truly long-term analysis of economic and political costs and benefits to develop an appropriate policy response to economic transformation taking place in Eastern and Central Europe.

Discussion

JAN VIT

In the years 1989 - 1990, when the political systems in Eastern and Central Europe collapsed, nobody was able to realize fully how difficult their economic transformation would be, and how painful it would be to find appropriate reform procedures.

I would like to report on my personal experiences of the transformation process in the former CSFR and now the Czech Republic. I will stress only those factors that, in my opinion, are the most important in regard to the integration of East and Central European countries into the international monetary system. This integration has two aspects, economic and institutional.

The cornerstone of the economic aspect of the problem is the exchange rate, i.e. how to reach a realistic exchange rate and how to create a system for its application. In other words, it is necessary to replace the administrative system of foreign exchange allocation with a form of convertibility. Of course, in practice this task is much broader. It is necessary to create uniform rules in the area of foreign exchange allocation, legislation in the area of the payment system, money and capital markets, etc. This may often be more difficult than basic economic decisions themselves.

Opinions as to how to achieve a realistic exchange rate are varied not only in east European countries. In principle, there are two ways possible: either stabilisation of the exchange rate at a realistic, maintainable level or a floating system. The first alternative, i.e.. a fixed exchange rate, is apparently possible only when a stabilisation period during the initial phase of economic reform is not necessary, and when this policy is accompanied by the gradual development of the market environment. This scheme was applied for the stabilisation of the exchange rate of the Czechoslovak and Czech crown. This was made possible by the fact that Czechoslovakia entered the economic reform with relatively sound state finances, low external debt, and a relatively low inflation rate.

The gross external debt of the Czech Republic totals $US 7.9 billion, which is less, for example, than in Hungary ($US 23.6 billion) and other countries such as Portugal, Greece and Turkey.

By adopting the fixed exchange rate scheme we did not feel the disadvantages of the floating exchange rate system, especially its sensitivity to speculative pressures, tendencies towards excessive devaluation, and hence a significant imported inflation.

As is well known, very tight monetary and fiscal policies were implemented in the initial phase of the transformation process. The exchange rate of the crown was made more realistic through devaluations, and a system of internal convertibility was introduced. In this way, the possible development of an inflationary spiral was prevented. After price deregulation, inflation was quickly controlled and the balance of payments stabilized.

The exchange rate has been stable in relation to the basket of freely convertible currencies since the beginning of 1991. This means nominal stability. However, there has been a real appreciation of the Czech currency as the inflation rate in OECD countries was lower than in the Czech Republic during the period in question. Therefore, the initial "pro-export" bias of the exchange rate has been eroded.

Table 1 Budget balance and inflation rates in selected countries.

	Czech Republic	Hungary	Belgium	Portugal	Spain	Greece
State budget balance 1992 (% of GDP)	- 0.9	- 7.0	- 6.7	- 5.6	- 4.6	- 13.4
Inflation rate as of mid-1993 (in % per year)	21.3*	20.9	2.4	5.5	4.9	15.8

* of which about one-half is the one-time impact of the tax reform

In this context, I would like to comment on the frequently pronounced opinion that the initial devaluation was extraordinarily high. In the case of Czechoslovakia, it was of vital importance to reduce the demand for foreign exchange to a level enabling a sustainable development of the balance of payments, given the low foreign exchange reserves at the beginning of the economic reform. If we had not succeeded in this, it would have resulted in the threat of either a series of subsequent devaluations with unpredictable inflationary impacts, or insolvency, and the loss of credibility among the general public, foreign investors, and international institutions. These risks led logically to the creation of a certain "safety measure" determined by the initial level of devaluation. Even today I am of the opinion that in a situation where estimates of price movements were, in principle, impossible, the introduced exchange rate measures were adequate for the conditions which existed at that time.

Another very relevant problem is how long a fixed exchange rate for the Czech currency is needed. If we consider the hitherto higher inflation level in our country than in the countries of our trading partners, we must recognize that sooner or later it will be necessary to contemplate further devaluations. However, in practice, there exists a certain "competition" between the decrease of the inflation rate and the use of the "pro-export room" created by the initial devaluation rate. The monetary policy of the Czech Republic is directed toward curbing the inflation rate, roughly to the average rate attained in the EC countries, without completely spending the aforementioned "limited room". If we succeed we can look forward to a relatively durable stability of the exchange rate.

On the other hand, this situation has created pressure in the microeconomic sphere, in particular, on exporters, to lower their production costs. In this area, enough room still exists.

Our experiences reveal that internal convertibility is only of a transitional nature and will require further deregulation toward free convertibility. We have seen how difficult it is to control semi-legal and illegal capital transactions which get around foreign exchange regulations. Further development will obviously lead to free convertibility being introduced sooner than anticipated. It is often reasoned that west European countries needed many years to reach full convertibility, and, that it is ridiculous, therefore, for us to want it in such a relatively short period of time. However, this argument forgets that the external environment was homogeneous at the time. Nowadays, to maintain "semi-convertibility" in a fully convertible environment is difficult.

Hitherto results have proved that our reform steps are, in principle, not wrong. I consider it a great success that the credibility of our currency has been renewed, even in the circumstances of the division of the CSFR and the currency split. We succeeded in fending of some speculative attacks on the exchange rate and foreign exchange reserves towards the end of 1992 and in early 1993.

Continued currency stabilization and integration into the international monetary system are also reflected in some new phenomena, which reveal that the process is apparently entering a new phase. For example, differences in interest rates have brought about an inflow of "hot" money from abroad with the aim to take profit from these interest differentials. For us this is a sign that foreign investors trust the stability of the Czech currency. The Czech corporate sector, including small and medium-sized enterprises, has also increased the volume of loans from abroad, given higher credit interest rates in the country, without fear of exchange rate risk. Presently, the volume of foreign financing of operational and investment requirements of the corporate sector amounts to approximately $US 1 billion.

Also with regard to the general public - and this is a very sensitive area - the tendency toward the stabilization of the demand for foreign exchange has been very pronounced. Czech citizens have the right to keep acquired foreign exchange and to freely dispose of it, with the only restriction requiring them to deposit it in their accounts at domestic commercial banks. The main source of foreign exchange are revenues from tourism, transfers, etc. This partial "dollarisation" of deposits has its historical roots. It reflects experience from the past when access to foreign exchange was limited, and, therefore, citizens were not willing to exchange acquired foreign exchange for crowns. However, the steep growth in foreign exchange savings of individuals in the years 1990 - 1992 was halted in the course of this year. Deposits in foreign exchange accounts levelled of at approximately $US 1.4

billion, with a recent tendency to decrease.

At the same time, the purchase of foreign exchange by individuals with domestic currency, mostly for the purpose of holidays abroad, is restricted. This year's limit is CZK 7,500 per person/per year (approximately US 250). This limit is not fully exploited. Only approximately 20 - 25 % of Czech citizens buy foreign exchange. During the first eight months of this year, sales of foreign exchange to Czech citizens by banks were down by $US 17 million compared with last year (a decrease of approximately 10 %)

Even in this area, there are some prerequisites for significant simplification of the foreign exchange regime. The abolition of foreign exchange limits and other administrative restrictions on the public are anticipated by 1995 at the latest. In other words, integration in this area has a relatively clear perspective.

I think that the development of integration of the Czech Republic into the international monetary system has definitely passed through its initial phase. It would be wrong, however, to see this process as one without problems, especially in the light of last year's shocks in the ERM. This brings up, on one hand, the question of the direction and rapidity of the liberalization of the capital account, and, on the other, of the necessity to build some braking mechanisms within the foreign exchange regime which would make speculative transactions involving the national currency more difficult. In practical terms, it will consist of the gradual deepening of the liberalization of capital imports, including its return transfers, while restrictions imposed on capital exports for residents will be abolished only very prudently.

The problem of speculative capital movement remains, though not only in the Czech Republic. The low development of the capital market could constitute a certain braking factor which, at least temporarily, makes quick movements of extremely high volumes of speculative capital more difficult.

However, integration into the international monetary system also has its institutional aspect. It does not, of course, relate only to the fact that central and east European countries entered early into international monetary institutions such as the IMF and the World Bank, and that the EBRD was founded.

More important are the effects of these institutional changes. I think that it is necessary to start from the fact that all central and east European countries needed both methodological and, in particular, financial support (more precisely, foreign exchange), to launch their reform steps. And this was provided. Even Czechoslovakia, whose economy was the most consolidated one at the time, urgently needed to strengthen its foreign exchange reserves in order to be able to launch its economic reform. Without this financial support, at least the first phase of the reform would have lasted much longer and been much more painful. For this reason, I assess the attitude of these organizations as positive.

This was just the first step. If we speak about the integration of the former COMECON countries into the international monetary system, we cannot forget the issue of international capital markets. The possibility to raise funds on these markets, especially through bond issues, is an integral part of the integration processes. However, of all former COMECON countries, only Hungary and the former Czechoslovakia had access (due to adequate credibility) to these markets. The only possible external sources of finances for all other countries were government credits and credits from international institutions.

On one hand, this increases the importance of these official sources, but, on the other, it bears evidence that the integration of Central and Eastern Europe into the international monetary system has many forms and does not always proceed with the same speed.

The list of countries that have access to private capital and institutional investors has not expanded so far. It remains limited to the Czech Republic, Hungary, and Slovakia which have already made use of the international capital market. Access to this market cannot be demanded, it must be earned by implementing trustworthy economic policies. This is also an integral part of the monetary integration.

In conclusion, allow me these comments. I have focused my remarks on the Czech Republic and its experiences of economic reform. I am fully aware of how difficult it is to make international comparisons, especially for the group of former east-block countries. For instance, the differences between Poland and the Republics in Central Asia, are greater than those between, let us say, Turkey and Holland. That is why our experiences cannot be considered as generally valid.

Further, I would like to add that when analyzing the transformation processes, their success is compared, in large part, to the development of the GDP. We have many doubts whether this is suitable. When I put aside the technical aspect of the problem, i.e. the reliability of data acquired during the period of the restructuring of our statistical systems, the fact remains that the abolition of central planning, the programme of privatization and other transformation processes, and, in particular, their rapidity, cast doubt on the comparability of the bases for the calculation of individual indexes.

As most important, I consider the fact that during the transformation process the GDP has been declining in all countries, no matter what form of economic reform is applied. This raises the question whether the effects on the development of the GDP of the collapse of central planning and the termination of COMECON (as the external part of central planning) were not the critical causes of the initial fall of the GDP irrespective of the adopted shape of economic reform.

4 Cooperation Across the Atlantic and Across the Rhine

DANIEL COHEN

1 Introduction

Macroeconomics of the past two decades is in large part the story of how a few specific shocks (the oil shock, the Reagan shock, the German shock) have been inefficiently propagated among industrialized countries.

Despite the variety of the shocks which had to be analyzed, most of the theory of policy coordination rested on essentially a single paradigm, the "beggar-my-neighbor" story, a paradigm which in the seventies and eighties became the centerpiece of models describing the consequences of the oil shock. These models describe two countries which are adversely hit by an inflationary shock. Both of them try to pass the inflation to the other by (vainly) attempting to over-appreciate their currency one against the other. (See Sachs (1983) and Miller and Salmon (1984); influential early analyses were those of Hamada (1985) and Canzoneri and Gray (1985)).

This standard paradigm takes no account of a crucial difference between two different types of international transmission mechanisms: one in which the two countries influence each other mainly through the aggregate demand effects of trade flows, and another where it is prices (rather than volumes) which are the main source of the propagation mechanism. Furthermore, not all shocks are as symmetric as the oil shock. Instead, many - the Regan shock and the German unification shock, for instance - are of an asymetric nature. In what direction should policy-coordination then be going?

Relying on previous work with Charles Wyplosz, I re-examine the appropriate role and nature of international policy coordination in light of the following differences between transatlantic and intra-European interactions. European countries are trading partners for which wide fluctuations of the real exchange rate have very costly demand effects. Europe and the US, on the other hand, are <u>relatively</u> more integrated by the effect of prices (oil prices, the value of the dollar, ...) on their economic activities than through the direct effects of trade flows. This distinction is documented in Cohen and Wyplosz (1991). In other words, European countries mainly interact through the direct effect of trade on their economies, while Europe and the United States interact through the effects of their policy decisions on each others' Philipps curves. This leads European policymakers to be too cautious with respect to the use of fiscal policy, when they are hit by a symmetric shock. Each individual European policymaker fears a trade disequilibrium which *ex post* never comes about, since all European countries move in a parallel fashion. On the other hand, it leads Europe and the US, when they are hit by a joint shock, to be too restrictive with respect to their monetary policy: each of them attempt to reduce the burden of inflation by (vainly) trying to appreciate one currency against the other. The end result is opposite to what would happened within Europe: there is too much fiscal accomodation, and too little monetary accomodation.

In order to be more specific upon the choices of policy instruments, I will spell out a simple model of policy making and policy coordination in Section 2. The reader who is impatient to read the conclusions can skip the next section and switch to Sections 3 and 4 in which I specifically address the debate over policy coordination in the past two decades.

2 A Framework of analysis

2.1 Monetary and fiscal policies in an open economy

Consider first a small country whose macroeconomic equilibrium is obtained by two equations, one being the Phillips curve (interpreted as a supply curve), the other one being a trade balance equilibrium (interpreted as a demand curve). Call π the inflation rate, z the real competitiveness of the country, Q output, A domestic absorption, and ε a random term which shifts the Phillips curve. We can then describe the equilibrium in this economy by the following two equations:

$$\pi = az + bQ + \epsilon \tag{1}$$

$$Q = A + hz \tag{2}$$

The intuition of these two equations is fairly simple. Real devaluations (increases in z) create inflationary pressures (equation (1)), and so do a growth of output (Q). On the other hand, real devaluations create a trade surplus and hence an increase in aggregate demand and output (equation (2)).

To simplify to the extreme the debate over policy instruments, we shall directly assume that monetary policy makes the inflation rate, π, a policy instrument, while fiscal policy makes aggregate absorption, A, another instrument. The macroeconomic equilibrium can then be obtained as in diagram 1.

Diagram 1

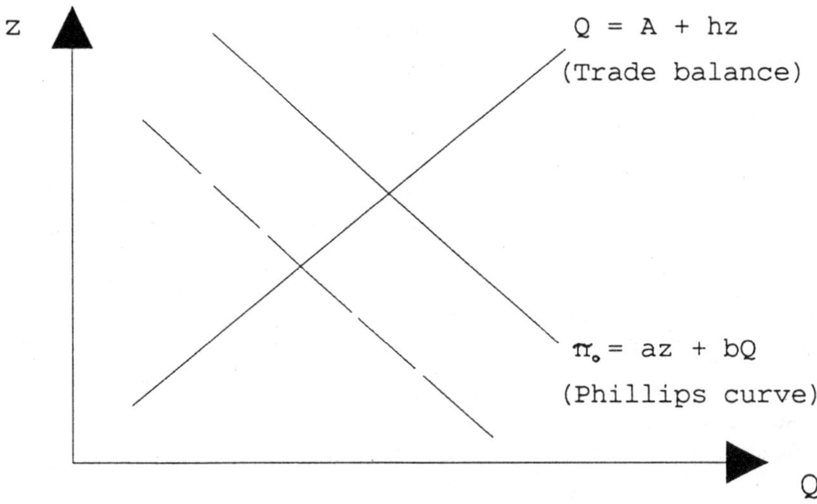

Consider a positive shock ε that creates inflationary pressures. If the shock is not accomodated, the new equilibrium is a "stagflation" point: there is a recession and simultaneously an inflation. The exchange rate is appreciated. Intuititively, one wants to think that the inflationary pressure, when not accommodated by a loose monetary policy, raises the interest rate and appreciates the currency. In our model, the channel is directly embedded in the way the Phillips curve is written.

When monetary and fiscal policies are geared towards alleviating the shock, two new effects are at work. By loosening monetary policy, the authorities may directly offset the external shock, at the expense of higher inflation. But the authorities can also expand output through a fiscal expansion. This raises output (through the demand expansion) and (further) appreciates the real exchange rate. Again, an intuitive explanation would involve the interest rate effect of a fiscal expansion.

When both instruments are used, the picture looks like in diagram 2. Both fiscal and monetary policies can help reduce the magnitude of the recession. Depending upon which one of the two is more active, the effect on the real exchange rate (and upon the trade balance) can go either way.

Diagram 2

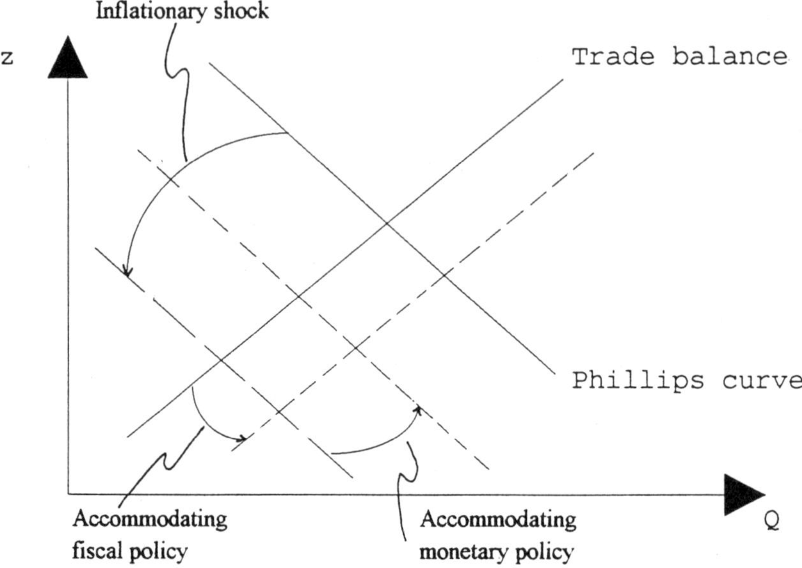

In order to be more specific about the direction of the change of the real exchange rate, one must first take account of the relative cost of using fiscal and monetary policy and of the ratio (a/h) which measures the relative impact of exchange-rate variations upon the Philipps curve and the trade balance, respectively. Let us focus on this term.

a. When (a/h) is big, the Phillips curve is flat (relatively to the Trade Balance Curve). In this case the policymaker has less of an incentive to accommodate the shock by an expansionary monetary policy, and will rely more upon fiscal policy. The reason is that monetary policy "mostly" determines (inflation and) the exchange rate, and that fiscal policy has strong effects on output.

b. When (a/h) is low, it is the trade balance schedule which is relatively flatter than the Phillips curve. In this case, fiscal policy is not a powerfull tool ofoutput stabilization. Indeed, when h is relatively big, the response of imports to domestic demand is large, so that a fiscal expansion is dissipated into higher imports rather than in an expansion of domestic output. In the limit, when h becomes infinitely large, the law of one price holds and the policy maker has no incentive to use fiscal policy at all (see Cohen (1989)).

2.2 Policy coordination

Let us now address the core question: how is policy coordination among a group of countries likely to affect the use of the monetary and fiscal instruments and, therefore, the real exchange rate and the trade disequilibrium?

In order to address this question, let us consider two identical countries 1 and 2 whose bilateral real exchange rate z, and whose real exchange rates with the rest of the world is respectively z_1 and $z_2 = z_1 - z$. Assume that the two countries' Phillips curves and trade balance eqations are now written respectively as

$$\pi_1(t) = a_1 z_1(t) + az(t) + bQ_1 + \epsilon_1(t)$$

$$\pi_2(t) = a_2 z_2(t) - az(t) + bQ_2 + \epsilon_2(t)$$

$$TB_1(t) = h_1 z_1(t) + hz(t)$$

$$TB_2(t) = h_2 z_2(t) + hz(t)$$

where ε_1 and ε_2 are two shocks which move each country's Phillips curve. We shall focus here on two extremes. The case when the shocks are symmetric, i.e, $\varepsilon_1 = \varepsilon_2$, and the case when the shocks are asymmetric, i.e $\varepsilon_1 = - \varepsilon_2$.

2.2.1 The symmetric case

When the two countries are hit by symmetric shocks, the equilibrium that they will eventually reach will also be symmetric. In particular, the end point will be characterized by $\Delta z = 0$ and $\Delta z_1 = \Delta z_2$. The real exchange rates of the two countries will not move, and their real competitiveness will not be affected. When they do *not* coordinate their policies, however, each country fails to internalize the fact that the other country moves in the same direction. This creates unnecessary constraints on policy making. In which direction do these constraints tip the balance of policy responses? In order to answer this question, one must distinguish two cases.

(i) When intra-regional trade (i.e. trade between country 1 and country 2) is "relatively" inelastic with respect to exchange rates.

Technically, this corresponds to the case when $(h_1/a_1) > (h/a)$. This inequality means that the influence of the bilateral real exchange rate on intra-regional trade (h) relative to its effect on the Phillips curve is small compared to the same ratio calculated with the elasticities with respect to the world exchange rate (h_1/a_1).

If a single policy maker were to determine the policies of both countries in the region, he would only take his decisions in view of the outside elasticities (since he would internalize the fact that intra-regional trade plays no role). In this case this means that the region's social planner would not wish to use fiscal policy as much as the individual domestic policy maker. Policy coordination would thus *loosen monetary policy* and *tighten fiscal policy* and hence bring *less exchange rate variation* and *smaller trade disequilibria*.

(ii) When intra-regional trade is "relatively" elastic to exchange rates.

This corresponds to the case where $(h/a) > (h_1/a_1)$. In this case the results go the other way around. Because internal trade is very exchange-rate elastic (h is big relatively to a), the domestic policy maker acting alone would not use fiscal policy very much (because he wrongly fears that this would create a trade disequilibrium originating within the zone).

In this case policy coordination would reduce monetary accomodation, increase the fiscal response, and raise trade disequilibria and exchange rate changes with respect to the rest of the world.

2.2.2 The asymmetric case

There is no need to present a detailed analysis of this case: the results are simply exactly opposite to those which were obtained in the preceding case. Indeed, in this case, each individual policy maker fails to internalize the fact that his partner within the zone moves in a direction which is exactly opposite to his own. In other words, he fails to internalize the fact that, say, the internal trade effects of his actions are actually twice bigger than what he actually thinks (because the other country within the zone magnifies his decision is the opposite direction). This leads to the following results.

(i) When intra-regional trade is relatively inelastic.

In this case, policy coordination would tighten monetary policy and loosen fiscal policy.

ii) When internal trade is relatively elastic.

This is just the opposite: policy coordination would loosen monetary policy and tighten fiscal policy.

Our results are summarized in the following box:

	Trade effects dominate within the region	Price effects dominate within the region
Symmetric shocks	SOS fiscal policy more active than NC SOS monetary policy tighter than NC	SOS fiscal policy less active than NC SOS monetary policy looser
Asymmetric shocks	SOS fiscal policy less active than NC SOS monetary policy looser than NC	SOS fiscal policy more active than NC SOS monetary policy tighter than NC

SOS = Socially efficient solution, NC = Nash (un-cooperative) solution

Rather than repeating the intuition for these results, we now turn to the implication of these results for analyzing the consequences of the major shocks of the past decade.

3 Policy coordination in the last two decades

Let us now review two major episodes of the past two decades: the responses to the oil shock and the response to German reunification.

3.1 The oil shock

This is the standard shock that has been examined in the literature. The oil shock is the prime example of a "stagflationary" shock which raises inflation and reduces output.

Let us first examine how policy coordination across the Atlantic should be designed in order to accomodate the shock. Both Europe as a whole and the US observe a downward shift of their Phillips curve, and neither is really concerned by transatlantic trade disequilibria. They respond by too loose a fiscal policy, and too tight a monetary policy. By doing so, they hope to transfer the burden of inflation to their transatlantic partner. To some degree, one can then see the Reagan-Volcker policy mix as an endogenous response to the (second) oil shock that follows that prediction. One surprise of many observers was that the trade deficit did not increase so much, despite the huge exchange-rate disequilibrium. As Krugman put it, following a line of Conan Doyle, the "dog (i.e., the trade balance) did not bark". This is consistent with the view that policy making across the atlantic paid little attention to trade disequilibria. But the failure to coordinate their response to the stagflation of the early eighties meant that policymakers moved too much in the direction of tightening monetary policy and exacerbated the fluctuation of the exchange rates. From that perspective, policy coordination focused on the exchange rates contained in the Plazza and the Louvre agreements was going in the right direction. It failed to impose fiscal discipline on the US, however, and was consequently only half right. Conversely, the mode of policy coordination that was open by the first oil shock, almost a decade earlier, by the Bonn summit was inadequate. By focusing on the "locomotive" theory that fiscal expansion was key to the recovery, they wrongly emphasized the need for fiscal stimuli. Exchange-rate coordination across the atlantic should have been the key issue.

From a European perspective, however, the oil shock should not have been accomodated in the same way. Indeed, the contention in this paper is that in the case of Europe each individual policymaker fears that any manipulation of the exchange rate will result into a massive trade disequilibrium with his other European partners. This leads the European policy maker to under-utilise fiscal expansion to fight the recession, and to be too laxist with respect to monetary policy. In brief, the European policymaker was not in a position to do what the US achieved: a tight monteary policy and a loose fiscal policy. From a strictly European perspective, the "locomotive" theory of policy coordination would have been appropriate. The proper policy mix would have been a <u>joint</u> fiscal expansion - which, since it was collective, would not have lead to any intra-european trade disequilibria - and a tight monetary policy - to offset its inflationary effects. Although it is not strictly speaking the same thing, the EMS can be viewed as such an attempt to put some monetary discipline within Europe. But it failed to be accompanied by the appropriate fiscal stimulus.

3.2 German reunification.

This shock can be characterized as an asymmetric shock which imposes inflationary pressures on Germany alone. As we noted in the discussion in section 2, asymmetric shocks call for opposite responses to those called for by symmetric shocks. Each individual policymaker fails to internalize the fact that the other party moves in a direction which is opposite to its own. In the case of Europe, for which trade disequilibria are very costly in terms of jobs, this implies that Germany, say, has been relying too much on fiscal looseness (and trade desequilibria) to alleviate the cost of the reunification. Policy coordination would have tigthtened fiscal policy in Germany (and loosened fiscal policy in France), and loosened (tightened) monetary policy in Germany (France).

Put differently, policy coordination, in that case, would have *reduced* imbalances in trade volumes, and *raised* inflation differentials. As one sees, this is just the opposite to what policy coordination within the EMS has imposed upon its members. This should come as no surprise. EMS is an institution which has been designed to cope with symmetric shocks of the oil shock type. It is inappropriate for dealing with asymmetric shocks. Let us now review more specifically that point.

4 The Arguments against EMU

The arguments in the 1980s in favor of EMU were made in a period when Europe was subject to shocks which were essentially symmetric: oil shocks, fluctuations of the dollar and of American interest rates. Coordinated European policy responses, and ultimately European Monetary Integration, may then have appeared to be natural inasmuch as the Single Market made it possible to militate for "one market, one money".

Yet, Europe of the 1990s does not resemble much the Europe of the first half of the eighties. It is no longer the United States which imposes high interest rates, and it is not Japan which imposes trade imbalances (through an undervalued Yen) on Europe. Europe has now become a zone of "strong" currencies with high interest rates because of its own disequilibria.

If one trusts the analysis that has been offered in this chapter, one sees that coordination should go in a direction opposite to the EMU: European countries should reduce imbalances in trade volumes, and raise inflation differentials. Hence the strains on the ERM.

Does that foreclose the EMU? I don't think so. For one thing, the German shock is either transitory or permanent. If it is permanent, then Germany will have to adjust domestically.[1] No appreciation of the currency can help offset a *permanent* loss of income. All that the country can do is reduce its standard of living correspondingly.

If the German shock is transitory, then the short-term cost of the EMU must be compared to the long run consequences of not having one. Even though Europe appears *today* to be more concerned with its idiosyncratic disturbances, it would be extremely short-sighted to believe that this will always be the case. The fluctuations of the dollar, of the yen, and of world interest rates will not long remain as insignificant as they are now. A single European currency will then be in a position to provide what the EMS was designed to accomplish: allow Europe as a whole to respond collectively to the world monetary disorders and avoid a futile competition among its own currencies.

NOTES

1. If an earthquake permanently destroys 10% of a country's wealth, having a currency of its own or not will change little to the welfare of the country.

REFERENCES

Canzoneri, M. and J.A. Gray (1985). "Monetary Policy Games and the Consequence of Non-Cooperative Behavior", International Economic Review, vol.26, pp. 547-564.

Cohen, D. (1989) - "Monetary and Fiscal Policy in an Open Economy with or without Policy Coordination", European Economic Review, March, Papers and Proceedings.

_____ and Ph. Michel (1988). "How Should Control Theory Be Used to Calculate a Time-Consistent Government Policy", Review of Economic Studies, LV, pp. 263-74.

Cohen, D. and C. Wyplosz (1989). "European Monetary Union: An Agnostic - Evaluation", in Macroeconomic Policies in an Interdependent World. In R. Bryant et. al., (eds.). Washington, D.C: The Brookings Institution.

Cohen, D. and C. Wyplosz (1991) - "France and Germany in the EMS: the Exchange Rate Constraint". In G. Alogoskoufis, R. Portes and L. Papademos (eds.), The Exchange Rate Constraint. Cambridge: Cambridge University Press.

Hamada, K. (1985). The Political Economy of International Monetary Independence. Cambridge, Massachusetts: MIT Press.

Mélitz, J. (1987). "Germany, Discipline and Cooperation in the EMS". In F. Giavazzi et al. (eds.), The European Monetary System. Cambridge: Cambridge University Press.

Miller, M. and M. Salmon (1985). "Policy Coordination and Dynamic Games". In W. Buiter and R. Marston (eds.), International Policy Coordination. Cambridge: Cambridge University Press.

Sachs, J. (1983) "International Policy Coordination in a Dynamic Macroeconomic Model", NBER, Working Paper No. 1166.

Discussion

SHIJURO OGATA

There seem to be two kinds of international policy cooperation. One is "passive" cooperation, which is activated or strengthened to deal with existing or emerging economic disturbances. The other is "positive" cooperation in which efforts are made to attain a more advanced stage of joint international economic management. The establishment and the reform of the Bretton Woods institutions, the establishment of the European Monetary System and the attempt to proceed to European Monetary Union may all belong to the latter.

If we look back upon recent international developments, however, we have to admit that there are signs which indicate some weakening of international policy cooperation. In the first place, there are more "passive" cases than "positive" cases. Major countries tend to strengthen their cooperation only after some crisis or some violent reaction of market forces. Secondly, there seems to be less willingness to cooperate on the part of major countries. There must be a number of factors behind such trends.

In the first place, in almost all major countries, their economic policy management is being conducted with emphasis on stability (rather than growth) and the preoccupation with domestic affairs (rather than global affairs) in spite of increasing international interdependence. Having been a central banker, I am fully aware of the importance of domestic price stability as the basis for a sustainable growth, but if stability orientation and domestic preoccupation are combined, the willingness to cooperate internationally can be weakened.

Such a trend is partly influenced by the bitter memories of many economic and financial excesses during the '70s and '80 when growth was encouraged in the name of international cooperation after the oil shock and after the Reagan-Volcker shock, if I borrow the terminology of Mr. Cohen. Such a trend is also due to the fact that in many major countries, the political leadership is weak and therefore inevitably inward-looking. Politicians are mainly seeking the support of voters without paying proper attention to the international implication of their own policies.

Secondly, the inflexibility of fiscal policy and the over-burdening of monetary policy seem to continue, not only in the countries with large fiscal deficits but also in the countries with relatively favorable fiscal positions, such as Japan. The inadequate policy mix of major countries must have contributed to international imbalances.

For instance, the so-called Reagan-Volcker shock can be interpreted at least partly as the product of the too easy fiscal policy and the too tight money policy of the United States and the opposite policy mix of Japan; both started due to the inflexibility of their respective fiscal policy. Japan is now facing another ' shock", which can be called " Clinton shock" the sharp rise of the yen on top of the prolonged recession, triggered by the repeated remarks of U.S. high officials welcoming the yen's appreciation as the most effective means of Japan's balance of payments adjustment, There are a number of factors, both in Japan and in its trading partners, for such large imbalances. But one of those factors is again the inflexibility of Japanese fiscal policy together with that of U. S. fiscal policy in opposite direction.

How should we overcome these problems? Frankly, there is no simple answer. But I would like to make the following modest suggestions.

First, the G-7 summit exercise should be improved. The present practice of intensive bureaucratic preparation of the conferences and communiques is not productive. But it is useful and necessary, once in a while, to have occasions to remind the ordinarily domestic oriented top leaders of major countries of the importance of international cooperation. What I would like to propose is to make the summit a more informal forum where these top leaders have face-to-face discussions, without too much bureaucratic assistance, and inform each other of the world's and respective countries' developments and problems, thereby mutually enlightening and encouraging each other in order to strengthen their respective leadership in the own countries and in the world.

Second, the role of the IMF and the World Bank should be strengthened. The Bretton Woods institutions have been effective with regard to the problems of their smaller member countries, but not so effective to their largest shareholders. I would like to propose to make the IMF the de facto secretariat to the G7 meetings, in connection with their surveillance of exchange rate policies, and the related international policy cooperation, if not in connection with other, more political agenda items. An international institution established to exercise surveillance over the exchange rate policies of member countries, the Fund should be entitled to get involved more directly in the discussions among major currency countries.

In addition, in order to let major countries listen to the IMF's recommendation more carefully, I would propose to set up a small advisory committee consisting of qualified persons of international repute, including those from major countries, so that the Fund can refer its draft recommendation of critical importance to this committee before presenting it to member countries in question.

Third, it is extremely important to build up reasonable and constructive public opinion: in many countries in order to obtain wider recognition of the reality of global interdependence and the need for stronger international cooperation. This kind of conference will definitely serve such a purpose, but this is a modest beginning. Efforts should be continued at academic, business and official levels across borders and across professional divisions.

In closing my short remarks, I could not but recall the last visit to Japan by the late Otmar Emminger at the end of 1985, the year of the Plaza Accord, the year of the drastic fall of the U. S. dollar. When he visited us at the Bank of Japan, he said that in 1978 he and others had to make decisions which were not the best for Germany but good for the world, apparently referring to the Bonn Summit. Looking into 1986 which was just coming, he told us that the coming year might be another year in which we would have to make decisions which might not be the best for individual countries but good for the world. Shortly after this visit, he died in the Philippines. Therefore, these words are his last words at least for me.

I am afraid that what is missing at present is what Emminger said at the end of 1985.

Discussion

TORSTEN PERSSON

It is a pleasure to make these comments against the backdrop of such a thought-provoking paper as the one by Daniel Cohen. His paper - like some of his earlier work with Charles Wyplosz - departs in two refreshing ways from what has been the main track in the literature on international policy cooperation or coordination, since the mid eighties. Rather than studying policy interactions between two symmetric countries, the paper allows for *asymmetries* both in economic structure and in the shocks that hit the countries. And it suggests two imaginative reinterpretations of the same formal model, either as portraying the interactions between the US and an aggregate of the European countries, or else as portraying intra-European interactions. Hence, the title of the paper.

Specifically, the paper derives and discusses a number of results regarding how the jointly optimal policy mix differs from the equilibrium policy stance in a setting of decentralized policy making, depending on economics structure and the type of shocks. A key insight is that the results hinge crucially on the relative strength of international spill-overs via prices and via trade volumes. The most interesting upshot of the analysis, in my view, is the perspective that it offers on the EMU-project.

In these comments, I will use the paper as a stepping-stone for discussing three issues. First, I will comment on what difference it makes whether the attempted cooperation is going for a discretionary one time deal or whether it takes place in a rules-based institutional framework of ongoing interaction. Second, in keeping with the theme of the conference, I will specialize the discussion to deal with systems for multilateral exchange rate pegging. And finally, I will try to draw some lessons for design of international monetary institutions generally, and the EMU specifically.

1 Cooperation via discretion or rules?

The crux of much of the literature on international policy coordination is that it stops at the level of suggesting that there may be prospective gains from coordinating the macroeconomic policies of two or more countries, without suggesting how such coordination may be enforced. After all, the "cooperative solution" require countries to pursue policies that run against their own individual short-run interests.

To discuss enforcement, it is useful to distinguish two stylized polar environments of international policy making, namely a discretionary framework versus a rules-based framework. What I mean by coordination in a discretionary setting is an attempt by some countries to cut a one-shot deal regarding the stance of their macroeconomic policies at a given time. Real-world examples would be the Bonn Summits, the Plaza and Louvre accords, and various other attempts by G-10 countries to agree. Coordination in a rules-based setting, by contrast, involves shaping repeated policy interactions in an explicit institutional framework. Here, the prime examples would, of course, include the Bretton Woods system and the EMS.

There are two reasons, I believe, why enforcement of cooperative outcomes are inherently easier in a rules-based framework. The first is that institutionalized repeated interactions between a given group of actors facilitates enforcement by reputational mechanisms, a well-known point from many situations of strategic interaction. The second reason is that under discretion there is no meaningful distinction between a design stage and an implementation stage: the participants are just trying to strike a deal in a given situation with apparent conflicts of interest. A rules-based framework, on the contrary, can be thought about as policy interaction, which is influenced by some rewards or sanctions embodied in an institution that was designed at some earlier point in time. At that institution-design stage, the future specific interests of the participating countries are much more open. This implies that any decisions regarding the enforcement mechanisms to be put in place are made under a "veil of ignorance", which is likely to promote the willingness to sustain cooperative outcomes. (For an articulation of this view in more detail, see Persson and Tabellini (1994).)

The recent analytical literature on international policy coordination has actually recognized the role of reputational mechanisms - see, for instance, the recent survey of the field in Canzoneri and Henderson (1991). But it has not paid much attention to the institutional mechanisms. One important reason why the policy coordination literature has not made more of an impact may indeed be that it most often stopped at the point of analysing international policy strategies, rather than taking the further step of asking how the domestic and international policy-making institutions shape the incentives for these strategies by providing explicit or implicit rewards or sanctions conditional on policies or policy outcomes.

The formal analysis in Daniel Cohen's paper does not shed any light on the distinction between policy making under rules and discretion; a static model as his, is not well geared towards addressing such questions. Nevertheless, as I will argue below, the discussion in the paper naturally leads one to think about the institution design questions, at least it led me to think about them.

2 Cooperation and asymmetries in fixed exchange rate regimes

One theme emphasized in the paper is the distinction between symmetric and asymmetric macroeconomic shocks hitting some economies that may, or may not, coordinate their macroeconomic policies. Faced with symmetric shocks, reasonably similar countries reach a better outcome if they can agree to pursue reasonably convergent monetary and fiscal policies, without trying to export some of their macroeconomic problems abroad via competitive depreciations or appreciations. As Cohen rightly argues, a multilateral fixed exchange rate arrangement might foster good policy outcomes under such circumstances, in that it requires convergent monetary policies and may make countries internalize the costs to other countries of short-run strategic policy making. The first ones to clearly articulate this argument were Canzoneri and Gray (1985). I would only add that the prospective benefits from coordination are much more likely to be realized in a multilateral institutionalized peg, where the participating countries really think about the exchange rate arrangement as a rule with some sanctions attached to strategic abuse of the system.

Whereas this kind of arrangement may be a virtue if shocks are symmetric, it becomes a vice in the wake of asymmetric shocks. This is because such shocks require a divergent policy response. Indeed, a coordinated response requires even wider diverging policies than what's in the individual interest of each country. A monetary arrangement that tie strong incentives to convergent policies is then worse than having no arrangement at all. Cohen portrays the strain and eventual breakdown of the

EMS in the aftermath of German unification - clearly an asymmetric shock - in these terms. One can tell a similar story about a U.S. fiscal policy shock - in connection with the Vietnam War and Johnson's Great Society program - playing a major role for the strain and eventual breakdown of the Bretton woods system.

Asymmetry in shocks is indeed a crucial consideration. But another asymmetry may also become central to the functioning and survival of fixed exchange rate system. (I abstain here from treating yet another set of asymmetries, which is well known from the literature on optimal currency areas, namely asymmetries in *structure* between the participating countries.) It emanates from the well-known "N-1 problem", essentially the question of what is to be the anchor of the system. The post-war exchange rate arrangements have resolved this issue by explicit or implicit agreements, where the task of defining the anchor was assigned to the U.S. Fed in the Bretton Woods system, whereas the German Bundesbank assumed it in the EMS. Clearly medium to long-run stability in the monetary policy of the central currency country was an important condition for the other pegging countries to go along with the agreement. A prime reason for the breakdown of both system was not only a large asymmetric shock, but an asymmetric shock that hit the central-currency country and challenged its attempts to maintain monetary stability.

The fiscal policy shocks to Germany and the US both implied a rise in the relative price of the central-currency country's goods. The Bundesbank was unwilling to let this happen via higher inflation in Germany, while the other countries were unwilling to devalue their currencies. This imposed on them contractionary monetary policies that eventually became very costly to sustain, speculative pressure developed, and the system broke down. Twenty years earlier, the Fed instead allowed U.S. inflation to rise in the late sixties. There was not a coordinated realignment of exchange rates until the Smithsonian agreement in 1971, at which point the dollar had instead become overvalued. But with an upcoming U.S. recession, the Fed was unwilling, or unable, to resume its role of providing monetary stability. In this case too, speculative pressure developed - albeit this time against the central currency country - and the system broke down.

These two episodes are thus different in that central-currency country maintained the anchor in one case, but let it go in the other. But they are similar in that failure to realign early imposed on the other countries undesirable macroeconomic outcomes - too much recession in the EMS case and too much inflation in the Bretton-Woods case.

3 International institution design

Based on the discussion above, an important aspect of a fixed exchange rate arrangement is its institutional underpinnings. The arrangement not only publicly pegs the relative price of two or more currencies, but also provides a set of perceived sanctions or rewards for sticking to the announced peg for some time. These perceived incentives will - for given parameters of structure and shocks - govern how hard the peg becomes: the possibilities range from the exchange rate being one out of several non-committing and unilaterally declared intermediate targets for a single country's monetary policy to full monetary union tied to membership in political union.

The developments in the EMS in the last decade can be thought about in terms of a trade-off, which is closely connected to these institutional considerations. On the one hand, a harder peg, with larger perceived costs of realignments, will make it less likely that the system implements desirable divergent policies in the wake of asymmetric shocks. On the other hand, a harder peg makes the system more useful as a commitment device for those member countries, whose attempts to follow low-inflation monetary policies are plagued by credibility problems. Institutional changes in the EMS - first the abolition of capital controls and next the plans for transition to monetary union - undoubtedly raised the perceived costs of following divergent policies leading up to a realignment. As pointed out by Cohen, the harder peg may have been well adapted to the kind of shocks hitting the member countries in the early eighties, but was ill adapted to the asymmetric shock hitting Germany at the end of the decade.

This kind of institution-design problem is essentially what is underlying the papers on the EMS by Giavazzi and Pagano (1988) and by Alesina and Grilli (1991). These papers portray the problem as necessarily trading off credibility against flexibility, much along the same lines as the literature, started by Rogoff (1985), on domestic credibility problems in monetary policy and prospective remedies by institutional reform. In the domestic context, delegating monetary policy to a conservative central banker gives more credibility in fighting inflation at the cost of less flexibility in stabilizing the economy. In the international context, delegating some decisions on monetary policy to the partners in the exchange rate arrangement gives more credibility to an inflation-prone country at the cost of less flexibility in stabilizing country-specific shocks. The upshot is, of course, that the peg should be harder - so that the "escape clause" of a realignment is triggered less often - the more important is the credibility problem relative to the frequency of country-specific shocks.

Even though this kind of logic seems impeccable, I think it misses some important questions. The first question is whether a half-way house between floating rates and full monetary union like the EMS of the early eighties is at all possible with today's high capital mobility. The thesis that destabilizing speculation may seriously threaten the stability of a fixed exchange rate arrangement was advanced by some sceptics, particularly Giavazzi and Giovannini (1989). The sceptics were subsequently proven right by the mayhem in European currency markets in 1992-93. Most wine tasters have always maintained that rosé wine combines the worst rather than the best of which and red wines. Some economists now seem to drift towards a similar thinking about arrangements like the EMS: they do not really entail any of the advantages of floating rates or monetary union, just their disadvantages. If that is the case, the stance one would take on the appropriate exchange rate arrangement for European countries largely depends on one's attitude towards of other aspects of European integration. For someone who is in favour of further economic and political integration, monetary union takes on additional benefits because it becomes part of a broader move towards a more federal structure. This is the stance that Daniel Cohen seems to take in the concluding section of his paper. But for someone who wishes to de-emphasize further integration in other areas, a route towards a more flexible exchange rate arrangement becomes natural.

Does the latter route mean giving up the possible gains of more credibility and better policy coordination that the enforcement by an international institution may entail? This is not clear. Credibility may be built at home by appropriate institutional reform. Furthermore, the recent "contract approach" to reform in Persson and Tabellini (1993) and Walsh (1994) shows that it may not be necessary to buy credibility at the price of lower flexibility. Applying a similar idea to the prospective gains from policy coordination. Persson and Tabellini (1994) show that under some circumstances cooperatives outcomes may indeed be implemented via appropriate domestic policymaking institutions without any supernational enforcement. These and other theoretical issues, as well as real world events, will keep economists interested in international monetary arrangements busy for some time to come.

REFERENCES

Alesina, A. and V. Grilli, 1992, "The European central bank: Reshaping monetary politics in Europe", in Canzoneri, M., V. Grilli, and P. Masson (eds.) Establishing a Central Bank: Issues in Europe and Lessons From the US. (Cambridge University Press).

Canzoneri, M. and J. Gray, 1985, "Monetary policy games and the consequences of non-cooperative behaviour", International Economic Review, 26, 547-64.

Canzoneri, M. and D. Henderson 1991, Monetary Policy in Interdependent Economies: A Game Theoretic Approach. (MIT Press).

Giavazzi, F. and A. Giovannini, 1989. Limiting Exchange Rate Flexibility. (MIT Press).

Giavazzi, F. and M. Pagano, 1988, "The advantage of tying ones hands: EMS discipline and central bank credibility". European Economic Review, 32, 1055-75.

Persson, T. and G. Tabellini, 1993, "Designing institutions for monetary stability", Carnegie-Rochester Conference Series, vol. 38.

Persson, T. and G. Tabellini, 1994, "Double-edged incentives: Institutions in macroeconomic policy", forthcoming in Grossman, G. and K. Rogoff (eds.) Handbook of International Economics, Vol III (North-Holland).

Rogoff, K., 1985, "The optimal degree of commitment to an intermediate monetary target", Quarterly Journal of Economics 100, 1169-90.

Walsh, C., 1994, "Optimal contracts for central bankers", forthcoming in American Economic Review.

5 Emerging Currency Blocks

JEFFREY A. FRANKEL AND SHANG-JIN WEI*

When countries in the 19th century joined the gold standard one-by-one, they were seeking to acquire more than just stability in the values of their currencies. They were moving toward closer integration, financially and economically, with the world economy. After World War I, the system fragmented into currency blocs and trading blocs: Sterling bloc, gold bloc, Central Europe bloc, and dollar bloc.[1] The allies who met at Bretton Woods in 1944 were determined not to repeat after World War II the fragmentation and instability that had characterized the interwar years. The ensuing period of growth in world trade and income indeed seemed to be closely associated with the common world monetary standard, the dollar standard.

The 1971-73 transition to floating exchange rates, among the dollar, yen, mark and pound, was only the beginning of a steady slide into currency entropy. The currencies of eighty smaller countries in the mid-1970s retained pegs to major currencies: the dollar, pound, French franc, or the SDR. Between 1975 and 1990, however, the number of countries pegging their currencies fell virtually monotonically. Exchange rate variability between most pairs of countries increased. Yet, despite fears that exchange rate uncertainty after 1973 would have an inhibiting effect, international trade continued to grow.

Recently, a new trend has begun to emerge. Some countries have sought to re-establish stability in their exchange rates. When they have done so, they have not always chosen to peg to the major currency to which they were most closely linked in the past. Rather, the emerging pattern that many observers see is a division of the world into three great blocs, reminiscent of the 1930s but drawn more along regional lines: a European bloc centered on the DM, an Americas bloc centered on the dollar, and an East Asian bloc, centered on the yen.

Formal regional economic arrangements have progressed the furthest in Europe. Within the European Community (EC), the European Monetary System (EMS) had succeeded in stabilizing exchange rates well enough by December 1991 that the members agreed on ambitious plans for European Monetary Union (EMU). Those plans were soon proved overly ambitious, but the long-run trend toward integration is nevertheless clear. The next successful project of the EC will most likely be enlargement to include those of the other Western European countries (members of EFTA -- European Free Trade Association) who wish to join. There is also talk of eventually including countries from Central and even Eastern Europe.

In the Western Hemisphere, there are some regional trading arrangements in place, such as the North American Free Trade Agreement (NAFTA), and others under discussion. There are, however, no formal monetary or financial arrangements analogous to the EMS or prospective EMU. Nevertheless, when a Latin American country like Argentina decides to peg its currency, the dollar is the currency to which it pegs. Many countries are heavily dollarized *de facto*.

In East Asia and the Pacific, formal regional arrangements are almost altogether absent.

This paper concerns two key aspects of the possible regionalization of economic relations, and the interaction between the two. They are trade links and currency links. That the two may be closely intertwined is evident in that a major motivation behind recent attempts to strengthen currency links within Europe is to reduce the extent to which exchange rate risk discourages imports and exports, and thereby to promote stronger trade links. Other important aspects, such as financial links within regions or the extent to which countries within a region share common economic disturbances, are not considered here.

1 Introduction

There is more talk of regionalization, of whether the world is breaking up into three great trading blocs or currency blocs (Europe, Western Hemisphere, and East Asia; or mark, dollar, and yen blocs), than there are attempts at hard quantitative analysis. Often studies simply report measures of the relative size of the blocs, such as shares of world trade, and measures of the extent of intra-regional trade, such as the fraction of countries' trade conducted with others in the region. But these are not measures of intra-regional bias, the extent to which countries are concentrating their economic activity with others in the region.[2]

The paper looks econometrically at three questions: (1) Is trade biased toward intra-regional partners, within each of the three potential major blocs? (2) Are exchange rates more stable within each of the three potential blocs than across them? (3) To the extent exchange rates are stabilized within a bloc, does that contribute to intra-bloc trade?

Frankel (1993) applied to the trading bloc question the natural framework for studying bilateral trade, the gravity model. The gravity model assumes that trade between two countries is proportional to the product of their sizes and inversely related to the distance between them. These two factors are presumably the source of the name, by analogy to the formula for gravitational attraction between two masses. It has a fairly long history.[3] There are only a few recent applications to a large cross-section of countries throughout the world, however.[4]

Frankel (1993) and Frankel and Wei (1994) found that: (1) there are indeed intra-regional trade biases in the EC and the Western Hemisphere, and perhaps in East Asia; but (2) the greatest apparent intra-regional bias was in none of these three, but in the APEC grouping, which includes the U.S. and Canada with the Pacific countries; (3) the bias in the East Asia and Pacific groupings did not increase in the 1980s as it did in Europe and the Americas; and (4) bilateral exchange rate variability may have had a small negative effect on bilateral trade in 1980, but there is little evidence of an effect in 1985 or 1990.[5]

This paper begins by considering an extension of the original gravity model estimation, allowing a role for linguistic links in trade. At the same time, we extend the results back in history, to 1965. Next, we look more carefully at the possible role of stabilization of bilateral exchange rates in promoting intra-regional trade. We examine the extent to which exchange rates have been stabilized within regional groupings such as the EC and EFTA. Then we test whether the stabilization of bilateral exchange rates promotes bilateral trade, on the entire data set, running from 1965 to 1990.

Besides these extensions, the paper focuses relatively more on Europe, including both the EC and EFTA, whereas the earlier papers focused relatively more on East Asia and the Pacific. In particular, a central motivating question is the extent to which stabilization of exchange rates within Europe has been a contributing factor to the increase in intra-regional trade there. One view, labelled "American" by Charles Wyplosz, is that stabilization of exchange rates within a region is not a prerequisite for trade integration, with the example of U.S.-Canadian integration frequently cited in support, whereas the "European" view is that it is a prerequisite.[6] The set-back that European Monetary Union received in the Exchange Rate Mechanism crises of September 1992 and August 1993 means that a return to the higher levels of exchange rate variability that held in the past is a real possibility. To what extent would that reduce intra-European trade?

The final section of the paper discusses the future of the dollar, mark and yen as international currencies.

2 Is Europe a trade bloc?

2.1 The gravity model

One cannot meaningfully investigate the extent to which regional policy initiatives are influencing trade patterns without holding constant for natural economic determinants. A systematic framework for measuring what patterns of bilateral trade are normal around the world is offered by the gravity model. A dummy variable can then be added to represent when both countries in a given pair belong to the same regional grouping. One can check how the level and time trend in, for example, Europe compares with that in other groupings. The variable to be determined is trade (exports plus imports), in log form, between pairs of countries in a given year. We have 63 countries in our data set, so that there are 1,953 data points (=63x62/2) for a given year.[7] The goal, again, is to see how much of the level of trade within each region can be explained by simple economic factors common to bilateral trade throughout the world, and how much is left over to be attributed to a special regional effect.

One would expect the two most important factors in explaining bilateral trade flows to be the geographical distance between the two countries, and their economic size. These factors are the essence of the gravity model.

Despite the obvious importance of distance and transportation costs in determining the volume of trade, empirical studies surprisingly often neglect to measure this factor. Our measure is the log of distance between two major cities (usually the capital) of the respective countries. We also add a dummy variable "Adjacent" to indicate when two countries share a common land border.

Entering GNPs in product form is empirically well-established in bilateral trade regressions. It can be justified by the modern theory of trade under imperfect competition.[8] In addition there is reason to believe that GNP per capita has a positive effect on trade, for a given size: as countries become more developed, they tend to specialize more and to trade more.

The equation to be estimated, in its most basic form, is:

$$\log(T_{ij}) = \alpha + \beta_1 \log(GNP_i GNP_j) + \beta_2 \log\left(\frac{GNP_i}{pop_i}\,\frac{GNP_j}{pop_j}\right)$$

$$+ \beta_3 \log(DISTANCE_{ij}) + \beta_4 (ADJACENT_{ij}) + \gamma_1 (EC_{ij})$$

$$+ \gamma_2 (WH_{ij}) + \gamma_3 (EASIA_{ij}) + u_{ij}.$$

The last four explanatory factors are dummy variables. *EC*, *WH*, and *EASIA* are three of the dummy variables we use when testing the effects of membership in a common regional grouping.

The results are reported in Tables 1, 2, and 3. These differ from the tables in Frankel (1993) principally by the explicit distinct consideration of (1) the EC, (2) EFTA, and (3) Europe overall, and the inclusion of terms to capture any possible trade-diversion effects in Europe. We found all four standard gravity variables to be highly significant statistically (> 99% level).

The adjacency variable indicates that when two countries share a common border, they trade with each other approximately twice as much as they otherwise would [exp(.7)=2]. The coefficient on the log of distance is about -.56, when the adjacency variable is included at the same time. This means that when the distance between two non-adjacent countries is higher by 1 per cent, the trade between them falls by about .56 per cent.

The estimated coefficient on GNP per capita is about .29 as of 1980, indicating that richer countries do indeed trade more, though this term declines during the 1980s, reaching .11 in 1990. The estimated coefficient for the log of the product of the two countries' GNPs is about .75, indicating that, though trade increases with size, it increases less-than-proportionately (holding GNP per capita constant). This presumably reflects the widely-known pattern that small economies tend to be more open to international trade than larger, more diversified, economies.

2.2 Estimation of trade-bloc effects

How large do intra-regional preferences appear to be in the data? If there were nothing to the notion of trading blocs, then the basic economic variables in our gravity regressions would soak up most of the explanatory power. There would be little left to attribute to a dummy variable representing whether two trading partners are both located in the same region. In this case the level and trend in intra-regional trade would be due solely to the proximity of the countries, and to their rate of overall economic growth.

But we found that dummy variables for intra-regional trade <u>are</u> highly significant statistically. If two countries are both located in the Western Hemisphere for example, in 1980 they traded with each other by an estimated 86 per cent more than they would have otherwise [exp(.62) = 1.86], after taking into account distance and the other gravity variables. The strongest bloc effect in our gravity estimates is not any of the three most often discussed, but is the Pacific bloc that includes the United States and Canada along with East Asia, Australia and New Zealand. (This dummy variable is labelled APEC, after the membership of the Asian Pacific Economic Cooperation forum.) The coefficient in 1980 suggests that two APEC members trade five times as much as a typical pair of countries [exp(1.6)=5.06]. The group of East Asian countries alone also constituted a significant distinct trade bloc, with a coefficient suggesting that it doubles trade between members [exp(.8) = 2.23].

Both coefficients declined a bit during the decade, reflecting that the rapid growth in Asian/Pacific trade which many observers have remarked was entirely the result of economic growth among the individual countries.[9]

The blocs that strengthened in the 1980s lay elsewhere, in the Americas and Europe. The Western Hemisphere coefficient started the decade with an implied 1.86 multiplier, as noted above, and rose to 2.46 [=exp(.9)]. The rise came entirely between 1985 and 1990. We turn now to Europe.

2.3 The European Community and EFTA

The results suggest that Europe may not even have been an operational trade bloc in 1980. The estimated coefficient on the EC is only of borderline significance (The point estimate of the effect on trade is 26 per cent [exp(.23)=1.26]). Furthermore, it diminishes when a dummy variable is added to capture the overall openness of European countries. This dummy variable is defined to equal one when <u>either one</u> of the two countries in a given pair is located in Europe, as opposed to both. The results indicate that, as of 1980, the high level of intra-regional trade in Europe can be mostly explained by a combination of proximity, high income, and openness (as compared to the average level of openness in the sample, which includes many LDCs).

By 1985 the EC dummy had become statistically significant. The coefficient implies that two EC members trade an extra 58 per cent with each other [exp(.46) = 1.58]. It is clear that it is the European Community in particular that is having an influence, as terms for EFTA or for Europe overall are not significant.[10] Furthermore, when the term is added to capture the greater openness of European countries, even though it is again significantly positive, the significance of the EC bloc effect rises a bit rather than falls.

Why did the EC strengthen in the early 1980s? One possibility is the accession of Spain, Portugal and Greece during this period, and of the United Kingdom, Ireland and Denmark not long before. (For ease of comparison across time, these countries are included in the definition of the EC grouping throughout the sample.) Another possible contributing factor, considered below, is the stabilization of exchange rates under the European Monetary System.

The EC coefficient in 1990 is a little larger than in 1985. The effect is 68 per cent [exp(.52)=1.68]. The EFTA and Europe effects are again insignificant. The major change relative to 1985 is that the coefficient on European openness, which was previously significantly greater than zero, is now less than zero, and borderline-significant. This finding bears on the famous distinction between trade-diversion and trade-creation in the literature on the welfare effects of customs unions.

The 1980 and 1985 results suggest that trade-diversion is not greater than zero, indeed that it is negative. One might wonder how the formation of a free-trade area like the EC could produce a negative "trade-diversion coefficient," or what we have called a positive openness coefficient. In theory, the reduction of trade barriers within the region should not encourage trade with other countries; if anything, it should discourage it. The answer is that countries in a given region may somewhat reduce barriers with respect to non-members, at the same time that they reduce or eliminate barriers internally. Indeed, the two policy changes may be related in a political economy sense. Some have argued that the constellation of political forces that allows liberalization with respect to trade with regional neighbors may be similar to what is required to allow liberalization more generally. The best example is Mexico's decision to negotiate the NAFTA soon after undertaking unilateral liberalization and joining GATT (Lawrence, 1991).

The 1990 result suggests a shift toward trade-diversion. While a typical European country now trades 68 per cent more with other European countries than can be explained by natural factors, it trades an estimated 11 per cent less with non-European countries. Further results, not reported here, suggest that the trade diversion takes place among the EFTA countries, not the EC countries.

2.4 Common languages

The earlier results were incapable of distinguishing between regional biases reflecting discriminatory trade policies, and those that might derive from historical, political, cultural and linguistic ties. We now add a dummy variable to represent when both countries of a pair speak a common language or had colonial links earlier in the century. We allow for English, Spanish, Chinese, Arabic, French, German, Japanese, Dutch, and Portuguese.[11] The results, reported in Table 4, show that two countries sharing linguistic/colonial links tended in 1965 or 1970 to trade roughly 65 per cent more than they would otherwise [exp(.5)=1.65]. The bloc variables remain significant even when holding constant for these links.

We tested whether some of the major languages were more important than the others. Chinese is the only one to qualify, and its apparent effect is probably spurious.[12] French, Spanish, and Arabic, if anything, have less effect than other common languages, though the differences are not very significant statistically. When all nine linguistic/colonial links are constrained to have the same coefficient, it is significant at the 99 per cent level.[13] The 1980 effect is again 65 per cent.

To summarize, allowing for the linguistic links has little effect on the statistical significance of the bloc coefficients, as was also true of earlier extensions.

3 Currency blocs

Does the stabilization of exchange rates within regions help promote trade within those regions? The question bears on the larger literature on the implications of fixed versus floating exchange rate regimes.

3.1 Stabilization of exchange rates within the blocs

Table 5 reports statistics on the nominal variability of exchange rates among various groupings of countries. Worldwide, monthly exchange rate variability rose in the 1980s, from a standard deviation of .33 per cent in 1980 to .38 per cent in 1990. The latter figure suggests that for a typical pair of countries, approximately 5 per cent of monthly exchange rate changes are larger than .76 per cent (two standard deviations, under the simplifying assumption of a log-normal distribution).

There is a tendency for exchange rate variability to be lower within each of the groups than across groups, supporting the idea of currency blocs. The lowest variability occurs within Europe. The 1980 statistic is a standard deviation of .04 per cent, and it falls by half during the course of the decade.

Even though the members of the EC correspond roughly to the members of the European Monetary System,[14] non-EC members in Europe show about as much stability in exchange rates (both vis-a-vis themselves and vis-a-vis other European countries) as EC members. The EC members show slightly more stability than the EFTA members in 1990, but slightly less in 1980. These results no doubt in part reflect that the United Kingdom and the Mediterranean countries have not been consistent members of the Exchange Rate Mechanism, especially not with the narrow margins set by the others. It also reflects, however, that such EFTA countries as Austria are loyal members of the currency club *de facto*, even though they are not *de jure*. We saw in the first part of the paper that the statistical significance of intra-European trade links applies only to the EC, not to EFTA. Observing that the EFTA members have stabilized bilateral exchange rates as much or more than EC members, one immediately suspects that the stabilization of exchange rates must not have been the dominant source of the intra-EC trade links.

The members of APEC also have a relatively low level of intra-regional exchange rate variability, especially considering the diversity of the countries involved. It too fell by half in the course of the 1980s. The level of exchange rate variability is a bit higher within East Asia considered alone. This reflects that the international currency of Asia is not the yen, but rather the dollar, as we will see below. Results on the determination of exchange rates for nine East Asian countries in Frankel and Wei (1994) show that all place very heavy weight on the dollar in their implicit baskets.[15]

The Western Hemisphere considered alone in Table 5 shows much higher levels of exchange rate variability than any of the other groupings (in 1985 and 1990).

3.2 The influence of the dollar, yen, and DM on the values of smaller currencies

We now examine the influences which the most important international currencies have on the determination of the values of currencies of smaller countries. One way that countries in a given area could achieve the lower levels of intra-regional bilateral exchange rate variability observed in Table 5 is to link their currencies to the single most important currency in the region. In a simple version of the currency-bloc hypothesis, one would expect that the dollar has dominant influence in the Western Hemisphere, the yen in East Asia, and the mark (or ECU[16]) in Europe.

The equation to be estimated is

$$\Delta\, (\textit{value of currency } i) =$$

$$\alpha + \beta_1 \Delta\, (\textit{value of \$}) + \beta_2 \Delta\, (\textit{value of yen}) + \beta_3 \Delta\, (\textit{value of DM}) + \epsilon,$$

where the change in the value of each currency is computed logarithmically. The goal is to see whether countries try to stabilize their currencies in terms of a particular major currency. Such an equation is exceptionally well-specified under a particular null hypothesis, namely that the value of the local currency is determined as a basket peg (perhaps a crawling peg, since we allow for a constant term). By "exceptionally well-specified", we mean that the coefficients should be highly significant and the R^2 should be close to 1.

In 1988, for example, there were 31 countries that were officially classified by the IMF as following a basket peg of their own design (plus another eight pegged to the SDR). They included Austria, Finland, Norway, Sweden, Iceland, and Thailand. (Some who claimed to define the value of their currency in terms of a basket, in fact followed an extremely loose link.) Most basket-peggers keep the weights in the basket secret, so that one can only infer the weight statistically from observed exchange rate movements. Previous tests have suggested that countries that are officially classified as basket-peggers in practice often exhibit a sufficiently wide range of variation around the basket index, or else alter the parity or weights sufficiently often, that they are difficult to distinguish empirically from countries classified as managed floaters.[17]

In applying equation (2) to a wide variety of countries, we realize that most do not even purport to follow a basket peg. Policy-makers in some countries monitor an index that is a weighted average of their trading partners, even though they allow the exchange rate to undergo large deviations from the index depending on current macroeconomic considerations or speculative sentiments. We can still meaningfully estimate the coefficients in the equation under the (restrictive) assumption that these local deviations - the error term - are uncorrelated with the values of the major currencies.

There is a methodological question of what numeraire should be used to measure the value of the currencies. Here we use the SDR as numeraire. Under the basket-peg null hypothesis, the choice of numeraire makes no difference in the estimation of the weights (though more generally it does make some difference).[18]

Table 6 reports estimates for nine EC currencies. The sample period is 1979-90, broken into three sub-samples. We also allow for the possibility of some effect of a fourth major currency, pound sterling, in memory of the role it once played as the world's international currency. We impose the constraint that the weights on the four currencies sum to 1 (by subtracting the change in the value of the pound from each of the other variables).

The EC countries, as expected, give heavy weight to the DM. In the case of Belgium, the other three major currencies get no weight, and the weight on the DM is insignificantly different from 1 during most of the period. France, Denmark and the Netherlands show some sign of a small weight on the dollar. For Italy the weight on the dollar is statistically significant, and estimated at just over 0.1; the weight on the mark is around 0.8. Greece gave heavy weight to the dollar during the sub-period 1979-82, but this diminished thereafter. Ireland and Portugal also give some weight to the dollar in 1987-90, but, as with the others, give dominant weight to the DM throughout. No European country gives significant weight to the yen.

The implicit coefficient on the pound is equal to 1 minus the sum of the three coefficients reported. For Ireland, for example, the implicit coefficient on the pound ranges between .1 and .2. The pound is not generally significant, however. Multicollinearity between the pound and DM is very high, as one would expect. When all four major currencies are entered on the righthand side without imposing the constraint that their coefficients sum to 1, the pound loses out to the mark, and is not significantly greater than zero for any of the EMS countries. (These results are not reported here, to save space.)

The DM also dominates among the six EFTA countries, shown in Table 7. Austria exhibits a very tight peg to the DM, as expected. (The R^2 is .98

or .99.) Switzerland also gives heavy weight to the DM. It, like some Nordics, appears to give significant weight to the yen as well at times. The four Nordic countries have a weight on the dollar which is highly significant statistically, though still less than the DM. The weight on the pound is seen also sometimes to be statistically significant for the Nordics, in the unconstrained estimation (not reported). But the pound gets less weight than either the DM or the dollar. Overall, the DM dominates.

Similar tests among five major Western Hemisphere currencies show the dollar dominant. Colombia is close to a dollar peg (though with a large significant trend depreciation). Canada, Chile, and Mexico also have dollar weights in the neighborhood of 1.0. Argentina is the only country that consistently appears to show a weight on another currency (.5 on the DM) that is significant and larger than the dollar weight (.2). Its estimated weight on the pound is similar (.2). However the pound is not significant for any of the Latin American countries.[19]

In each region considered thus far, Europe and the Western Hemisphere, almost all countries give dominant weight to the major currency of the region. This pattern is broken in East Asia, however.[20] The weight on the dollar is very high in most countries. Only in Indonesia, and to a lesser extent Singapore, is there significant evidence of a yen weight exceeding 10 per cent. Each of the Asian countries is more properly classed in a dollar bloc than in a yen bloc. It is not a coincidence that many Asian/Pacific countries call their currencies "dollar." Nor, given the economies of scale in the use of an international currency, is it surprising that the dollar is the choice of Asia, as the rest of the world. (International currencies are discussed further in section 5 below.[21])

We have also tried regression tests that do not impose the constraint that the weights on the major currencies sum to one (and that also exclude the pound). The results are similar: the DM reigns supreme in Europe, the dollar in the Western Hemisphere, and the dollar -- not the yen -- is also dominant in East Asia. A t-test does not reject the constraint that the sum of the three coefficients is 1 for the Western Hemisphere and Asian countries, but often does reject this constraint for the European countries, perhaps reflecting the absence of the pound and French franc.[22]

3.3 An attempt to estimate the effect of exchange rate variability on trade

One rationale for a country to assign high weight to a particular currency in determining its exchange rate is the assumption that a more stable bilateral exchange rate will help promote bilateral trade with the partner in question. This is a major motivation for exchange rate stabilization in Europe. There have been quite a few time-series studies of the effect of exchange rate uncertainty on trade overall,[23] but fewer cross-section studies of bilateral trade. One exception is De Grauwe (1988), which looks at ten industrialized countries. Two others are Abrams (1980) and Brada and Mendez (1988). We will re-examine the question here using a data set that is more recent as well as broader, covering 63 countries. The updating of the data set turns out to be qualitatively important. A problem of simultaneous causality should be noted at the outset: if exchange rate variability shows up with an apparent negative effect on the volume of bilateral trade, the correlation could be due to the government's deliberate efforts to stabilize the currency vis-a-vis a valued trading partner, as easily as to the effects of stabilization on trade. Therefore we will also use the method of instrumental variable estimation to tackle the possible simultaneity bias.

Volatility is defined to be the standard deviation of the first difference of the logarithmic exchange rate. We start with the volatility of nominal exchange rates and embed this term in our gravity equation (1) for 1980, 1985 and 1990. The results are reported in Table 8, which does not include the trade bloc dummies. Most of the standard gravity coefficients are similar to those reported in the earlier results without exchange rate variability (Tables 1-4). Nominal exchange rate variability appears to have a statistically significant negative effect on the volume of trade in 1980; but the negative effect disappears in 1985 if we hold constant for distance and adjacency, and also in 1990 (whether we hold constant for the two geographic variables or not).

A presumably more relevant measure of exchange rate uncertainty is the volatility of the real exchange rate, which takes into account the differential inflation rates in the two countries in addition to movements in the nominal exchange rate. Table 8 also reports the gravity equation with real exchange rate volatility included. It has a statistically significant negative effect in every year, even when holding constant for the geographic variables. From these results, it would appear that the conventionally hypothesized effect of exchange rate uncertainty on trade is borne out.

We know that stabilization of bilateral exchange rates is correlated, not only with whether countries are neighbors, but also with whether they are located in the same continental area. When we add the bloc variables back into the equation, the statistical significance of the exchange rate variability term falls somewhat. OLS regressions are presented in Table 9. In addition to adding variables for the major continental groupings, this table extends the results by adding the EFTA bloc variable, and by measuring volatility as the <u>level</u> of the standard deviation rather than its log. The latter change allows the experiment of asking how much trade would go up if exchange rate variabilities like those reported in Table 5 were reduced to zero. The magnitude of the coefficients on the variability in level form is not, of course, to be compared with the magnitude in log form.[24]

In 1980, the coefficient(s) for the volatility term are still negative and statistically significant at the 99% level. In comparison to the earlier gravity results that did not include a role for exchange rate volatilities, the EC and Western Hemisphere bloc dummy variables appear with lower coefficients, suggesting that a bit of the bloc effect may have been attributable to exchange rate links. In 1985, the volatility parameter(s) are no longer significant (with the point estimate turning slightly positive). Clearly, much of the apparently significant effect of exchange rate variability in Table 8 was a spurious stand-in for the effect of regional trading arrangements like the EC. In 1990, the coefficient on real volatility returns to a negative sign, and is statistically significant, but only at the 90 per cent level. (Henceforth we concentrate our discussions on the regressions involving the real exchange rates.)

By way of illustration, these point estimates can be used for some sample calculations. They suggest that if the level of EC exchange rate variability that prevailed in 1980, a standard deviation of 0.050 per cent in Table 5, had been eliminated altogether, the volume of intra-EC trade would have increased by .77 per cent (=15.26 x.0504). In 1990, when both the standard deviation and its coefficient were smaller, the estimated effect on trade of eliminating real exchange rate variability within the EC would have been only .15 per cent (=8.04x.019).

Worldwide, the average level of exchange rate variability in 1990 was still .376 per cent. The estimated effect of adopting fixed exchange rates worldwide was thus 3.02 per cent (=8.04x.376).

The exchange rate disruptions of September 1992 and August 1993 may herald a return to the level of variability among the EMS countries that prevailed in 1980. Table 5 shows that this would represent an approximate doubling of the standard deviation of exchange rates, relative to the stability that had been achieved by 1990. What would be the predicted effects on trade? The estimate in Table 9 suggests that trade would fall by .25 per cent (=8.04x(.050-.019)).[25]

Even if the stabilization of exchange rates achieved in Europe in the 1980s indeed raised trade on the order of .25 per cent, that is tiny compared to the 1/3 increase in trade bias estimated in our gravity model of Section 2 during the decade (1.68/1.26 = 1.34). The exchange rate stabilization effect is only 7/10 of one per cent of the increase in the bias, which is in turn only half the total estimated 68 per cent European intra-regional trade bias in 1990.[26]

Interpretations of the estimates in Table 9, small as they may be, are complicated by the likelihood of simultaneity bias in the above regressions. Governments may choose deliberately to stabilize bilateral exchange rates with their major trading partners. This has certainly been the case in Europe. Hence, there could be a strong observed correlation between trade patterns and currency linkages even if exchange rate volatility does not depress trade.

To address this problem, we use the method of instrumental variable estimation, with the standard deviation of relative money supply as our instrument for the volatility of exchange rates. The argument in favor of this choice of instrument is that relative money supplies and bilateral exchange rates are highly correlated in theory (they are directly linked under the monetary theory of exchange rate determination), and in our data as well,[27] but monetary policies are less likely than exchange rate policies to be set in response to bilateral trade patterns. The results are reported in Table 10.

In 1980, the volatility parameter is still negative and significant at the 95% level. But the magnitude is much smaller than without using the instrument, suggesting that part of the apparent depressing effect of the volatility was indeed due to the simultaneity bias. Strong confirmation comes from an examination of the trade bloc coefficients for the EC and the Western Hemisphere: when the simultaneity is corrected, the presence of the volatility variable no longer reduces the trade bloc coefficient.

In 1990, the volatility parameter in Table 10 turns again into a positive number. The results suggest that if exchange rate volatility has depressed bilateral trade in the past, its negative effect diminished over the course of the 1980s. This sharp change is somewhat surprising.

Theoretical models of the behavior of the firm often produce the result that, because of convexity in the profit function, exports can be an increasing function of exchange rate variability. Only when the firm is sufficiently risk-averse does the intuitive negative effect on trade emerge. Several empirical studies have taken this possibility seriously, and perhaps we should as well.[28] Before we put too much weight on the econometric findings for 1985 and 1990, it would be desirable to look at more data. Our final tests, reported in Tables 11-13, extend the results 15 years further back in history. The OLS results show a negative trade effect of exchange rate volatility (whether nominal or real) that is highly significant in 1965, 1970, and 1975, as well as 1980. Only in 1985 and 1990 does it turn positive. The Instrumental Variables results, reported in Table 13, show the same sign pattern across the years (though the negative effect is only statistically significant in 1965). One possible explanation is the rapid development of exchange risk hedging instruments.

In short, these results, while less robust than most of the other gravity equation findings, are generally consistent with the hypothesis that real exchange rate volatility has depressed bilateral trade a bit in the past. More specifically, they would appear to be a piece of evidence that the stabilization of exchange rates within Europe helped to promote intra-European trade from 1965 to 1980. But the evidence for a negative trade effect, which starts out relatively strong in 1965, diminishes steadily in the 1970s and 1980s. The proliferation of currency options, forward contracts, and other hedging instruments may explain why even the small effect that appears once to have been there has more recently disappeared.

4 Summary of conclusions regarding Europe

Trade within Europe was at a high level even before the 1980s, and increased rapidly during that decade. Much of the tendency to trade intra-regionally can be explained by natural economic factors: the size of the GNPs, the levels of GNP/capita, the proximity of the countries, the sharing of common borders and common languages, and the openness of the economies. Some of the increase in intra-regional trade in the 1970s and 1980s can be explained by an increase in GNP per capita (though to a lesser extent than in Pacific Asia). There was also a highly significant increase in the degree of intra-regional trade bias in the course of the 1980s, most readily explained by deliberate policy initiatives of the European Community. (The same was true in the Western Hemisphere.) Our estimates in Table 3 suggest that a country joining the EC would have experienced an increase in trade with other members of 68 per cent by 1990.[29] No such effect is observed for EFTA.

We have considered in this paper the possibility that the stabilization of exchange rates was a significant contributor to the increase in intra-regional trade. The standard deviation of exchange rates fell among EFTA countries by about half in the 1980s, and among EC countries by slightly more. Among both groups, the currencies in effect linked themselves to the mark, much as Western Hemisphere (and East Asia) currencies in effect link themselves to the dollar.

We have found some possible cross-section evidence that real exchange rate variability has had an effect on trade volume. There is much more evidence that this factor is statistically significant in the period 1965-1980 than in 1985 or 1990. A possible explanation is the spread of hedging instruments. Even when the estimated effect is at is peak, however, it explains only a very small fraction of the intra-regional trade bias. It does not appear that the stabilization of European exchange rates in the 1980s played a large role in the increase in intra-regional trade.

5 The future of the dollar, mark and yen as international currencies

The dollar remains easily the world's most important vehicle currency, reserve currency, and all-around international currency. It has, however, sustained some recent loss of position vis-a-vis other major currencies. In this section we briefly consider the extent to which the dollar, yen, mark, and other currencies are used as international currencies. We then proceed to consider what conditions are likely to determine the use of these currencies in the future.

5.1 Measures of the use of international currencies

The tables in Frankel (1992) offer statistics on the relative importance of the major currencies in a number of categories: invoicing foreign trade, denominating international financial flows, pegs for smaller countries' currencies, reserve holdings of central banks, and foreign exchange trading. The dollar is easily the leading currency by all measures, but its relative role declined during the course of the 1980s.[30] The estimated fraction of trade invoiced in dollars (for overall trade reported by the six largest market economies plus OPEC) declined from 32.8 per cent in 1980 to 25.7 per cent in 1987.[31] The frequency of dollar-denomination shrank from 83 per cent in the early 1980s to 65 per cent in 1990 in the case of external bank loans, from 63 per cent to 52 per cent in external bond issues, and from 74 per cent to 53 per cent in eurocurrency deposits. Turning from private-sector use of international currencies to public-sector use, the proportion of fixed-rate currencies that pegged to the dollar declined from 54 per cent in 1980 to 50 per cent in 1990, while the share of central banks' holdings of foreign currency reserves allocated to dollars declined from 69 per cent in 1980 to 56 per cent in 1990.

Two other currencies are in a close contest for second place after the dollar: the yen has surpassed the mark by some measures, but is still behind by others. The question of fourth place also depends very much on the criterion used. The pound does rather well in foreign exchange trading and external bank loans, the Swiss franc in international bond issues, the French franc and SDR in the number of countries that peg their currency to them, and the ECU (European Currency Unit) in international reserve holdings among European central banks.

The ECU has been put forward by the EC as a rival to the others. If and when Europe's individual central banks disappear into monetary union, their holdings of ECUs will disappear, while today's holdings by <u>other</u> central banks of marks, francs and pounds will presumably be replaced by holdings of ECUs that are at least as large. The prospects for the ECU as an international currency, however, suffered at least as sharp a setback in September 1992 as did the EMS and the prospects for eventual EMU. The Euromarket in ECU bonds all but dried up. It seems unlikely that the ECU will be widely used outside Europe until after EMU is achieved, whenever that is.

5.2 Conditions for an international currency

What are the conditions for a currency to become an international currency? One can think of four major sorts of factors.

(1) History. There is much inertia in the system, and for good reason. An individual (exporter, importer, borrower, lender, or currency trader) is more likely to use a given currency in his or her transactions if everyone else is doing so. For this reason, the world's choice of vehicle currency is characterized by multiple stable equilibria. Krugman (1984) showed how there can be multiple equilibria in use of an international currency, developing some less formal ideas of earlier authors such as Kindleberger (1981), McKinnon (1979), and Swoboda (1969). The pound remained the world's leading international currency somewhat longer than purely contemporaneous economic factors might have dictated. In the present context, this favors the continued central role of the dollar.

(2) Patterns of trade and finance. The currency of a country that has a large share in international trade and finance has a natural advantage. By such measures, Japan should clearly be number 2, after the U.S. and before Germany, in light of the large size of the Japanese economy. If the measure of being a vehicle currency is how often it is used in the invoicing and financing of international trade, then other aspects of the pattern of trade may also be relevant.[32]

(3) Financial markets that are not only free of controls, but also deep and well-developed. The large financial marketplaces of New York and London benefit the dollar and pound relative, for example, to the deutschemark.

(4) Confidence in the value of the currency. Even if an international currency were used only as a unit of account, a necessary criterion would be that its value not fluctuate erratically. An international currency is also used as a form in which to hold assets: (i) firms hold working balances of the currencies in which they invoice, (ii) investors hold bonds issued internationally, (iii) central banks hold currency reserves, and (iv) households and small businesses in hyperinflation-prone countries may hold foreign cash. (Even though relatively few Latin American countries are literally pegged to the dollar, dollar currency circulates throughout the region, and many countries offer dollarized bank accounts.) Here confidence

that the value of the currency will be stable, and particularly that it will not be inflated away in the future, is critical.

The dollar lost 47 per cent of its purchasing power between 1973 and 1990, as compared to a 24 per cent loss during the time period 1948-72 (calculated from the CPI, logarithmically). The monetary authorities in Japan, Germany, and Switzerland, established good track records of price stability in the 1970s and 1980s, though Germany's has deteriorated a bit since unification in 1990, and the U.S. record has begun to look better.

A negative for the dollar is the fact that the United States began to acquire large and growing international debts in the 1980s. It is sometimes said that net creditor status is a necessary requirement for a country to have an international currency. Even if the Federal Reserve does not succumb to the temptations or pressures to inflate away the U.S. debt, the continuing U.S. current account deficit could induce a further depreciation of the dollar. Such fears work to make dollars unattractive. The loss of key currency status and the loss of international creditor status have sometimes been associated - along with such non-economic factors as political prestige and military power - in discussions of the historical decline of great powers.

5.3 Advantages of having an international currency

One can think of four advantages to a country of having its currency play a large role in the world.

(1) Convenience for the country's residents. It is certainly more convenient for a country's exporters, importers, borrowers and lenders to be able to deal in its own currency than foreign currencies. The global use of the dollar, as with the global use of the English language, is a natural advantage that American businessmen tend to take for granted.

(2) More business for the country's banks and other financial institutions. There need be no firm connection from the currency in which banking is conducted to the nationality of the banks (nor from the nationalities of the savers and borrowers to the nationality of the intermediating bank). Nevertheless, it stands to reason that U.S. banks have a comparative advantage at dealing in dollars, Japanese banks at dealing in yen, etc.

(3) Seigniorage. This is perhaps the most important advantage of having other countries hold one's currency. They must give up real goods and services, or ownership of the real capital stock, in order to add to the currency balances that they use. This was the basis of European resentment

against the U.S. basic balance deficit in the 1960s, and against the dollar standard to the extent that the European need to acquire dollars was the fundamental origin of the deficit.

(4) Political power and prestige. Britain's gradual loss of key currency status was simultaneous with its gradual loss of political and military pre-eminence. As with most of the other benefits and conditions mentioned above, causality here flows in both directions. The benefits of "power and prestige" are decidedly nebulous. Nevertheless, the "responsibilities commensurate with Japan's new status as a great economic power" that many Americans have urged on Japan in the abstract, will - when realized in the concrete - increasingly be seen as Japanese gains at U.S. expense.

5.4 Disadvantages of having an international currency

One can think of two disadvantages from the viewpoint of a key-currency country. They explain why Japan and Germany have in the past been reluctant to have their currencies held and used widely.

(1) Larger fluctuations in demand for the currency. It is not automatically clear that having one's currency held by a wide variety of people around the world will result in greater variability of demand. Perhaps such instability is more likely to follow from the increase in the degree of capital mobility described under condition (3) in Section 5.2, than from key currency status *per se*. In any case, central banks are particularly concerned that internationalization will make it more difficult to control the money stock. This problem need not arise if they do not intervene in the foreign exchange market; but the central bank may view letting fluctuations in demand for the currency be reflected in the exchange rate as being just as undesirable as letting them be reflected in the money supply.

(2) An increase in the average demand for the currency. This is the other side of seigniorage. In the 1960s and 1970s, the Japanese and German governments were particularly worried about the possibility that if assets were made available to foreign residents, an inflow of capital would cause the currency to appreciate and render exporters uncompetitive on world markets. While Japan has become much more confident about its ability to export (it could hardly think otherwise!), talk of further substantial appreciation is not always welcome.

5.5 Conclusion: the future of the dollar

From a microeconomic perspective, it is clear that there are large economies of scale with respect to transactions costs in the choice of vehicle currency. As McKinnon (1979), Kindleberger (1981) and Krugman (1984), among others, have pointed out, an implication is that it is more efficient for the world economy to have a single vehicle currency. Assuming that world trade and finance continue to become more highly integrated, the importance of international transactions costs and the need to economize on them should grow.

Regardless whether or not U.S. economic performance in the future lags behind Japan's, the dollar - not the yen - will remain the premier currency of the Pacific. Regardless whether European monetary integration in the future regains the momentum of the late 1980s (which to an American seems unlikely), Europe's lot is as a smaller economic bloc than the vast Pacific. European firms will not be able, with the rest of the world using dollars, to insist on using the mark or the ECU in most of their overseas dealings. Thus the dollar will almost certainly persist as the world's unit of account in the twenty-first century. And, as well, English as the world's language.

Table 1. EFTA and EEC as trade blocs, 1980

GNP	GNP/cap.	Dist	Adja	WH2	EAEC2	APEC2	EUR2	EUR1	EEC2	EFTA2	EFTA-EEC	adj-R^2/SEE	#obs
.73**	.29**	-.56**	.71**	.52**	.78**	1.49**			.23			.71/1.20	1708
.02	.02	.04	.18	.15	.27	.18			.18				
.73**	.29**	-.56**	.71**	.53**	.78**	1.49**			.23	.06		.71/1.20	1708
.02	.02	.04	.18	.15	.27	.18			.18	.32			
.73**	.29**	-.56**	.71**	.52**	.78**	1.49**	-.01		.23			.71/1.20	1708
.02	.02	.04	.18	.15	.27	.18	.16		.18				
.73**	.29**	-.56**	.71**	.52**	.78**	1.49**	-.02		.25	.07		.71/1.20	1708
.02	.02	.04	.18	.15	.27	.18	.17		.22	.35			
.73**	.27**	-.53**	.75**	.63**	.76**	1.61**		.20**	.23			.71/1.20	1708
.02	.02	.04	.18	.15	.27	.18		.07	.18				
.73**	.27**	-.53**	.75**	.63**	.76**	1.61**		.20**	.23	.06		.71/1.20	1708
.02	.02	.04	.18	.15	.27	.18		.07	.18	.32			
.73**	.27**	-.54**	.75**	.62**	.76**	1.61**		.20**	.22		-.02	.71/1.20	1708
.02	.02	.04	.18	.15	.27	.18		.07	.18		.17		

Notes: 1. **, (*), (#), (##) denote "significant at the 99%, (95%), (90%) and (85%) levels, respectively.
2. All regressions have an intercept, which is not reported here. All variables except the dummies are in logs.

Table 2. EFTA and EEC as trade blocs, 1985

GNP	GNP/cap.	Dist	Adja	WH2	EAEC2	APEC2	EUR2	EUR1	EEC2	EFTA2	EFTA-EEC	adj-R^2/SEE	#obs
.76**	.25**	-.70**	.75**	.34*	.57*	1.25**			.46**			.74/1.17	1646
.02	.02	.04	.18	.16	.26	.18			.18				
.76**	.25**	-.70**	.75**	.34*	.57*	1.25**			.46**	-.07		.74/1.17	1646
.02	.02	.04	.18	.16	.26	.18			.18	.32			
.76**	.25**	-.68**	.75**	.35*	.58*	1.26**	.10		.39$^{\#}$			.74/1.17	1646
.02	.02	.04	.18	.15	.27	.18	.16		.21				
.76**	.25**	-.69**	.75**	.35*	.58*	1.26**	.13		.37$^{\#\#}$	-.16		.74/1.17	1646
.02	.02	.04	.18	.15	.27	.18	.17		.22	.34			
.76**	.23**	-.67**	.79**	.45**	.56*	1.38**		.20**	.46**			.74/1.17	1646
.02	.02	.04	.18	.15	.26	.19		.07	.18				
.76**	.23**	-.67**	.79**	.45**	.56*	1.38**		.20**	.46**	-.05		.74/1.17	1646
.02	.02	.04	.18	.15	.26	.19		.07	.18	.32			
.76**	.22**	-.66**	.79**	.46**	.57*	1.39**		.20**	.49**		.14	.74/1.17	1646
.02	.02	.04	.18	.15	.26	.19		.07	.18		.16		

Notes: 1. **, (*), (#), (##) denote "significant at the 99%, (95%), (90%) and (85%) levels, respectively.
2. All regressions have an intercept, which is not reported here. All variables except the dummies are in logs.

Table 3. EFTA and EEC as trade blocs, 1990

GNP	GNP/cap.	Dist	Adja	WH2	EAEC2	APEC2	EUR2	EUR1	EEC2	EFTA2	EFTA-EEC	adj-R^2/SEE	#obs
.75**	.09**	-.55**	.79**	.93**	.66**	1.25**			.52**			.77/1.07	1647
.02	.02	.04	.16	.14	.24	.18			.18				
.75**	.10**	-.55**	.79**	.93**	.66**	1.33**			.52**	-.05		.77/1.07	1647
.02	.02	.04	.16	.14	.24	.16			.16	.29			
.75**	.09**	-.54**	.79**	.94**	.67**	1.34**	.17		.40*			.77/1.07	1647
.02	.02	.04	.16	.14	.24	.16	.14		.19				
.75**	.09**	-.54**	.80**	.94**	.67**	1.34**	.20		.37$^{\#}$	-.19		.77/1.07	1647
.02	.02	.04	.16	.14	.24	.16	.15		.20	.31			
.75**	.11**	-.56**	.77**	.89**	.67**	1.25**		-.11$^{\#\#}$	.51**			.77/1.07	1647
.02	.02	.04	.16	.14	.24	.17		.07	.16				
.75**	.11**	-.57**	.77**	.88**	.67**	1.25**		-.11$^{\#\#}$	.50**	-.07		.77/1.07	1647
.02	.02	.04	.16	.14	.24	.17		.07	.16	.29			
.75**	.10**	-.55**	.78**	.90**	.68**	1.26**		-.10	.56**		.19	.77/1.07	1647
.02	.02	.04	.16	.14	.24	.17		.07	.16		.15		

Notes: 1. **, (*), (#), (##) denote "significant at the 99%, (95%), (90%) and (85%) levels, respectively.
2. All regressions have an intercept, which is not reported here. All variables except the dummies are in logs.

Table 4. Linguistic Links in Trade
(Total Trade, 1965-1990)

	1965	1970	1975	1980	1985	1990
GNP	.63**	.64**	.72**	.74**	.53**	.76**
	(.02)	(.02)	(.02)	(.02)	(.02)	(.02)
GNP per capita	.27**	.37**	.28**	.74**	.06*	.10**
	(.02)	(.02)	(.02)	(.02)	(.02)	(.02)
Distance	-.45**	-.54**	-.70**	-.57**	-.36**	-.55**
	(.04)	(.04)	(.05)	(.04)	(.05)	(.04)
Adjacent	.53**	.65**	.50**	.65**	.68**	.75**
	(.17)	(.17)	(.18)	(.18)	(.20)	(.16)
WH2	-.07	-.19	.16	.57**	.47*	.89**
	(.18)	(.17)	(.18)	(.18)	(.21)	(.17)
EAEC2	1.56**	1.64**	.95**	.92**	-.37	.63*
	(.29)	(.30)	(.32)	(.27)	(.29)	(.25)
APEC2	.26	.62**	.79**	1.17**	1.36**	1.15**
	(.21)	(.21)	(.22)	(.19)	(.20)	(.17)
EEC2	.26	.08	-.07	.22	1.56**	.53**
	(.16)	(.17)	(.18)	(.18)	(.19)	(.16)
EFTA2	.05	.02	-.05	.06	.10	-.01
	(.30)	(.29)	(.32)	(.32)	(.35)	(.29)
English	.22	-.09	.22	.42	-.14	.32
	(.30)	(.30)	(.32)	(.31)	(.34)	(.29)
Spanish	-.60#	-.24	-.12	-.31	-.47	-.07
	(.34)	(.33)	(.36)	(.35)	(.40)	(.33)
Chinese	.76	1.77*	.63	.77	.58	1.35*
	(.59)	(.82)	(.90)	(.60)	(.65)	(.54)
Arabic	-.29	-.68*	-.42	-.64#	-.68	-.31
	(.33)	(.33)	(.35)	(.35)	(.43)	(.34)
French	-.29	-.39	-.24	-.20	-.42	-.27
	(.32)	(.32)	(.35)	(.34)	(.40)	(.32)
Common language	.51#	.50*	.28	.37	.76*	.12
	(.28)	(.28)	(.30)	(.30)	(.33)	(.28)
adj-R^2	.69	.71	.72	.72	.53	.77
SEE	1.05	1.07	1.17	1.18	1.26	1.06
#obs	1194	1274	1453	1708	1343	1573

Notes: (1) Standard errors are in parentheses. (2) **, (*), and (#) denote significance at the 99%, (95%), and (90%) levels, respectively. (3) All variables except the dummies are in logs. (4) The variable "common language" reflects a common linguistic link (German, Japanese, Dutch, Portugese and the five languages in the table).

Table 5. Mean volatility of monthly changes in exchange rates (100xStandard deviation of the first difference of the logs.)

"Entire World" (63)		
1980	.333	
1985	.389	
1990	.356	
Western Hemsiphere		
	Among members (36)	With the Rest-of-the-World (344)
1980	.082	.231
1985	.891	.757
1990	.920	.363
EC		
	Among members (45)	With the Rest-of-the-World (375)
1980	.050	.233
1985	.052	.255
1990	.019	.241
EFTA		
	Among members (45)	With the Rest-of-the-World (239)
1980	.040	.215
1985	.020	.226
1990	.021	.222
Europe		
	Among members (105)	With the Rest-of-the-World (527)
1980	.044	.244
1985	.040	.265
1990	.021	.254
EAEG		
	Among members (15)	With the Rest-of-the-World (237)
1980	.102	.234
1985	.073	.221
1990	.045	.235
APEC		
	Among members (28)	With the Rest-of-the-World (237)
1980	.083	.229
1985	.061	.221
1990	.039	.240

Note: Numbers of observations in parentheses.

Table 6. Currencies in the European community
a) Weights assigned to foreign currencies in determining changes in value
(Constrained estimation)

Time period	Const.	USD	Yen	DM	adj.R*/DW	#obs	SEE
France-Franc							
79.1-82.12	-.005*	-.010	.074	.872**	.737/2.31	47	.013
	(.002)	(.071)	(.056)	(.070)			
83.1-86.12	-.003##	.066	-.074	.853**	.788/1.95	48	.012
	(.002)	(.062)	(.086)	(.085)			
87.1-90.12	-.003	.054*	-.023	.897**	.911/1.80	48	.005
	(.001)	(.026)	(.038)	(.044)			
79.1-90.12	.003**	.031	.033	.868**	.800/2.09	143	.011
	(.009)	(.029)	(.033)	(.038)			
Italy-Lire							
79.1-82.12	-.006**	.118*	.052	.782**	.747/2.13	47	.011
	(.002)	(.060)	(.047)	(.059)			
83.1-86.12	-.004**	.144**	.085	.857**	.866/2.15	48	.008
	(.001)	(.045)	(.063)	(.062)			
87.1-90.12	-.001	.120**	-.055	.808**	.879/1.67	48	.006
	(.001)	(.027)	(.039)	(.046)			
79.1-90.12	-.003**	.121**	.050#	.821**	.818/1.85	143	.009
	(.001)	(.025)	(.028)	(.033)			
Belgium-Franc							
79.1-82.12	-.005*	-.042	.043	.897**	.756/1.76	47	.013
	(.002)	(.070)	(.055)	(.069)			
83.1-86.12	-.007	.017	-.015	.958**	.975/1.84	48	.004
	(.001)	(.022)	(.030)	(.030)			
87.1-90.12	.001	.021#	-.035#	.966**	.980/1.91	48	.003
	(.000)	(.013)	(.019)	(.022)			
79.1-90.12	-.002**	-.001	.015	.931**	.887/1.64	143	.008
	(.001)	(.023)	(.025)	(.030)			

Notes: All Currencies are measured in terms of SDR (USD 0.42, DM 0.19, Yen 0.15, FF 0.12, UK£ 0.12). (**), (*), (#), (##) denote significant at 99%, 95%, 90%, 85%.

Table 6 cont.. Currencies in the European community
a) Weights assigned to foreign currencies in determining changes in value
(Constrained estimation)

Time period	Const.	USD	Yen	DM	adj.R*/DW	#obs	SEE
Denmark-Krone							
79.1-82.12	-.005**	.018	.122**	.873**	.853/2.07	47	.009
	(.001)	(.051)	(.040)	(.051)			
83.1-86.12	-.001	.041	-.026	.955**	.942/2.46	48	.001
	(.001)	(.032)	(.045)	(.045)			
87.1-90.12	-.000	.052*	.002	.951**	.913/1.90	48	.006
	(.001)	(.026)	(.038)	(.045)			
79.1-90.12	-.002*	.019	.061*	.913**	.895/1.90	143	.008
	(.001)	(.021)	(.024)	(.028)			
Netherlands-Guilder							
79.1-82.12	-.000	-.040##	.053##	.924**	.968/2.20	47	.005
	(.001)	(.025)	(.035)	(.034)			
83.1-86.12	-.004**	.144**	.085	.857**	.866/2.15	48	.008
	(.001)	(.045)	(.063)	(.062)			
87.1-90.12	-.000	.000	-.014	.998**	.982/2.94	48	.003
	(.000)	(.012)	(.018)	(.021)			
79.1-90.12	-.000	-.007	.000	.935**	.960/2.14	143	.009
	(.000)	(.013)	(.014)	(.017)			
Ireland-Pound							
79.1-82.12	-.003*	.057	.022	.825**	.861/2.21	47	.008
	(.001)	(.044)	(.034)	(.043)			
83.1-86.12	-.004*	-.056	.152##	.713**	.770/1721	48	.013
	(.002)	(.067)	(.094)	(.093)			
87.1-90.12	-.000	.078**	-.046##	.822**	.927/2.00	47	.005
	(.001)	(.021)	(.032)	(.037)			
79.1-90.12	-.002**	.036	.017	.813**	.829/1.95	143	.009
	(.001)	(.026)	(.029)	(.033)			

Table 6 cont.. Currencies in the European community
a) Weights assigned to foreign currencies in determining changes in value
(Constrained estimation)

Time period	Const.	USD	Yen	DM	adj.R*/DW	#obs	SEE
Portugal-Escudo							
79.1-82.12	-.010**	.211*	.064	.510**	.225/1.95	47	.020
	(.003)	(.109)	(.085)	(.108)			
83.1-86.12	-.013**	.035	.175	.471**	.441/1.83	48	.020
	(.003)	(.106)	(.147)	(.145)			
87.1-90.12	-.003**	.152**	.034	.636**	.689/1.80	48	.005
	(.001)	(.022)	(.032)	(.037)			
79.1-90.12	-.008*	.136**	.050	.548**	.430/1.79	143	.017
	(.001)	(.047)	(.052)	(.061)			
Spain-Peseta							
79.1-82.12	.016	1.92	.074	-.108	-.060/2.39	47	.557
	(.082)	(3.03)	(2.37)	(2.99)			
83.1-86.12	-.016*	-1.687**	.367	2.125**	.758/2.06	48	.044
	(.007)	(.237)	(.330)	(.325)			
87.1-90.12	-.034	-1.266	.413	3.421	-.051/2.28	48	.593
	(.087)	(2.777)	(4.106)	(4.767)			
79.1-90.12	-.006	-.421	.376	1.487	-.012/2.31	143	.460
	(.039)	(1.289)	(1.432)	(1.680)			
Greece-Drachma							
79.1-82.12	-.011**	.427**	.074	.383**	.122/1.82	47	.018
	(.003)	(.099)	(.078)	(.098)			
83.1-86.12	-.017**	.186	.069	.688**	.150/1.71	48	.036
	(.005)	(.191)	(.266)	(.262)			
87.1-90.12	-.000	.078**	.046**	.822**	.927/2.00	48	.005
	(.001)	(.021)	(.032)	(.037)			
79.1-90.12	-.011*	.230**	.073	.543**	.215/2.01	143	.024
	(.002)	(.066)	(.073)	(.086)			

Table 7. Currencies in EFTA
a) Weights assigned to foreign currencies in determining changes in value
(Constrained estimation)

Time period	Const.	USD	Yen	DM	adj.R*/DW	#obs	SEE
Austria-Schilling							
79.1-82.12	-.001*	-.014	-.007	1.035**	.987/2.03	47	.003
	(.000)	(.017)	(.013)	(.016)			
83.1-86.12	-.000	.016	-.010	.994**	.992/2.59	48	.002
	(.000)	(.012)	(.017)	(.016)			
87.1-90.12	-.000	.011	.005	1.005**	.951/2.31	48	.004
	(.001)	(.021)	(.031)	(.036)			
79.1-90.12	.000	.008	-.008	1.011**	.981/2.28	143	.003
	(.000)	(.009)	(.010)	(.012)			
Finland-Markka							
79.1-82.12	-.003	.266**	.110	.477**	.256/1.80	47	.018
	(.003)	(.100)	(.078)	(.098)			
83.1-86.12	-.001	.138**	.097	.558**	.911/2.01	48	.005
	(.001)	(.028)	(.039)	(.039)			
87.1-90.12	-.001	.188**	.012	.509**	.711/1.79	48	.007
	(.001)	(.035)	(.052)	(.060)			
79.1-90.12	-.000	.182**	.088*	.526**	.577/1.90	143	.012
	(.001)	(.033)	(.036)	(.043)			
Norway-Krone							
79.1-82.12	-.003$^{\#}$	.280**	.097$^{\#}$	.489**	.463/1.37	47	.012
	(.002)	(.066)	(.051)	(.065)			
83.1-86.12	-.004*	.066	.129	.583**	.654/2.17	48	.014
	(.002)	(.072)	(.100)	(.099)			
87.1-90.12	.001	.281**	.077	.434**	.523/1.60	48	.008
	(.001)	(.039)	(.058)	(.067)			
79.1-90.12	-.002	.198**	.083*	.529**	.568/1.99	143	.012
	(.001)	(.033)	(.037)	(.043)			

Notes: See Table 6.

Table 7 cont.. Currencies in EFTA
a) Weights assigned to foreign currencies in determining changes in value
(Constrained estimation)

Time period	Const.	USD	Yen	DM	adj.R*/DW	#obs	SEE
Sweden-Krona							
79.1-82.12	-.007#	.240#	.136	.354*	.080/1.84	47	.027
	(.004)	(.145)	(.113)	(.143)			
83.1-86.12	-.001#	.245**	.104**	.482**	.910/2.05	48	.004
	(.001)	(.023)	(.031)	(.041)			
87.1-90.12	-.000	.290**	.048	.473**	.713/1.41	48	.006
	(.001)	(.026)	(.038)	(.045)			
79.1-90.12	.003*	.246**	.115*	.430**	.328/1.72	143	.016
	(.001)	(.044)	(.049)	(.058)			
Switzerland-Franc							
79.1-82.12	-.002	-.115	.121#	1.041**	.729/1.63	47	.017
	(.002)	(.091)	(.071)	(.090)			
83.1-86.12	-.001	-.157*	.366**	.629**	.800/1.87	48	.013
	(.002)	(.067)	(.093)	(.092)			
87.1-90.12	-.001	.029	.100	.817**	.682/1.73	48	.013
	(.002)	(.060)	(.089)	(.103)			
79.1-90.12	-.000	-.070#	.147**	.888**	.731/1.72	143	.014
	(.001)	(.040)	(.045)	(.053)			
Iceland-Krona							
79.1-82.12	-.034**	.751**	-.080	.277##	.007/2.23	47	.033
	(.005)	(.183)	(.143)	(.181)			
83.1-86.12	-.213**	.428#	-.060	.759*	.071/1.83	48	.042
	(.006)	(.222)	(.309)	(.305)			
87.1-90.12	-.011**	.245*	-.077	.442*	.142/2.13	48	.021
	(.003)	(.100)	(.148)	(.172)			
79.1-90.12	-.021**	.392**	-.015	.514**	.054/1.90	143	.035
	(.003)	(.097)	(.108)	(.126)			

Table 8 Exchange Rate Volatility and Bilateral Trade
(OLS estimation)

	Volat.	GNPs	GNP/cap	Dist.	Adj.	adj.R*	SEE
1980							
Nominal	-.077**	.78**	.32**			.63	1.39
Ex Rate	(.026)	(.02)	(.02)				
	-.064**	.78**	.24**	-.69**	.39##	.71	1.25
	(.023)	(.02)	(.02)	(.05)	(.22)		
Real	-.148**	.76**	.31**			.66	1.35
Ex Rate	(.033)	(.02)	(.03)				
	-.088**	.76**	.25**	-.67**	.60##	.74	1.19
	(.030)	(.02)	(.03)	(.05)	(.23)		
1985							
Nominal	-.159**	.75**	.29**			.65	1.37
Ex Rate	(.022)	(.02)	(.02)				
	.009	.80**	.22**	-.77**	.74**	.73	1.19
	(.021)	(.02)	(.02)	(.04)	(.19)		
Real	-.263**	.72**	.27**			.69	1.32
Ex Rate	(.028)	(.02)	(.03)				
	-.041##	.78**	.24**	-.76**	.60##	.76	1.15
	(.030)	(.02)	(.03)	(.05)	(.22)		
1990							
Nominal	.016	.77**	.13**			.67	1.30
Ex Rate	(.016)	(.02)	(.02)				
	.066**	.80**	.07**	-.69**	.92**	.76	1.10
	(.014)	(.02)	(.02)	(.04)	(.17)		
Real	-.133**	.79**	.17**			.75	1.16
Ex Rate	(.026)	(.02)	(.02)				
	-.079**	.81**	.09**	-.62**	.51##	.81	1.01
	(.023)	(.02)	(.02)	(.04)	(.21)		

Notes: (1) Standard errors are in parentheses. (2) **, *, # and ## denote "statistically signifincant" at the 99%, 95%, 90% and 85% levels, respectively.

Table 9 Exchange Rate Volatility and Bilateral Trade
(OLS estimation)

	Volat.	GNPs	GNP/cap	Dist.	Adj.	WH	EEC	EFTA	EAEC	APEC	adj.R*	SEE
1980												
		.74** (.02)	.29** (.02)	-.56** (.04)	.72** (.18)	.52** (.15)	.23 (.18)		.88** (.27)	1.51** (.17)	.71	1.23
Nominal Ex Rate	-56.11** (7.45)	.77** (.02)	.24** (.02)	-.74** (.05)	.24 (.21)	.13 (.23)	-.14 (.18)	-.08 (.32)	.96** (.36)	1.31** (.19)	.74	1.17
Real Ex Rate	-15.26** (5.25)	.74** (.02)	.27** (.02)	-.70** (.05)	.48* (.22)	.17 (.20)	-.09 (.18)	-.22 (.38)	.90* (.37)	1.40** (.22)	.76	1.14
1985												
		.76** (.02)	.25** (.02)	-.70** (.04)	.75** (.18)	.33** (.16)	.44* (.17)		.59* (.26)	1.28** (.17)	.74	1.17
Nominal Ex Rate	.23 (.49)	.77** (.02)	.24** (.02)	-.72** (.04)	.61** (.19)	.26## (.17)	.45* (.18)	-.02 (.31)	.79* (.36)	1.18** (.19)	.75	1.16
Real Ex Rate	.09 (.53)	.77** (.02)	.25** (.02)	-.77** (.05)	.46* (.22)	-.05 (.20)	.26## (.18)	-.19 (.31)	.72* (.36)	1.13** (.21)	.78	1.12
1990												
		.75** (.02)	.09** (.02)	-.56** (.04)	.79** (.16)	.92** (.14)	.47** (.16)		.69* (.24)	1.36** (.15)	.77	1.07
Nominal Ex Rate	5.23** (.58)	.78** (.02)	.09** (.02)	-.66** (.04)	.53** (.16)	.67** (.14)	.41** (.16)	-.03 (.28)	.68* (.32)	1.35** (.17)	.80	1.02
Real Ex Rate	-8.04# (4.39)	.79** (.02)	.12** (.02)	-.61** (.04)	.35# (.20)	.53** (.17)	.29 (.17)	-.09 (.27)	.91* (.27)	1.12** (.17)	.83	.97

Notes: See Table 8.

Table 10 Exchange Rate Volatility and Bilateral Trade
(Instrumental Variable Estimation)

	Volat.	GNPs	GNP/cap	Dist.	Adj.	WH	EEC	EFTA	EAEC	APEC	adj.R*	SEE
1980												
Nominal Ex Rate	-.15E-04** (.07E-04)	.73** (.02)	.27** (.02)	-.55** (.04)	.74** (.18)	.60** (.15)	.23 (.18)	.07 (.32)	.91** (.27)	1.48** (.17)	.71	1.20
Real Ex Rate	-.19E-04** (.07E-04)	.73** (.02)	.27** (.02)	-.55** (.05)	.76** (.18)	.64** (.15)	.23 (.18)	.07 (.32)	.90** (.27)	1.48** (.17)	.71	1.20
1985												
Nominal Ex Rate	.28E-05 (.73E-05)	.76** (.02)	.25** (.02)	-.70** (.04)	.75** (.18)	.32* (.16)	.45** (.18)	-.06 (.32)	.58* (.26)	1.29** (.17)	.74	1.17
Real Ex Rate	.41E-05 (.75E-05)	.76** (.02)	.25** (.02)	-.70** (.04)	.75** (.18)	.31* (.16)	.45** (.17)	-.06 (.32)	.58* (.26)	1.29** (.17)	.74	1.17
1990												
Nominal Ex Rate	.18E-04* (.07E-04)	.76** (.02)	.11** (.02)	-.56** (.04)	.78** (.16)	.84** (.14)	.49** (.16)	-.07 (.29)	.66* (.24)	1.38** (.15)	.77	1.07
Real Ex Rate	.23E-04** (.08E-04)	.76** (.02)	.11** (.02)	-.56** (.04)	.75** (.16)	.80** (.14)	.49** (.16)	-.07 (.29)	.65* (.24)	1.38** (.15)	.78	1.06

Notes: See Table 8.

Table 11 Effects of Exchange Rate Volatility: Nominal Rates
(Total Trade, 1965-1990)

	NV	GNP	GNP/cap	Dist.	Adj.	WH	EEC	EAEC	APEC	# obs.	adj.R*	SEE
1965	-3.81** (.60)	.63** (.02)	.27** (.02)	-.40** (.04)	.78** (.17)	.05 (.16)	.20 (.16)	1.59** (.31)	.60** (.22)	1115	.70	1.04
1970	-2.47** (.09)	.64** (.02)	.36** (.02)	-.51** (.04)	.69** (.17)	.01 (.14)	.08 (.21)	1.60** (.29)	.70** (.17)	1231	.72	1.06
1975	-1.49* (.74)	.72** (.02)	.27** (.02)	-.68** (.05)	.53** (.17)	.26# (.15)	-.10 (.18)	.87** (.33)	.87** (.23)	1401	.72	1.18
1980	-7.65** (.08)	.76** (.02)	.27** (.02)	-.62** (.04)	.64** (.18)	.44** (.15)	.01 (.16)	.81** (.26)	1.35** (.18)	1653	.72	1.18
1985	.13 (.34)	.76** (.02)	.25** (.02)	-.71** (.04)	.73** (.18)	.34* (.16)	.45* (.18)	.60* (.28)	1.21** (.19)	1589	.74	1.17
1990	2.24** (.27)	.76** (.02)	.12** (.02)	-.60** (.04)	.68** (.16)	.71** (.14)	.51** (.16)	.67** (.25)	1.39** (.17)	1519	.80	1.05

Notes: Standard errors are in parentheses.
**, *, # denote significant at 1%, 5%, and 10% level, respectively.
All variables except the dummies are in logarithms.

Table 12 Effects of Exchange Rate Volatility: Real Rates
(Total Trade, 1965-1990)

	RV	GNP	GNP/cap	Dist.	Adj.	WH	EEC	EAEC	APEC	# obs.	adj.R*	SEE
1965	-3.02** (.67)	.72** (.02)	.24** (.03)	-.53** (.05)	.59** (.18)	.02 (.15)	.04 (.17)	.99* (.50)	.44# (.26)	773	.76	.94
1970	-2.72** (.83)	.65** (.02)	.36** (.02)	-.50** (.04)	.77** (.16)	.02 (.13)	.08 (.16)	1.80** (.32)	.67** (.21)	1053	.76	.99
1975	-1.57* (.82)	.72** (.02)	.27** (.02)	-.67** (.05)	.58** (.18)	.27# (.15)	-.06 (.18)	.85** (.32)	.90** (.22)	1316	.74	2.21
1980	-6.97** (.08)	.74** (.02)	.26** (.02)	-.62** (.04)	.73** (.18)	.42** (.15)	.01 (.18)	.76** (.26)	1.35** (.18)	1503	.75	1.13
1985	.12 (.37)	.76** (.02)	.25** (.02)	-.71** (.04)	.73** (.18)	.30# (.15)	.40* (.17)	.60* (.27)	1.16** (.18)	1500	.75	1.14
1990	3.19** (.27)	.76** (.02)	.12** (.02)	-.57** (.04)	.80** (.16)	.74** (.14)	.57** (.16)	.71** (.25)	1.38** (.17)	1494	.78	1.04

Notes: Standard errors are in parentheses.
**, *, # denote significant at 1%, 5%, and 10% level, respectively.
All variables except the dummies are in logarithms.

Table 13 Effects of Exchange Rate Volatility: Real Rates
Instrumental Variable Estimation
(Total Trade, 1965-1990)

	NV	GNP	GNP/cap	Dist.	Adj.	WH	EEC	EAEC	APEC	# obs.	adj.R*	SEE
1965	-38.03* (.28)	.82** (.05)	-.07 (.12)	-.50** (.12)	1.09** (.47)	1.10$^{\#}$ (.60)	-.17 (.35)	1.28 (.92)	.26 (.46)	393	.51	1.40
1970	-4.54 (11.73)	.66** (.02)	.33** (.04)	-.51** (.08)	.69** (.18)	.16 (.43)	.00 (.18)	1.71** (.43)	.74** (.23)	921	.76	.97
1975	-2.05 (1.54)	.72** (.02)	.25** (.02)	-.69** (.05)	.51** (.20)	.42* (.17)	-.12 (.24)	.90* (.35)	1.09** (.24)	1076	.73	1.14
1980	-.28 (3.22)	.74** (.02)	.26** (.03)	-.67** (.05)	.62** (.19)	.49** (.15)	.00 (.22)	.79* (.32)	1.49** (.20)	1187	.74	1.13
1985	.18 (.46)	.78** (.02)	.21** (.02)	-.74** (.05)	.66** (.20)	.33$^{\#}$ (.17)	.39$^{\#}$ (.20)	.70$^{\#}$ (.36)	1.22** (.21)	1163	.76	1.12
1990	3.89** (.59)	.77** (.02)	.11** (.02)	-.61** (.04)	.70** (.17)	.55** (.17)	.59** (.16)	.52$^{\#}$ (.27)	1.39** (.17)	1319	.79	1.03

Notes: Standard errors are in parentheses.
**, *, # denote significant at 1%, 5%, and 10% level, respectively.
All variables except the dummies are in logarithms.

APPENDIX

List of Countries Used in the Gravity Equations Showing Regional Groupings and Main City. The distance between countries was computed as the great circle distance between the relevant pair of cities.

Americas (WH, 13)

Canada	Ottawa
US	Chicago
Argentina	Buenos Aires
Brazil	Sao Paolo
Chile	Santiago
Colombia	Bogota
Ecuador	Quito
Mexico	Mexico City
Peru	Lima
Venezuela	Caracas
Bolivia	La Paz
Paraguay	Asuncion
Uruguay	Montevideo

European Community (EC, 11)

Germany	Bonn
France	Paris
Italy	Rome
UK	London
Belgium	Brussels
Denmark	Copenhagen
Netherlands	Amsterdam
Greece	Athens
Ireland	Dublin
Portugal	Lisbon
Spain	Madrid

Other countries (23)

South Africa	Pretoria
Turkey	Ankara
Yugoslavia	Belgrade
Israel	Jerusalem
Algeria	Algiers
Libya	Tripoli
Nigeria	Lagos
Egypt	Cairo
Morocco	Casablanca
Tunisia	tunis
Sudan	Khartoum
Ghana	Accra
Kenya	Nairobi
Ethiopia	Addis Abeba
Iran	Teheran
Kuwait	Kuwait
Saudi Arabia	Riyadh
India	New Delhi
Pakistan	Karachi
Hungary	Budapest
Poland	Warsaw
Australia	Sydney
New Zealand	Wellington

European Free Trade Area (EFTA, 6)

Austria	Vienna
Finland	Helsinki
Norway	Oslo
Sweden	Stockholm
Switzerland	Geneva
Iceland	Reykjavik

East Asia (EAEG, 10)

Japan	Tokyo
Indonesia	Jakarta
Taiwan	Taipei
South Korea	Seoul
Malaysia	Kuala Lumpur
Philippines	Manila
Singapore	Singapore
Thailand	Bangkok
China	Shanghai

Note: APEC consists of East Asia, Australia, New Zealand, Canada, and the US.

NOTES

*. The author would like to thank Matthew Canzoneri, Hans Genberg, Morris Goldstein, Jacques Polak, and other conference participants for useful comments.

Parts of it draw on parts of an earlier paper, "Trade Blocs and Currency Blocs," which was presented at the Centre for Economic Policy Research Conference on *The Monetary Future of Europe*, at El Pazo de Marinan, La Coruna, Spain, and appeared as an NBER Working Paper 4335, 1993. The authors thank Benjamin Chui and Xiong Bai Fan for research assistance, Tamim Bayoumi and Richard Portes for comments on the earlier draft (including pointing out an error), Joe Gagnon for other comments, Warwick McKibbin for help in obtaining data, and the Center for International and Development Economics Research (funded at U.C. Berkeley by the Ford Foundation) for research support. Some of the work was carried out while Frankel was a Visiting Scholar at the Research Department of the International Monetary Fund, and Wei was a Visiting Scholar at the Federal Reserve Bank of San Francisco; but the views expressed are not those of any institution.

1. The country membership in the four currency blocs did not coincide perfectly with the membership in four sets of preferential trading arrangements. Eichengreen and Irwin (1993), using an approach similar to that of the present paper, find that exchange rate variability had a significant effect on trade in the 1930s, but that in the case of the British Commonwealth countries, for example, preferential trading arrangements were a more important source of intra-bloc trade than was the adoption of a common sterling standard.
2. Frankel (1991) presented a back-of-the-envelope measure of intra-regional bias: the ratio of the intra-regional trade share to the share of world trade. Anderson and Norheim (1992) use similar calculations of "intensity of trade indexes."
3. The results of one extensive early project along these lines were reported in Tinbergen (1962, Appendix VI, pp.262-293) and Linneman (1967). Foundations for the gravity model are offered in papers surveyed by Deardorff (1984, pp. 503-06) and Wang and Winters (1992).
4. Three others are Wang and Winters (1991), Hamilton and Winters (1992), and Havrylyshyn and Pritchett (1991). The focus of these papers was on potential Eastern European trade patterns.
5. NBER Working Paper No. 4335 considered some econometric extensions of the original gravity model estimation - allowing for heteroscedasticity and zero-valued observations - to see how that the basic results held up.
6. Eichengreen and Wyplosz (1993, p.136-37).
7. The list of countries, and regional groupings, is given in an Appendix.
8. The specification implies that trade between two equal-sized countries (say, of size .5) will be greater than trade between a large and small country (say, of size .9 and .1). This property of models with imperfect competition is not a property of the classical Heckscher-Ohlin theory of comparative advantage. Helpman (1987) and Helpman and Krugman (1985, section 1.5). We have also tried to capture classic Heckscher-Ohlin effects, first by including bilateral absolute differences in GNP/capita figures, and then by including some factor endowment variables with data (for a subset of 656 of our 1,953 pairs of countries) generously supplied by Gary Saxonhouse (1989). There is a bit of support for these terms [reported in the conference version of this paper]. The other coefficients are little affected.

9. Indeed, the East Asian bloc effect virtually loses significance in 1985 and 1990, if one allows for the greater openness of East Asia in general, and Hong Kong and Singapore in particular, simultaneously with the APEC bloc effect. See Table 5 in Frankel (1993).
10. This is the same result found by Hamilton and Winters (a significant coefficient of .7 on the EC and zero on EFTA). But it is the opposite of the conclusion one might draw from simple statistics on the magnitudes of intra-regional trade in the EC 12 and Western Europe as a whole, if one did not hold constant for proximity. Grant, Papadakis and Richardson (1992, p.48).
11. Havrylyshyn and Pritchett (1991) found that three languages are significant in the gravity model - Portuguese, Spanish and English, in decreasing order of magnitude. In a study of poor countries, Foroutan and Pritchett (1992) found that French, Spanish and English are statistically significant.
12. Most of the burgeoning trade between Taiwan and China shows up in the statistics twice, because it is recorded as passing through Hong Kong. An attempt to correct the data for the effect of the ban on direct trade results in the Chinese language term becoming no stronger than the other languages. Frankel and Wei (1993).
13. Reported ibid. The coefficients are .50, .54, and .32, in 1980, 1985 and 1990, respectively.
14. Of the EC 12, only Greece had not joined the Exchange Rate Mechanism by early 1992 (though Italy and the United Kingdom dropped out soon thereafter).
15. Only Singapore and Indonesia, and at times Malaysia and Thailand, appear to put significant weight on the yen, and the weight is usually less than .1, as against .9 to 1.0 on the dollar.
16. We have made the decision in this paper to focus on the mark rather than the ECU. One reason for this decision is that the ECU appears to have suffered a major set-back as an international currency subsequent to the foreign exchange crisis of September 1992. The ECU bond market, for example, largely dried up.
17. Why do countries keep the weights secret? It allows the governments to devalue their currencies secretly when they so desire. But secret weights undermine the governments' ability to commit credibly to a low inflationary monetary policy. (Lowell, 1992.)
18. The earlier tests on Asian currencies tried the Swiss franc and purchasing power over local goods as numeraires, in addition to the SDR [Frankel and Wei (1994) and Frankel (1993), respectively].
19. Table 7 in the NBER Working Paper 4335, or Table 6 in Frankel and Wei (1993).
20. The results in Table 8 in the NBER Working Paper 4335, or Table 7 in Frankel and Wei (1993), correspond to those reported here for the other regions. They confirm those in Frankel (1993) and Frankel and Wei (1994), which were produced with different numeraires.
21. See also Alogoskoufis and Portes (1992) and Frankel (1992).
22. Reported in NBER Working Paper 4335, Appendix tables 4-7.
23. For example, Hooper and Kohlhagen (1978), Kenen and Rodrik (1986), Akhtar and Hilton (1984), Cushman (1986) and Peree and Steinherr (1989). The literature is surveyed in Edison and Melvin (1990).
24. The regressions with the volatilities measured in log form are available in Table 13 of Frankel and Wei (1994). There the coefficient on real exchange rate volatility again loses significance in 1985, although remaining negative in sign.
25. Estimates based on a logarithmic specification for the standard deviation may be more appropriate for this question, what would happen to the level of trade if exchange rate variability among the EMS countries now returns to the level that prevailed in 1980. Of our various logarithmic estimates, the preferred one is the instrumental variables

estimate for the effect of the log of real exchange rate variability in 1980: .01. This point estimate would imply that a doubling of exchange rate variability would reduce trade within Europe by a mere 0.7 per cent (= .01(ln 2)).

26. It is also only a fraction of the total increase in intra-regional trade; recall from the first part of the paper that changes in such variables as GNP explain much of the variation in intra-regional trade flows.
27. "First-stage" regressions of exchange rate variability against our measure of variability in relative money supply changes are usually significant statistically (reported in Appendix Table 4 of the conference draft of this paper).
28. For example, Gros (1987) or Caballero and Corbo (1989).
29. This figure does not even take into account the outcome of more recent measures toward greater integration associated with 1992.
30. This pattern continued a trend begun in the 1970s; see Kenen (1983).
31. This computation is based on Thomas and Wickens, 1991, p.14.
32. The fact that much of Japan's imports are raw materials and that much of its exports go to the Western Hemisphere, for example, helps explain why a disproportionately small share of trade is invoiced in yen as opposed to dollars.

REFERENCES

Abrams, Richard, 1980. "International Trade Flows Under Flexible Exchange Rates," Economic Review, Federal Reserve Bank of Kansas City, March, 3-10.

Akhtar, M. Akbar, and Spence Hilton, 1984, "Effects of Exchange Rate Uncertainty on German and U.S. Trade," Federal Reserve Bank of New York Quarterly Review 9, no.1 (Spring),7-16.

Alogoskoufis, George, and Richard Portes. 1992. "European Monetary Union and International Currencies in a Tripolar World," in Establishing a Central Bank: Issues in Europe and Lessons from the US, M.Canzoneri, V.Grilli and P. Masson, eds, Cambridge University Press, 273-300.

Anderson, Kym, and Hege Norheim. 1992. "History, Geography and Regional Economic Integration," GATT Secretariat Conference, Geneva, Oct.; forthcoming in Regionalism and the Global Trading System, K.Anderson and R.Blackhurst, eds., London: Harvester Wheatsheaf, 1993.

Bayoumi, Tamim, and Barry Eichengreen. 1992. "One Money or Many? On Analyzing the Prospects for Monetary Unification in Europe and Other Parts of the World," International Monetary Fund and University of California at Berkeley, August.

Brada, Josef, and Jose Mendez. 1988. "Exchange Rate Risk, Exchange Rate Regimes and the Level of International Trade," Kyklos 41, no.2, p.198.

Caballero, Ricardo, and Vittorio Corbo. 1989. "The Effect of Real Exchange Rate Uncertainty on Exports: Empirical Evidence," The World Bank Economic Review, 3, no.2, May, 263-278.

Cushman, David. 1986. "Has Exchange Risk Depressed International Trade? The Impact of Third-Country Exchange Risk" Journal of International Money and Finance, 5, September, 361-379.

Deardorff, Alan. 1984. "Testing Trade Theories and Predicting Trade Flows," in R.Jones and P.Kenen, eds., Handbook of International Economics vol. I. Amsterdam, Elsevier Science Publishers. Ch.10: 467-517.

De Grauwe, Paul. 1988. "Exchange Rate Variability and the Slowdown in Growth of International Trade." IMF Staff Papers 35, pp.63-84.

Edison, Hali, and Michael Melvin. 1990 "The Determinants and Implications of the Choice of an Exchange Rate System," in William Haraf and Thomas Willett, Monetary Policy for a Volatile Global Economy, AEI Press, Washington.

Eichengreen, Barry. 1990. "One Money for Europe? Lessons from the US Currency Union, Economic Policy, April, 117-189.

Eichengreen, Barry, and Douglas Irwin, 1993, "Trade Blocs, Currency Blocs and the Disintegration of World Trade in the 1930s," U.C. Berkeley, June.

Eichengreen, Barry, and Charles Wyplosz, 1993, "The Unstable EMS," Brookings Papers on Economic Activity 1, 51-143.

Foroutan, Faezeh and Lant Pritchett. 1992. "Intra-Sub-Saharan African Trade: Is It Too Little?" World Bank, December.

Frankel, Jeffrey. 1991. "Is a Yen Bloc Forming in Pacific Asia?" in Finance and the International Economy, The AMEX Bank Review Prize Essays, edited by R. O'Brien, Oxford University Press, UK.

Frankel, Jeffrey. 1992. "On the Dollar," Pacific Basin Working Paper No. PB91-04, Federal Reserve Bank of San Francisco. In The New Palgrave Dictionary of Money and Finance, MacMillan Press Reference Books, London.

Frankel, Jeffrey. 1993. "Is Japan Creating a Yen Bloc in East Asia and the Pacific?" NBER working paper no. 4050. In Regionalism and Rivalry: Japan and the U.S. in Pacific Asia, edited by Jeffrey Frankel and Miles Kahler, University of Chicago Press, Chicago, forthcoming, September.

Frankel, Jeffrey, and Shang-Jin Wei. 1993 "Is There A Currency Bloc in the Pacific?" July 12-13, Kirribilli, Australia; in Exchange Rates, International Trade and Monetary Policy, edited by A. Blundell-Wignall and S.Grenville, Reserve Bank of Australia, Sydney.

Frankel, Jeffrey, and Shang-Jin Wei. 1994. "Yen Bloc or Dollar Bloc? Exchange Rate Policies of the East Asian Economies", *Third Annual NBER - East Asia Seminar on Economics*, held in Sapporo, Japan, June 17-19, 1992; forthcoming in Macroeconomic Linkage, Takatoshi Ito and Anne Krueger, editors, University of Chicago Press, Chicago.

Gagnon, Joseph, 1989, "Exchange Rate Variability and the Level of International Trade," International Finance Discussion Papers No. 369, Federal Reserve Board, Dec.

Grant, Richard, Maria Papadakis, and J.David Richardson, 1992, "Global Trade Flows: Old Structures, New Issues, Empirical Evidence," *Twentieth Pacific Trade and Development Conference*, Washington, D.C. September 10-12.

Gros, Daniel, 1987, "Exchange Rate Variability and Foreign Trade in the Presence of Adjustment Costs," draft.

Hamilton, Carl, and L.Alan Winters. 1992. "Opening Up International Trade in Eastern Europe," Economic Policy (April).

Havrylyshyn, Oleg, and Lant Pritchett. 1991. "European Trade Patterns After the Transition." *Policy, Research and External Affairs Working Paper Series* No. 748, August, World Bank.

Helpman, Elhanan. 1987. "Imperfect Competition and International Trade: Evidence from Fourteen Industrial Countries," Journal of the Japanese and International Economies 1: 62-81.

Helpman, Elhanan and Paul Krugman. 1985. Market Structure and Foreign Trade, Cambridge, MA, MIT Press.

Hooper, Peter, and Steven Kohlhagen. 1978. "The Effect of Exchange Rate Uncertainty on Prices and Volume of International Trade." Journal of International Economics 8, Nov., pp.483-511.

International Monetary Fund, 1983, "Exchange Rate Volatility and Trade," Research Department, Dec. 9.

Kenen, Peter, 1983, The Role of the Dollar as an International Currency, Occasional Papers No. 13, Group of Thirty, New York.

Kenen, Peter, and Dani Rodrik, 1986, "Measuring and Analyzing the Effects of Short-term Volatility in Real Exchange Rates," Review of Economics and Statistics, 311-315.

Kindleberger, Charles P., 1981, International Money, George Allen & Unwin, London.

Krugman, Paul, 1984, "The International Role of the Dollar: Theory and Prospect," in Exchange Rate Theory and Practice, edited by John Bilson and Richard Marston, Chicago: University of Chicago Press, 261-78.

Lawrence, Robert. 1991c. "Emerging Regional Arrangements: Building Blocks or Stumbling Blocks?" in Finance and the International Economy, *The AMEX Bank Review Prize Essays*, edited by R.O'Brien. United Kingdom: Oxford University Press.

Linneman, Hans. 1966. An Econometric Study of International Trade Flows, North-Holland, Amsterdam.

Lowell, Julia. 1992. "Do Governments Do What They Say (And Do We Believe Them?): Two Essays on National Debt and Exchange Regime Policies," Ph.D. Thesis, Department of Economics, University of California, Berkeley.

McKinnon, Ronald, 1969, Private and Official International Money: The Case for the Dollar, Essays in International Finance, No. 74, Princeton University, April

Peree, Eric, and Alfred Steinherr, 1989, "Exchange Rate Uncertainty and Foreign Trade," European Economic Review 33: 1241-1264.

Saxonhouse, Gary, 1989, "Differentiated Products, Economies of Scale, and Access to the Japanese Market," in R. Feenstra (ed.), Trade Policies for International Competitiveness, University of Chicago Press: Chicago, 145-174.

Swoboda, Alexander, 1969, "Vehicle Currencies in the Foreign Exchange Market: The Case of the Dollar," in R.Aliber, ed., The International Market for Foreign Exchange, Praeger, New York.

Thomas, S.H. and M.R. Wickens, 1991, "Currency Substitution and Vehicle Currencies: Tests of Alternative Hypotheses for the Dollar, DM and Yen," Discussion Paper No. 507, Centre for Economic Policy Research, London, Jan.

Tinbergen, Jan, 1962, Shaping the World Economy, The Twentieth Century Fund: New York.

Wang, Zhen Kun, and L.Alan Winters, 1991, "The Trading Potential of Eastern Europe," Centre for Economic Policy Research Discussion Paper No. 610, November, London, UK.

Discussion

MATTHEW CANZONERI

Frankel and Wei have begun the ambitious task of merging two separate literatures - one on trade blocks, and the other on currency blocks. This is a very welcome development in light of the EC view that a common currency is required to complete its single market program and the North American view that there is no such requirement.[1] Frankel and Wei are among the first to provide a formal empirical analysis of these competing views.

Merging two literatures can be difficult because the literatures will generally come from very different perspectives. Frankel and Wei have done an admiral job, but occasionally I feel that they have let the different perspectives of steer them away from the main issues. Let me first discuss the results presented in the paper, then I will take a few minutes to speak more generally about the Transatlantic debate.

1 Frankel and Wei's Three Questions

Frankel and Wei organize their analysis around three empirical questions: (1) Do trade blocks exist? (2) Are there coinciding currency blocks? (3) Does monetary integration foster trade blocks?

Question 1: Do trade blocks exist?

Frankel and Wei first show that a gravity model gives a good account of bilateral trade, and we are asked to assume that the gravity model explains the "normal" amount of trade one would expect between any two countries. Then, Frankel and Wei add regional dummies to see if the countries within a given region trade more than the gravity model would predict. If so, a trade block is said to exist.

Frankel and Wei show that trade blocks so defined certainly do exist, but they are probably not the blocks you or I would have suspected. Their figures show that two EC countries trade 50% more than normal, but that two East Asian countries trade two times more than normal, that two Western Hemisphere countries trade two and a half times more than normal, and that two Pacific block countries trade a whopping five times more than normal. (The Pacific block includes the East Asian countries, the US and Canada, Australia and New Zealand.) The numbers for the EC seem high, but perhaps plausible; they certainly make a strong case for labeling the EC a trading block. The real question is: why are the numbers for the other blocks so much higher. Their implausibility may cast some doubt on the methodology, and therefore the results for the EC.

Tamim Bayoumi has suggested that the fault may lie in the specification of the distance variable in the gravity equation. Long sea miles probably do not imply the same transportation costs as miles across congested land masses. In addition, there may be nonlinearities in transportation costs and in the other factors that the distance variable may be a proxy for. If so, this variable may be overstating the detrimental effects of "distance" for the Pacific block countries, and the Pacific block dummy may just be undoing the effect. The coefficient on the Western Hemisphere dummy may have the same positive bias.

I do not know how to correct this bias, but I would suggest refocusing the study on the three blocks that people generally have in mind: I would replace the Western Hemisphere block with a US-Canada-Mexico block, think carefully about what to put in the East Asia block, and ignore the Pacific block. I think this would increase the interest in the comparisons, and it might limit the bias coming from a possible misspecification of "distance" in the gravity equation.

The main drawback to this method of defining trade blocks is that it does not identify the factors that produce above normal trade. One would like to go on to replace the regional dummies with variables that reflect the actual factors at work. Conscious governmental decisions may have played a role in the EC block, but this explanation is implausible for the other blocks the authors have defined. Would it be possible to develop an index of integration policies within a given region? If so, it could be added to the gravity model, and we could see how much of the trade bias is attributable to this factor. Are there other, more fundamental, factors at work? Frankel and Wei added a dummy for a common language, and it proved to be quite significant. This dummy variable may represent a wide range of cultural or institutional factors, and it would be interesting to try to be more specific. One could develop proxies (or indices) for legal systems, political processes, etc. But for present purposes, the most intriguing factor to consider is the degree of monetary integration. This is what Frankel and Wei go on to do.

Question 2: Are there coinciding currency blocks?

First, we need a measure of the degree of monetary integration. Frankel and Wei use the standard deviation of monthly exchange rate changes, as an inverse measure. In one sense, it is very hard to object to this: A common currency is equivalent to a system of multiple currencies with rigidly fixed exchange rates. The variability of exchange rates is therefore a results oriented measure of the degree of monetary integration, and indeed the literature on currency blocks has focused on it.

On the other hand, exchange rate variability may not be a very good measure of the fundamental progress that is actually being made in the area of monetary integration. The European experience provides an illustration. First, exchange rates fluctuations are limited; then, capital controls are lifted and financial markets become integrated across borders; then, money demands become unstable (reflecting the underlying integration of goods markets) and there may be speculative attacks based more on political factors than on realized policy actions. At this stage, exchange rate variability increases. Then, there may be a final push to credibly fixed rates or a common currency, or the whole process may take several steps backward. In other words, there may be what Andrew Crockett (1991) calls an "inherent dynamic" to regional integration, and in this process, exchange rate variability may not be a close - or even monotonic - measure of the fundamental progress that is being made. I will come back to this point several times in what follows.

First, Frankel and Wei look at the volatility of exchange rates inside and outside the trade blocks. They conclude that there "is a tendency for exchange rate variability to be lower within each of the groups than across groups." The big exception is the Western Hemisphere block, which has exchange rate variability that is twice the world average and ten times the EC average. The only sense in which the Western Hemisphere is becoming a currency block is the process of dollarization: some 2/3 of the stock of US currency is thought to reside outside the country, and presumably a lot of it is in Latin America. This raises a host of issues that are not captured in the authors' analysis, which is another reason to think about replacing the Western Hemisphere block with a US-Canada-Mexico block.

Next, Frankel and Wei regress changes in the exchange rates of smaller countries on changes in the exchange rates of the three major currencies. The stated goal is "to see whether countries (in a given block) try to stabilize their currencies in terms of a particular major currency." They conclude that most EC countries and some EFTA countries (most notably Austria) are in mark zone, while the Western Hemisphere and Asian countries form a dollar zone. The yen does not seem to be a key currency in this sense.

The authors clearly view their equations as policy reaction functions, but they are open to another interpretation. Exchange rates are endogenous variables, not policy instruments; they move in response to a variety of factors. Elsewhere, I have shown that if two countries experience a common shock they should find that their exchange rates move in tandem vis a vis some third currency.[2] If European countries share many of the same shocks, perhaps because of the integrated nature of their economies, then we would expect to see their exchange rates moving in tandem with the DM. In other words, these equations might simply be showing the integrated nature of the region, as reflected in a commonality of shocks.[3]

My point, once again, is that exchange rate variability may not be a very good measure of the degree of monetary integration. If the goal is to see whether monetary policies are coordinated across a given region, why not use the policy instruments? Regress the policy actions of the followers on the policy actions of the three potential leaders.

Having identified trade blocks with currency blocks, the next step is to ask if monetary integration fosters trade.

Question 3: Does monetary integration foster trade blocks?

If, as Frankel and Wei assume, exchange rate variability is the appropriate measure of monetary integration, then the question becomes: does exchange rate variability impede trade flows? This question has been the subject of numerous studies over the past two decades; the usual finding is that there is little or no effect. Frankel and Wei take a new approach: they put exchange rate variability into the gravity equations. They find that it had a small negative effect in the early '80s, but that it was gone by 1990. (Actually, they get a significantly positive effect in 1990, suggesting some sort of misspecification.)

Throughout the paper, Frankel and Wei try to assess the robustness of their results, and here they investigate a possible reverse causation problem. They worry that monetary authorities might try to smooth exchange rate fluctuations with important trading partners. Their response is to use an instrumental variables procedure, but their choice of instrument is very controversial. They use the standard deviation of relative money supplies as an instrument for exchange rate volatility on the grounds that "monetary policies are less likely than exchange rate policies to be set in response to bilateral trade patterns". There is a large empirical literature on sterilized intervention that suggests monetary and exchange rate policies are really one and the same thing; however, Frankel may wish to differ with this conclusion based on his recent work with Katherine Dominguez. (See for example Dominguez and Frankel (1989).) I am tempted to interpret the instrumental variable regressions in a somewhat different way, namely as an attempt to cleanse the exchange rate movements of the extra non-policy shocks I discussed earlier. Be that as it may, the results are not much different.

Frankel and Wei go on to investigate the effects of real exchange rate variability on trade flows. This may be an interesting exercise, and it is in keeping with the literature, but it does seem tangential to the main theme of the paper. Suppose we found that real exchange rate variability has a detrimental effect on trade. Would we then have concluded that monetary integration does foster trade blocks? To do so, we would have had to argue that real exchange rate volatility is a better measure of monetary integration than nominal exchange rate volatility, which has little or no effect. That seems hard to do. I would, of course, be in favor of trying other more measures of monetary integration, since I have already argued that nominal exchange rate variability may not capture the process very well.

Frankel and Wei focus their analysis on the effects monetary integration on the level of trade flows, and this is an important factor in determining whether one market requires one money. However, the question has been looked at from other perspectives as well, and it may be appropriate for me to take a few moments to outline the more general debate, as I see it.

2 Does One Market Require One Money?

Feldstein's (1991) discussion of the question is typical of what I would call the "American view". Feldstein reviews the well known criteria for an optimal currency area that were developed by Robert Mundell[4]; then, citing only one empirical study, he asserts that the EC does not qualify. There is not much explicit discussion of North America, but the US-Canada case is often held out as a counterexample to the general proposition, and I think it is a case that proponents of the proposition would do well to study. Feldstein goes on to assert that the real arguments for a common currency in Europe are entirely political.

Feldstein makes no attempt to ask whether the US qualifies on the Mundell criteria: for example, should multiple currencies be introduced to decouple Texas and its energy problems from the rust belt and its long term decline, or from New England and its differing views on social policy? I sometimes see the American view as a rather satisfied acceptance of the status quo, perhaps reflecting the political realities in North America: NAFTA will not have a common currency any time soon, and the governors of Massachusetts and Texas will not be allowed to formulate their own monetary policies. It seems pointless to analyze these things on my side of the Atlantic, except in the most abstract terms.

In Europe by contrast, the integration of markets for goods and services is much deeper, and economists are faced with a number of very practical questions. I think the best way to characterize what I would call the European view is to return to Crockett's (1991) "inherent dynamic" of regional integration, and to ask where the natural stopping point might be.

I would describe the "dynamic" as follows: First, free movement of goods and labor is allowed. Then, banking and other financial services are allowed to move across borders, because they are important intermediate inputs that increase the efficiency of trade. At the same time, capital is allowed to move freely, because it is a necessary complement to cross border banking services and it allocates savings and investment efficiently. Finally, a regional payments mechanism is developed to allow the fast and safe transactions necessary for efficient cross border trade. All of these financial activities may be expected to increase the efficiency of trade within the region, and one can argue that the single market program is not complete without them.

One can also argue that all of these financial activities require some coordination on the regional level. Someone has to supervise and regulate banking institutions to insure safety of the system and to arbitrate national disputes. Someone has to decide how much deposit insurance will be required, and how cross border differences will be arbitrated. If the principle of "mutual recognition" is imposed to let competition work out the differences, then someone has to see that competition in laxity does not go too far. Someone has to set up the regional payments mechanism, and to insure its liquidity. Currently, this coordination is done at the national level, and it is done in a variety of ways, but a central bank is usually involved in at least some of the activities.

Moreover, one can argue that all of these financial activities may be expected to make the formulation of monetary policy more difficult at the national level. It appears that the integration of goods markets and the free mobility of capital is making the EC choose between a common currency and system of essentially free floating exchange rates. As we have seen, the empirical literature suggests that exchange rate volatility has little effect on trade, but I do not think that this view is generally accepted in Europe (or even by academic economists, who exhibit a strong proclivity to study and restudy the issue). Whatever the effect on trade, it has been argued that exchange rate volatility makes regional fiscal programs - the CAP, for example - unmanageable. The integration of goods markets and free capital mobility also seems to be making national money demands more unpredictable, which complicates the formulation of domestic monetary policy. As banking institutions move across borders, the "lender of last resort" responsibilities of the national monetary authorities will become intertwined, and unwanted liquidity spillovers may infringe on a neighboring country's domestic monetary policies. Finally, it is not clear who would provide liquidity for the regional payments mechanism, or how this liquidity might impinge on monetary policy at the national level.

So, the question is this: after you have allowed all of the financial integration that is necessary to support an efficient trade block, can you still retain a system of national currencies and a significant degree of decentralized monetary policymaking? I certainly do not have an answer to this question, and indeed we will probably never be able to answer it confidently. However, formal analyses of the various steps along Crockett's "inherent dynamic" of regional integration will be illuminating and helpful to policymakers, whatever decision the politicians finally make about financial arrangements. Frankel and Wei take us a good step in that direction.

NOTES

1 The EC Commission's view is apparent in the title of its document One Market, One Money. There is no such presumption in discussions of NAFTA.
2. See Canzoneri (1982).
3. This interpretation seems much less plausible for the other blocks the authors study.
4. Hans Genberg (1989) provides a nice review of ideas.

REFERENCES

Canzoneri, Matthew, "Exchange Intervention Policy in a Multiple Country World", Journal of International Economics, November, 1982, 267 - 291.

Crockett, Andrew, "Financial Market Implications of Trade and Currency Zones", in Policy Implications of Trade and Currency Zones, A Symposium Sponsored By the Federal Reserve Bank of Kansas City, 1991.

Dominguez, Kathryn and Jeffrey Frankel, "Does Foreign Exchange Intervention Matter? Disentangling the Portfolio and Expectations Effects for the Mark", working paper, 1989.

Feldstein, Martin, "Does One Market Require One Money?", in Policy Implications of Trade and Currency Zones, A Symposium Sponsored By the Federal Reserve Bank of Kansas City, 1991.

Genberg, Hans, "Exchange Rate Management and Macroeconomic Policy: A National Perspective," Scandinavian Journal of Economics, 91 (2), 439-469, 1989.

Discussion

MORRIS GOLDSTEIN*

1 Introduction

Jeff Frankel is to be commended for providing us with a rich empirical paper that adds to our understanding of natural trading blocks and regional trade biases, of the influence of larger currencies on smaller ones, and of the effects of exchange rate variability on trade flows. These are all areas where economists talk a good game, but often on the basis of rather limited empirical evidence to support their diagnoses and policy prescriptions. In this and in a series of related papers, Jeff has been working productively to help close that gap.

In my remarks I plan to do three things. First, I want to raise some questions about both the gravity model of bilateral trade flows and about Jeff's findings with respect to regional trade biases. Second, I want to offer an assessment of the effect of exchange rate uncertainty on trade. And finally, I want to make a capsule argument as to why we have not seen - and are not likely to see in the future - a fixed exchange rate regime encompassing the three major currencies.

2 Gravity, Familiarity, Multinationals, Relative Prices, and Trade Biases

In trying to identify what part of observed bilateral trade flows are natural and what part represent regional biases, Jeff adopts a straightforward strategy: use the gravity model to hold constant the natural determinants of trade flows, and then use a dummy variable representing alternative regional or country groups to pick up regional or trade blocks biases.

The gravity model, while it does not derive from any rigorous microeconomic foundation, captures one important empirical regularity about trade flows that is missing from other theories, namely, the tendency for countries to do more trade, other things equal, with countries that are geographically close to them than with those that are far away. Still, there are a number of questions about the interpretation and specification of the gravity model that are relevant to assessing the robustness of Jeff's results.

One question relates to the interpretation of "<u>distance</u>" in the model. In a number of places in the paper, Jeff implies that distance is a proxy for <u>transportation costs</u>. To be sure, transportation costs do go up with distance and transportation costs are important for evaluating the welfare effects of trade blocks.

Nevertheless, I am doubtful that distance can be associated exclusively with transportation costs for at least two reasons. To begin with, if distance were simply proxing for transportation costs, we should expect to see the influence of distance declining over time. From rough figures, it would seem that there has been a secular fall in transportation and insurance charges. For example, the ratio of c.i.f. to f.o.b. world imports has fallen steadily from about 1.08 in 1975 to about 1.05 in 1990; the same time-series calculation for industrial-country imports tells a similar story.[1] In addition, the past two decades have witnessed a considerable "downsizing" of products. Radios that used to require large vacuum tubes now fit in your pocket, thick bundles of heavy copper telephone wire have been replaced by thin fibre optic cables, and so on. It has been estimated (Greenspan (1988)) that pounds shipped by vessel and air per real dollar of U.S. exports have fallen by 2 1/2 per cent per year over the past two decades. Helpman and Krugman (1985) likewise find important economies of scale in transportation costs, especially for manufactured goods. Yet in Jeff's regressions, there is no discernable tendency for the estimated coefficient on the distance variable to decline between 1980 and 1990 (see his Tables 1 to 3); indeed, the estimated coefficient on distance increases as between 1980 and 1985. If distance means transportation costs, how can we explain these results?

Second there are plenty of indications from related spheres of international exchange among countries that market participants are more inclined to trade with participants and institutions that are familiar to them than with those who are not. Under this interpretation, distance is a proxy for information, for familiarity, and perhaps also for perceived risk. Consider the literature on "home bias" in investor portfolios, that is, on comparisons of actual with optimally internationally diversified portfolios (Tesar and Werner (1982) and French and Poterba (1990)).[2] A few facts. U.S. investors hold about 94 percent of their equities in the form of U.S. securities; for none of the other G-5 countries is the corresponding home share less than 85 percent. The 300 largest pension funds in the world have only about 7 percent of their assets denominated in foreign-currency instruments. When these actual portfolios are compared to those that would be optimal (using traditional mean-variance analysis), actual international diversification turns out to be much too low. Moreover, while data limitations on international capital flows make it difficult to verify, there is strong suspicion that there is a "neighborhood" or regional bias as well as a home bias. Just what accounts for these home or regional biases has not yet been fully determined. The list of possible candidates includes transactions costs, externally-imposed prudential limits on foreign assets, uncertainties about expected returns, and higher (than warranted) risk perceptions about foreign assets due to relative unfamiliarity with those markets and institutions. My own preference leans heavily toward the last factor. In discussions with portfolio managers during the Fund's annual capital market missions, there is little doubt that even today - and despite the trend toward increasing international diversification - investors are most comfortable and knowledgeable about investments in their own back yards - or at least in their neighbor's back yard. U.S. investors, for example, seem to be more aware of what is going in Latin America than would investors say, in Japan, and vice versa for investments in East Asia.[3]

My point is that the interpretation of distance is ambiguous in gravity models and that, more generally, information and familiarity factors count for bilateral trade flows. Jeff has made a useful start in controlling for some of these factors by adding a dummy variable for a common language or earlier colonial links. But there are other possibilities worth investigating. I would not be surprised if bilateral trade flows are larger the greater the number of former nationals of one country living in the other. Affinities for consumption patterns and product varieties from the old country, business alliances with relatives and former colleagues, workers' remittances, and banks continuing to service their customers when they go abroad, should all work in that direction. Thus, for example, if Asians living in the United States represented a larger share of the (U.S.) population in 1990 than in 1975, then, other things equal, one might expect bilateral trade between the United States and Asia - relative to other U.S. bilateral flows - to be higher in the latter period than in the former. This would not be captured by the dummy representing colonial or language ties. Yet it would be a "natural" determinant of bilateral trade flows and failure to account for it would presumably result in an upwardly biased coefficient on the APEC regional bias variable.

Two other factors - one institutional and one theoretical - are also missing from the gravity model and could affect the robustness of Jeff's conclusions. I refer here to the <u>trade of multinational corporations</u> and to <u>relative prices of traded goods.</u>

Approximately 25 percent of U.S. imports and about 10 percent of U.S. exports represent transactions between multinational companies and their affiliates abroad. Of U.S. imports from Japan, roughly three quarters is apparently accounted for by intrafirm trade of either U.S. or Japanese multinationals. While data on intrafirm trade for other countries is not as complete, there is little doubt that a non-trivial share of all world trade in manufactures (certainly more than 10 percent) represents trade between multinational companies and their foreign affiliates (Goldsbrough (1981)). Moreover, while distance (or familiarity) has a role in determining the location of direct foreign investment, there are surely other factors involved (see Lizondo (1991)).

Even if Goldsbrough (1981, p.573) is going too far when he concludes that "international trade flows are to a great extent determined by the location of the affiliates of multinational firms and worldwide production facilities," some recognition of intrafirm trade is probably warranted in bilateral trade equations. At the same time, the existence of such trade raises thorny questions for the modelling of bilateral trade flows. For example, should Jeff's equations include a dummy variable for those country pairs that are known or suspected of having relatively large parent/affiliate flows? Is intrafirm trade a "natural" determinant of trade or does it itself represent a regional or trade policy bias? On the last matter, suppose a multinational firm sets up an affiliate abroad to get around actual or expected trade barriers that would otherwise limit exports to that country. If bilateral trade between two countries then changes because of the presence of that affiliate, should we conclude that regional trade bias has changed?

This brings me to relative prices of traded goods. A striking difference between gravity models and other models of trade flows is that the former ignores relative price considerations while the latter do not. In some specifications of a gravity model, omitting relative prices could be a serious error. Suppose, for example, that the dependent variable were bilateral exports. In that case, we would definitely want to include relative export prices in the equation. Moreover, we would need to include not only the bilateral real exchange rate in the equation but also third-country real exchange rates. Consider, for example, the determination of U.S. exports to Latin America. We would expect those exports to be affected not only by the real exchange rate between the United States and developing countries in Latin America, but also by say, the real exchange rate between the United States and Europe: if U.S. products had become more competitive in Europe (relative to Latin America), some U.S. exports would presumably be switched to Europe. In Jeff's specification of the gravity model, this omission of relative prices is less serious because his dependent variable is (the log of) the <u>sum</u> of exports and imports. Since movements in relative prices affect exports and imports in opposite directions, relative price effects will come closer to cancelling out. But it is not clear that the influence of relative traded goods' prices will cancel out completely: differences in price elasticities across countries, across commodities, and over time, may prevent such neutrality (Goldstein and Khan (1985)). In addition, imports in many developing countries are best modelled as a function of the availability of foreign exchange receipts, the largest component of which is export earnings (Masson et. al. (1990)). This sets up the possibility that changes in bilateral export flows (due to relative price considerations) could induce changes in imports in the <u>same</u> direction, thereby diminishing the natural offsetting (to relative price changes) from opposite movements in exports and imports. For both of these reasons, it would be useful to reestimate these bilateral trade flow equations (either separately for exports and imports or for the sum) with the inclusion of some appropriate relative price terms, so that we could be assured that the split between the natural and unnatural determinants of trade was not being seriously affected by their omission.

Thus far, I have talked exclusively about the interpretation and specification of the model that generates the estimated trade block effects. There is also an issue about how those trade block effects should themselves be interpreted. In particular, I don't think they can necessarily be regarded as <u>independent</u> of one another. A good analogy is the inappropriateness of attempting to gauge the effect of unionization on wages by comparing the wages of workers in union versus non-union firms. The rub here is that managers in non-union firms will set wages in part with the view to discouraging their workers from becoming unionized. Thus, unionization affects both union and non-union wages and the difference between the two captures only part of the overall effect of unionization. Estimating trade block effects is in some ways similar. If one group of countries is discriminatory and discourages trade with outsiders, this may create incentives for other groups to form their own fortresses. Thus, each block's <u>own</u> trade bias doesn't necessarily capture all of the effects of its discriminatory policies; it can create trade biases elsewhere as well.

To <u>sum up</u>, Jeff Frankel is surely right to argue that we will not be able to get a good handle on regional or trade-block biases by simply looking at comparisons of shares and/or growth rates of intraregional trade. Instead, we need a framework that separates the natural from he unnatural determinants of bilateral trade flows. For that purpose, I would agree with Jeff that the gravity model has a definite - even seductive - appeal: it requires data on only a few variables (distance and national products) that are readily available for a large number of countries, thus allowing estimation from huge cross-section samples on the direction of trade. It also seems to fit the data quite well. Nevertheless, I believe that alternative specifications of the gravity model, as well as other models, should be tried (even though they have more demanding data requirements) so that we can get a better picture of how "robust" are these estimated trade biases.[4]

3 The Effects of Exchange Rate Variability on Trade

In the third section of the paper, Jeff uses his bilateral trade flow equations to test for the impact of exchange rate variability on trade. In brief, he finds that real exchange rate variability does depress trade and that this effect is decreasing over time. He also uses these estimates to calculate how much intra-EC and world trade would be increased by a decrease in exchange rate variability. Allow me to offer two reactions to those findings.

First, I believe that the results from time-series estimates of the effects of real exchange rate variability on trade are more reliable that those from cross-section studies. I say that because we have a much better idea of how to hold "other things equal" in time-series studies of import and export demand than we do in cross-section studies. Levels of real income (at home or abroad), cyclical conditions, and relative traded goods prices provide together a very satisfactory explanation of those trade volume flows, at least for differentiated goods (see Goldstein and Khan (1985)). In contrast, and as outlined above, the explanation of bilateral trade flows in a cross-section framework is more problematic. The large changes in the variability of nominal and real exchange rates as between the fixed and floating rate periods - or even during the floating rate period itself - also provide us with plenty of time-series variation in exchange rates with which to test for this uncertainty effect. The fact that the lion's share of the time-series studies has not been able to find a significant effect of exchange rate variability on trade (Edison and Melvin (1990), IMF (1984)) suggest to me that this effect is very unlikely to be important. Less formally, the observations that trade forecasters in the major industrial countries have not changed their trade equations much over the past ten years, that there has been no wholesale decline in the size of estimated price elasticities for imports and exports (as might be the case if increased uncertainty were depressing volume responses), and that proposals for a free trade area between the United States and Canada (which have considerable trade with one another and a floating exchange rate between them) have not been accompanied by calls for a monetary union, likewise make me sceptical that exchange rate variability is seriously disrupting international exchange. Jeff's conclusion that the stabilization of European exchange rates in the 1980s did not play a "large role" in the increase in intra-regional trade, is consistent with this broad appraisal.

Second, I think one needs to be cautious in using cross-sections estimates of the effect of exchange rate variability to make predictions about how trade - or even more, welfare - would respond in the future to a change in variability. For one thing, as Jeff recognizes, the availability and use of hedging instruments have expanded enormously over the past decade. For example, it used to be difficult to arrange forward exchange cover for maturities say, two years or longer. The use of currency swaps now permits such cover for periods extending to 7, 10, or even 20 years. Jeff's finding that the (retarding) effect of exchange rate variability is declining over time is consistent with these institutional developments and suggests that the private sector adapts (at least partially) to increased volatility in asset prices in ways that may well make any given degree of volatility less costly in the future than it was in the past. More fundamentally, it is not legitimate to assume that a decrease in exchange rate variability would necessarily leave unaffected other policy variables that influence the volume of international trade or capital flows. To take the most obvious example, if exchange rates were less free to move to accommodate changes in real economic conditions across countries, it is quite possible that recourse to capital controls - or perhaps to protectionist trade measures - would increase. In short, we need a much more general-equilibrium simulation of how a reduction in exchange rate variability would be achieved - and the policy and market reactions to that reduction - before we could draw welfare implications from it.

4 A Fixed Exchange Rate Area for the Major Industrial Countries?

Jeff's paper analyzes the stabilization of small-country exchange rates within currency blocks but does not address prospects for stabilizing exchange rates - or creating a common currency area - among the three largest currencies themselves. Since this is a conference devoted to the "future of the international monetary system," how should we evaluate prospects for a restoration of fixed exchange rates - or even establishment of a common currency - among the Big Three? To my mind, those prospects are dim - and for two good reasons.

First, there can be only one monetary policy for a group of countries that seek to keep their bilateral exchange rates fully fixed. This could be the monetary policy of the dominant country to which other members of the group passively adjust, or it could be the monetary policy that is agreed by some common mechanism. But it cannot be separate monetary policies for different members of the group. For the three largest countries, there is simply little evidence of a willingness to subordinate the domestic requirements of monetary policy to the constraints implied by a fixed exchange rate. And so long as these key countries do give the highest priority to internal balance in the implementation of monetary policy, tight and ambitious exchange rate commitments will lack the credibility they need to be effective, since market participants will learn that when push comes to shove, interest rate adjustments necessary to defend exchange rate targets are not forthcoming.

Ask yourself the following questions. Would the U.S. Federal Reserve be willing to follow the Bundesbank or the Bank of Japan in the formulation of its monetary policy - or vice versa? Would the U.S. authorities have been willing over the past two years to forego the large reductions in interest rates that were undertaken to help move the U.S. economy out of recession, in order to satisfy a fixed exchange rate or target zone obligation? Would the Japanese authorities have been willing at the tail end of the 1980s to forego the interest rate increases needed, inter alia, to deflate the bubble in asset prices and real estate values, if an exchange rate target had suggested an alternative course of action? Or look to the EMS where the political stakes surrounding exchange rate policy have been higher than elsewhere. Still, in last fall's crisis, Germany was not willing to reduce interest rates significantly before it had more assurance that inflationary pressures (in Germany) were under better control, and Italy, the United Kingdom, and Sweden each decided in the end that the costs of keeping interest rates well above what would otherwise be required on domestic grounds were too high to tolerate. And in July's recurrence of the crisis, there was again a decision that it would be too costly on domestic grounds (for both Germany and other ERM members) to implement a pattern of interest rates that would have been necessary to sustain existing parities; instead, a widening of exchange rate bands was viewed as the lesser of two evils. So long as monetary policy in each of the Big Three countries continues to be ruled primarily by domestic considerations, the feasible set of exchange arrangements among them is limited - and fixed rates are not part of that feasible set.

Second, there remain legitimate doubts that fixed exchange rates could accommodate the kinds of large, medium-term, country-specific real shocks that might well arise in the future. In this connection, the experience of the EMS in adapting to the shock of German unification is not encouraging. That shock, in combination with other factors, meant that the monetary policy that the anchor country saw as appropriate to its own circumstances (including its fiscal policy stance) increasingly became inappropriate for others members of the group, whose cyclical positions and inflationary pressures, *inter alia*, were different from those in Germany. Agreement on an early, generalized realignment of nominal exchange rates to help adjust to these differing circumstances of members proved elusive. Moreover, other adjustment mechanisms (factor mobility) were not sufficient to deal with the adjustment problem. Because it has been over twenty years since the break-up of Bretton Woods, there is no recent period of observation to gauge how the three largest economies would react to large, country-specific shocks under fixed rates. There is, however, an empirical literature that has simulated the shock-absorbing properties of alternative exchange rate regimes, drawing on the historical record of shocks across countries. My reading of that literature suggests that the economic performance of the three largest countries would have suffered in the 1970s and 1980s if they had attempted to fix their exchange rates within narrow bands (Frenkel, Goldstein, and Masson (1989)). It is of course possible that the future could be prone to fewer, or less severe, shocks than the past, but I see no compelling reason why that should be so. Thus, until other mechanisms for dealing with country-specific shocks are better developed, this consideration too makes it unlikely that we will see a fixed exchange rate regime, or a common currency, among the Big Three in the foreseeable future.

NOTES

* The views expressed are solely those of the author and do not represent the views of the IMF.

1. Barbone (1988) constructs a more sophisticated measure of transportation costs by regressing the ratio of cif imports to fob imports on a polynomial in distance (with separate treatment of manufactured and non-manufactured goods) and on a time trend.
2. This literature, along with that dealing with other measures of the integration of capital markets, is reviewed in Goldstein and Mussa (1993).
3. In some cases, of course, familiarity breeds contempt - rather than confidence. A gross outlier in Jeff's gravity model results must be bilateral trade between the United States and Cuba. They are close together but hardly trade at all. This is an indication that political differences, once they get to extremes, also affect the size of trade flows.
4. De Grauwe [1988] and Marquez [1992, 1993] offer alternatives to the gravity model for explaining bilateral trade flows.

REFERENCES

Barbone, Luca, "Import Barriers: An Analysis of Time-Series, Cross-Section Data," OECD Economic Studies, OECD, Paris, Autumn 1988.

De Grauwe, P., "Exchange Rate Variability and the Slowdown in Growth of International Trade," IMF Staff Papers, 1988.

Edison, H., and M. Melvin, "The Determinants and Implications of the Choice of an Exchange Rate System," in W. Haraf and T. Willett (eds)., Monetary Policy for a Volatile Economy, AEI, Washington, D.C., 1990.

French, K., and J. Poterba, "Investor Diversification and International Equity Markets," American Economic Review, May 1991.

Frenkel, J., M. Goldstein, and P. Masson, "Simulating the Effects of Some Simple Coordinated Versus Uncoordinated Policy Rules," in R. Bryant and others (eds)., Macroeconomic Policies in an Interdependent World, Brookings Institution, Washington, D.C., 1989.

Goldsbrough, D., "International Trade of Multinational Corporations and Its Responsiveness to Changes in Aggregate Demand and Relative Prices," IMF Staff Papers, September 1981.

Goldstein, M., and M. Khan, "Income and Price Effects in Foreign Trade," Chapter 20 in R. Jones and P. Kenen (eds)., Handbook of International Economics, North-Holland, 1985.

Goldstein, M., and M. Mussa, "The Integration of World Capital Markets," in Federal Reserve Bank of Kansas City, Changing Capital Markets: Implications for Monetary Policy, Kansas City, 1993, forthcoming.

Greenspan, A., "Goods Shrink and Trade Grows," Wall Street Journal, October 24, 1988.

Helpman, E., and P. Krugman, Intra-Industry Trade, MIT Press, Boston, 1985.

International Monetary Fund, Exchange Rate Volatility and World Trade, IMF Occasional Paper No. 28, Washington, D.C., 1984.

Lizondo, S., "Foreign Direct Investment," in M. Goldstein et al, Determinants and Systemic Consequences of International Capital Flows, IMF Occasional Paper No. 77, Washington, D.C., March 1991.

Marquez, J., "The Anatomy of Trade Elasticities: Choices and Consequences," International Finance Discussion Paper No. 422, Board of Governors of the Federal Reserve System,

Washington, D.C., January 1992.

____, "The Econometrics of Elasticities or the Elasticity of Econometrics: An Empirical Analysis of the Behavior of U.S. Import," Board of Governors of the Federal Reserve System, April 1993, unpublished.

Masson, P., et al, MULTIMOD Mark II: A revised and Extended Model, IMF Occasional Paper No. 71, Washington, D.C., December 1990.

Tesar, L., and I. Werner, "Home Bias and Globalization of Securities Markets," University of California at Santa Barbara, unpublished, 1993.

6 The IMF and the World Bank at Fifty

STANLEY FISCHER*

The vitality of the International Monetary Fund and World Bank Group and their central roles in the world economy testify to the foresight of the founding fathers who designed them as two of the three bulwarks of the postwar international monetary system. This remains true even though neither institution operates as planned at Bretton Woods in 1944, and even though the third institution, the International Trade Organization, was stillborn - not to reappear until fifty years later, as the impending World Trade Organization.

The IMF was set up to police an adjustable peg exchange rate system which disappeared in 1973 and it has had no effective responsibility for the international monetary system since then. The Fund's last loan to a high income industrialized country was made in 1977. Increasingly it has become a specialized development agency, one that was in danger of losing its rationale during the debt crisis but that has been revived by its new mission in the reforming formerly centrally planned economies.

The IBRD has remained closer to its original design. Originally it was thought that the Bank would channel funds to the developing countries by guaranteeing their obligations, but for good reasons it has rather lent to them directly, placing its own bonds in the international capital markets. The World Bank Group has grown beyond its original design, first by the addition in 1956 of an affiliate, the International Finance Corporation (IFC), which helps finance the private sector in developing countries, and then through the creation - at the initiative of the United States - in 1960 of the International Development Association (IDA). IDA lends on concessional terms to the poorest countries. In most years loan commitments made by IDA amount to one third to one quarter of the commitments made by the IBRD; net disbursements made by IDA are usually more than half those of the IBRD, and in some years exceed those of the IBRD. IDA plays a key role in enabling the Bank Group to continue lending to the poorest countries. Another affiliate, the Multilateral Investment Guarantee Agency (MIGA), was set up in 1988.[1]

Fifty years after Bretton Woods it is natural to review the role and performance of the international institutions, and to discuss the major questions about their futures. Among the big issues are:[2]

- Is there a demand for the services the agencies provide?

- If so, should these services be provided by the Fund and the Bank?

- Should the goals of the agencies be redirected, for instance by requiring the IMF to take more responsibility for the international monetary system, and the Bank to return to its roots as a project lender?

- Should the overlap of activities between the agencies be reduced by sharpening the division of responsibilities between them?

- Should the Bank and the Fund be merged?

There is also a host of more specific questions about each agency. For instance, in the case of the Bank, whether it should be downsized, whether it should put more people in the field, and how to enhance its interactions with the regional development banks.

Of course the Bank, the Fund, and the international economy have been evolving and reforming over the past fifty years. A host of interlocking agencies and groupings, among them the GATT (soon to become the WTO), the FAO, other UN agencies, the G-7, the G-10, the G-24, the regional development banks, the OECD, the European Community, and other regional trade blocs have grown up and help run the international economy. A full review of the institutional structure of the world economy would take all these organizations into account, ask why and whether they should exist, and whether there is a better way of achieving their goals. Such a review would have to distinguish between an optimal institutional structure designed from the ground up, which we can safely assume would not look like the present system, and the best improvements that can be made starting from the current structure rather than from the near tabula rasa of 1944.

In this paper I focus narrowly, on the World Bank Group and the IMF, and refer to other agencies and institutions only as they relate to the functions of the Bretton Woods twins. I start by describing the initial functions, current structures and operations of the IMF and the World Bank. In these sections I discuss questions and make suggestions about current modes of operation. I then go on in Section 3 to discuss the major issues set out above. Readers familiar with the current structures of the Fund and the Bank should concentrate on Section 3.

1 The International Monetary Fund

Table 1 sets out the six functions of the Fund specified in Article I of its Articles of Agreement. There has been substantial progress in several of these areas since 1945. Trade has expanded more rapidly than output almost every year in that period; payments restrictions have essentially disappeared among the major countries, and have been greatly reduced even among many developing countries;[3] and Fund resources are indeed routinely utilized by developing country members. Progress in expanding trade owes more to other institutions than to the Fund; the Fund has been too accepting of current account restrictions for several major members, such as India; but its role in promoting current account convertibility has generally been constructive.

To a considerable extent, the Fund does serve as specified in clause (i), as an institution through which countries consult on international monetary problems. There is probably no forum in which more serious regular discussion of international financial issues takes place than the Fund's Executive Board. However, the important decisions are made elsewhere, through consultations by the G-7.[4] This should not be a surprise, for the Fund Board is an unwieldy group in which to negotiate. Because the big decisions are made outside the Fund, Executive Directors of the large countries tend to be middle level government officials rather than independent decision-makers.

Discussions in the Fund Board are confidential. While this gives the Executive Directors the freedom to speak frankly, the Fund keeps far too much of its information from the public. Some discussions, of problems such as devaluations and the debt strategy where expectations of a policy change can become self-justifying, have to remain confidential. But background papers prepared for the great majority of Board discussions, including the Fund's reports on Recent Economic Developments in member countries, should be made available to the public within a few weeks of the Board discussion. This would enhance the quality of economic policy discussion in member countries. Publication of the World Economic Outlook represents an important step forward, but publication and public provision of information should become the rule rather than the exception.

There is an important issue of whether the Fund management and staff should be taking more of the initiative in identifying and proposing solutions to problems in the international system. Two considerations should be noted. First, the management of the Fund or the Bank is ultimately controlled by the Board, and needs to retain the confidence of the governments they represent; thus management cannot lead where it knows the Board is certain not to follow. But there is a great deal of space for leadership between playing the role of Don Quixote and the passive acceptance of prevailing G-7 views.

Second, the Fund may not have a solution. Consider for instance the reform of the international monetary system, a topic which is central to the Fund's mission. Ultimately Fund staff would probably like to return to a fixed or adjustable peg system, but there is absolutely no prospect that the major countries will move in that direction soon; nor does the recent European experience commend that course unless policies and the structure of economies become far more coordinated than they are now. The Fund is also generally anxious to strengthen the role of the SDR in the international system. While the SDR serves as a convenient composite unit of account, the Fund has not presented any persuasive argument in favor of expanding its role in the current international system.[5] Thus at this time the Fund staff appears to have little to contribute in the area of international monetary reform.[6]

In the international debt crisis, the Fund first helped form and then dutifully followed the G-7's policy line from 1982 until at least 1987. Then the Managing Director began to speak out with increasing bluntness, contributing to the general change in attitude and approach that led to the Brady Plan in 1989. In this case, the Managing Director timed his dissent so as to get ahead of the official strategy, but only when the strategy clearly was not working. Since it was obvious to many by 1986 that the Baker Plan was not succeeding, the Managing Director could have moved earlier. Indeed, he may have, for we do not know what his confidential advice to G-7 policymakers was at the time.

Turning now to the current structure of the Fund, a simplified balance sheet is presented in Table 2, and the administrative budget in Table 3. With total assets of $140 billion, the Fund is large as international agencies go. However, it is difficult to appraise its size relative to potential demands for resources, since only a subset of countries are potential borrowers, and only a subset of the Fund's resources are likely to be available to be borrowed.[7] Note that the Fund has relied almost entirely on its own resources for lending to its members: borrowing by the Fund from member countries has been small relative to the scale of its assets, but it has potential access under the GAB (General Arrangements to Borrow) to $26 billion of borrowed resources. Note also the attraction of Fund gold sales, which are perenially advanced as a solution to some shortage of funds:[8] with its gold valued at SDR35 per oz, the Fund would on paper make a capital gain of over $30 billion if it could sell all its gold at $350 per oz.[9]

The Fund is generally thought of as running a tight ship. Administrative expenses in financial year 1992 were $350 million, for a staff of about 1750.[10] Most of these expenses were for personnel, with travel expenses accounting for 15 percent of costs. The Fund's net income amply covers expenses.

The Fund's resources are deployed in three main lines of activity: surveillance and analysis of the economies of member countries and the international system; lending; and technical assistance and training.

1.1 Surveillance

The term surveillance derives from the Fund's responsibility under Article IV to exercise "firm surveillance over the exchange rate policies of its members". On the argument that domestic policies affect exchange rates, the Fund staff conducts annual Article IV consultations with members that cover the full range of domestic macroeconomic policies. The resultant Article IV report typically provides a highly competent, informative, data-packed, macroeconomic analysis of the economy. These reports are discussed by the Board either annually or every second year.

The importance of the exercise varies from country to country. In the smaller and less developed countries, the Fund's analysis may well be not only the best, but also the only, thorough analysis of the macroeconomy.[11] It is not uncommon in such countries for the Fund's report to be leaked by one agency or the other (the central bank or the finance ministry) either because that agency has been commended, or in support of a particular policy view. Article IV consultations receive less attention in the more developed countries. That is a pity, because the Fund's analysis could contribute to improving the domestic policy debate.

To increase the influence of the reports in both developing and industrialized countries, the Fund should work towards making them available to the public within a short time of their being written. No doubt it will be argued that publication will affect the frankness of the reports. While that danger exists, the professional quality of the staff should ensure that the basic message gets across - certainly the World Economic Outlook (WEO) manages to say what it wants on the major issues. It should be possible even now to find some countries that are both self-confident enough and that sufficiently value informed public discussion to agree to the timely publication of the Article IV report on their country. Once a few countries take the lead, others will follow.

In addition to the Article IV reports, the Fund staff twice a year presents the WEO to the Board. This is the opportunity for the Fund to discuss the global economy, both the policies of the major countries individually, and systemic problems such as the debt crisis and the economics of socialist transition. Staff papers on special topics are also discussed from time to time.

How effective are these surveillance and analytic exercises? The Fund Board is quoted on this issue in the 1992 Annual Report (p.15): "the effectiveness of Fund Surveillance has less to do with strengthening the principles of surveillance and more to do with the willingness of member countries to consider fully the views expressed by the international community - through the forum of the Fund - in formulating and adopting their macroeconomic and structural policies".

Powerful countries have shown little overt inclination to change their basic economic policies because of the views of the international community. Continued complaints by the rest of the G-7 seem to have had very little impact on the United States' willingness to deal with its twin deficits; the wishes of its ERM partners had little visible effect on German monetary policy; and the examples could be multiplied.

However, it is far too absolutist a position to argue that the Fund's analytic exercises therefore have no impact on individual country policies and on systemic problems, such as the debt crisis. Peer pressure, "arm twisting by public exposure", "pointing the finger of public shame",[12] does have some impact. Continued international pressure on the United States to cut its deficit helped keep that issue in public view; Germany in fact tried to keep the ERM alive for longer than its own preferences would have dictated; and academic analyses as well as brute facts helped bring about a change in the debt strategy. And even if finger pointing were ineffective, it is better to speak up than to acquiesce in error.

The influence of Fund surveillance on policy will have as much to do with the quality of the analysis as with the forum in which it is presented. The WEO is generally well regarded. Most Article IV reports are well regarded, though there is a view that reports on some countries are unduly responsive to the views of the authorities. By presenting analyses of unquestionably high quality, and objectivity, on individual countries and other issues, and by making its reports public, the Fund will increase its influence on policy. To do that it has to ensure that the analytic quality of its staff remains very high, and is indeed enhanced, and that the staff receives the backing of management for presenting its own views. The Fund could further increase the quality of its analysis and its influence by engaging in more public interchange with academics and others who analyze policy in member countries.

To increase the effectiveness of surveillance, the Fund should pursue two goals: it should ensure that it becomes the world's premier macroeconomic policy analysis institution; and it should ensure that it is seen and understood to be the best such unit. It cannot do the latter while hiding behind the shelter of confidentiality.

1.2 Lending

For over a decade the Fund has lent exclusively to developing countries. Lending exploded during the debt crisis of the early 1980s, with the outstanding stock of Fund credit rising from SDR10 billion in 1980 to over SDR37 billion in 1985; the outstanding stock then declined through 1990, and has subsequently risen somewhat.

Tables 4-6 provide information on Fund lending, both the volume, and the different forms in which assistance is provided. The Structural Adjustment Facility (SAF) and Extended SAF (ESAF) both lend at highly subsidized terms, with an interest charge similar to that of IDA. However, since the term of the lending is much shorter than that of IDA, the repayment burden from loans through these facilities is greater than for IDA loans. While the volume of lending under SAF and ESAF is relatively small (Table 4), these facilities make it possible for the poorest countries to borrow from the Fund at a low interest rate and for a longer period than under a normal standby.

Net resource flows to the developing countries in 1991 amounted to \$131 billion[13], \$73 billion of that in the form of official development finance. This is a base against which to scale the Fund's net disbursements of \$1.6 billion seen in Table 4. However, disbursements understate the significance of some Fund loans, for in many cases the availability of that portion of the loan which is not yet disbursed gives the borrower the confidence to proceed with adjustment measures. It is also true that the Fund can make a crucial difference with a very big loan to a country that has decided to stabilize; for instance, in March 1992 the Fund reached an extended agreement for \$3 billion with Argentina; in 1989 it made a loan in excess of \$5 billion to Venezuela. Loans of this size, whether drawn or not, are not available other than through the Fund.

In addition, the Fund's loans come with a stabilization and often a reform program, and with conditionality. The conditionality usually relates to monetary, fiscal, and exchange rate policy, and is often criticized for being mindlessly contractionary. This criticism has to be evaluated on a case-by-case basis. Certainly in many cases the Fund is only trying to get a country to stabilize the macroeconomy while living within its budget constraint. But in some circumstances, the description of the budget constraint may be too unimaginative. For example, during the debt crisis, debt relief came onto the Fund's agenda very late.

One description of the difference between the Fund's financial programming approach to stabilization, and the World Bank's two-gap model approach, is that the Fund asks what resources are available and tailors the program to that availability, whereas Bank economists ask what resources are needed to achieve a target growth rate, and then go out to find the money.[14] Needless to say, this is a caricature, but it does capture a subtle difference in attitude that affects the two institutions.

What is the record of success of Fund loans? Khan (1990) evaluated the effects of Fund programs between 1973 and 1988. He concluded that Fund programs unambiguously reduced the current account deficit,[15] and tended to reduce inflation, though the inflation effect was not statistically significant. The programs reduced the growth rate in the year they went into operation, but this effect was moderated (though not reversed) over time.

Despite this very mixed verdict, I judge that the Fund's lending activities to developing countries are frequently productive. Further, the Fund's ability to move large amounts of funding quickly is extremely valuable to a country seeking to stabilize, as it was to Poland, and may yet be to Russia.

It has also to be recorded that the Fund's lending to countries with deep-seated structural problems, many of them in Africa, has not been successful. The notion underlying a standby, that the balance of payments will be corrected within a few years, is not relevant to these countries. It is for that reason that the Fund has had steadily to lengthen the term of its loans. Because countries in Africa, and some of the heavily indebted countries, did not return to equilibrium quickly, the Fund's loans were in effect repaid by the World Bank.

There is a strong case for the Fund to concentrate on short-term macroeconomic stabilization, and to stay away from the long-run development problems that should be the focus of World Bank activities. The Fund itself seems to have drawn this conclusion, as it has slowed the pace of its lending to Africa.

1.3 Technical Assistance

The Fund provides a broad range of technical assistance to its members.[16] The IMF Institute runs regular courses and seminars in Washington for middle- and senior-level officials. In 1991/92, 639 participants took part in the Washington courses. Most of the courses are on financial programming and policy, i.e. on the Fund's approach to balance of payments and monetary policy issues, with an admixture of material on adjustment. Other courses covered money and banking statistics, balance of payments methodology, and government finance statistics. The Institute also conducted courses abroad, the majority of them in the last few years in the reforming formerly centrally planned economies.

Technical assistance was provided to member countries by the Departments of Monetary and Exchange Affairs (formerly Central Banking), Fiscal Affairs, Legal, and Statistics. A variety of statistics suggests that this is a major activity: in 1991-92 68 person-years of assistance to 79 countries and 3 regional organizations were provided by the Monetary and Exchange Affairs Department; Fiscal Affairs helped 82 countries; Legal helped 29 countries; and Statistics 37 countries. Much of the assistance has been sent to Eastern Europe and the former Soviet Union.

Evaluation of these programs is not publicly available.[17] One criticism that has been levied, especially with regard to the former Soviet republics, is that the Fund's technical experts do not spend enough time with the recipients to leave a deep imprint on their systems. Certainly in many developing countries there is a deep need for longer term technical assistance, for experts who remain in the country for at least a year, to try to ensure that the methods they teach take hold.

As international development continues on two tracks, with much of the world's population in Asia enjoying the fruits of rapid growth, and with others, in South Asia and especially in Africa, growing more slowly or not at all, the need for technical assistance for the countries with impaired institutional capacity becomes more urgent. It is likely that the international community and agencies will increasingly contribute to the slower-growing economies through technical assistance. It is therefore a serious priority to begin to evaluate these programs and their effects more systematically.

1.4 Summary

The Fund undertakes three main lines of activity, surveillance and analysis, lending, and technical assistance. Evaluation of the effectiveness of each has at best been partial. Given that the Fund does not now lend to industrialized countries, and that it should be cutting back its lending to countries whose problems are not short-term, its lending is likely to continue at a lower level than in the early 1980s.[18] Increasingly, in future, the Fund is likely to assist members through its surveillance or analytic activities, and through technical assistance. In both these areas, it can make a major contribution to the efficient operation of individual economies and the international system. While the quality of the Fund's analytic and policy-advising contributions appears on average to be high, there is a need for more openness and more daring in these areas. Not enough is known at present about the quality of the Fund's technical assistance programs.

2 The World Bank Group

The purposes of the World Bank as set out in the Articles of Agreement lack the crispness of those stated for the Fund. The emphasis is on the promotion of reconstruction and development by encouraging international investment, private if possible, but public if necessary. Since the great bulk of lending has been for projects, and since the Bank finances the foreign exchange costs of projects, it can be said to have promoted development by encouraging international investment, though most of the investment has been by the public sector. IFC loans and investments more directly support the private sector in developing countries. Adjustment loans, formally introduced in 1980, and since then accounting for about 20-25 percent of lending, are less directly linked to international investment - though policy changes that improve economic performance in a country are likely to lead to greater foreign investment.

The IBRD's balance sheet (Table 7) shows assets of $140 billion, almost identical to those of the Fund. This is however a misleading figure, for IDA has assets in excess of $80 billion (Table 8),[19] so that IBRD/IDA assets exceed $220 billion. IFC assets, less than $10 billion, have to be added to obtain the asset value of the World Bank Group, which a year ago were about $230 billion.

By contrast with the Fund, the IBRD is a market borrower, which jealously guards its AAA rating. The Bank does not borrow more than its callable capital, so the question of whether the rating derives from the guarantees provided by the callable capital or from the quality of the portfolio cannot be answered. However, the experience of the IFIs (international financial institutions) with arrears in the last few years suggests that their portfolios are quite secure. This is not because their borrowers are safe bets, but because the major donors have made certain that arrears with the IFIs are cleared immediately when a formerly recalcitrant country returns to the fold. It has also become clear that developing countries cannot stay out of the international system; in the end, all the defaulters want to come back into the system, and the system has been sufficiently imaginative to help them come back in on condition of good behavior.[20]

About a third of Bank lending is through IDA. These funds are contributed by the donors, the wealthier countries, with IDA being replenished on a three year cycle. Mason and Asher wrote in 1973 that the Bank would have to find a more secure way of financing IDA, but now, as the tenth replenishment struggles to closure, it is clear that the donors prefer the short leash of the three year cycle to a longer cycle. The present arrangement enables the donors to pressure the Bank more effectively on issues such as the environment and poverty than appears to be possible through the regular Board channel.

IDA can be thought of as an efficient way for donors to provide conditional aid to developing countries, using the expertize of the World Bank to try to ensure that the aid is used productively. However, as the pressure on aid budgets increases, countries seeking to preserve bilateral aid programs may cut back on IDA contributions.

Because IDA credits are very long-term, the flow of repayments has so far been small. Less than a decade from now, reflows will increase to more than $2 billion a year, making possible a substantial nominal increase in IDA lending - provided the donors do not take the opportunity to reduce their contributions correspondingly. Indeed, IDA has already precommitted SDR one billion of reflows to be relent in the next IDA period. These reflows, together with contributions of profits from the IBRD, have made an increase in IDA resources possible at a time when direct donor contributions have not risen.

The Bank has three times as many staff members as the Fund. In June 1992 there were 6000 staff members, 766 long-term consultants, and over 500 other employees. As Table 10 shows, Bank personnel costs are almost three times those of the Fund, though its travel budget is relatively smaller. Despite the general impression that the Bank staff is too big (presumably for the work that it does), it would be difficult to establish that the Bank suffers from more than the usual levels of bureaucratic waste and inefficiency. The 1987 reorganization did downsize the Bank somewhat and increases in staff size have been kept small since then, though it has expanded to deal with the challenges of the formerly centrally planned economies. As in the case of the Fund, the Bank's income more than covers its expenses.

The Bank's activities can be categorized into lending, technical assistance, analysis and research, and aid coordination.

2.1 Lending

In recent years the Bank has lent about $20 billion per annum, a sizable amount relative to the flow of resources to the developing countries. But net flows from the Bank have been smaller, with net disbursements in fiscal year 1991/1992 being $10 billion, while net transfers in that year were negative (Table 11). The negative net transfers were accounted for mainly by large repayments from Latin America. It is also the case that in real terms, IBRD lending has barely increased over the past five years, despite the opening up of lending to Eastern Europe and the former Soviet Union.

Through 1980, almost all Bank lending was for projects, although program lending was permitted, and had indeed taken place, for instance to India in 1965. The Bank lends for an enormous range of projects. Whereas the Fund made 36 loans in 1992, the Bank made 222. The projects are classified under 12 major headings, including agriculture and rural development, industry, education, energy, telecommunications, and so forth. This range of projects demands that the Bank maintain either a high level of expertize in a variety of areas, or access to a wide range of consultants.

Even before the debt crisis broke, the Bank moved to introduce adjustment lending - policy-based, rapidly disbursing loans. The Bank justified this form of lending as responding to the needs of the borrowers at a time when private flows were declining, and as a way for the Bank to have a say about the macroeconomic policies issues that were affecting the outcomes of its projects. During the 1980s adjustment loans played an important role in the debt crisis and accounted for an important share of bank lending. Because the loans disburse fast, adjustment lending in some years accounted for as much as 50 percent of disbursements to Latin America.

Adjustment lending was needed to deal with the debt crisis, and was supported by the G-7. But since the conditionality for adjustment lending had to relate to macroeconomic policies, the Bank's role brought it into potential conflict with the Fund and its conditionality. The Fund, ever fearful of being dominated by the much larger Bank, sought to establish its primacy in dealing with macroeconomic policy conditionality in member countries. The conflict burst into the open when, at U.S. urging, the World Bank made an adjustment loan to Argentina in September 1988, at a time when the Fund was not willing to lend. With a G-10 report on the roles of the Bank and the Fund in the debt crisis in preparation, the two agencies reached an accord in March 1989 that set out procedures for dealing with conflicts, and that murkily divided responsibilities for short- and long-term macroeconomic policies between the Fund and the Bank. There have been few reports of conflicts since then, but that may be more because Eastern Europe and the FSU came along and provided enough work for everyone than because the accord provided the right formulae for cooperation.[21]

As in the case of the Fund, the potential importance of the Bank's lending depends on its ability to affect member countries' policies and growth. The Bank has carried out three major studies of the effectiveness of adjustment lending,[22] and a recent important study (the Wapenhans report) of the effectiveness of its project lending. The evaluations of adjustment lending have shown it to have an overall positive effect on exports and on growth, and a negative effect on investment.[23] Concerns over adjustment lending have more recently shifted to the question of whether adjustment, as defined in the mid-1980s, is sufficient for the restoration of growth, or whether it is necessary also to focus more on longer-term growth determinants that are not entirely market determined, such as institution building and the creation of human capital, as well as directly on poverty alleviation.

The Wapenhans report was critical of the declining quality trend that it saw in Bank projects, the success rate of which had fallen from more than 80 to 70 percent during the 1980s. It attributed this to the loss of Bank technical expertize (equivalently to the excessive increase in the number of economists) and to inadequate attention to project supervision. Bank management has promised the Board that it will remedy the situation, and is beginning to change the composition of the staff and supervisory practices to this end. It has also shifted the focus of Bank activities from new lending to the management of the entire portfolio, and to the overall contribution of the Bank to the country's development.

The optimal success rate for projects must be less than 100 percent, and too many resources can be put into project supervision. Thus the mere fact that success rates have declined is not conclusive evidence that Bank project lending needs to be reformed. But given that it is the borrowers who are left to pay off the loans, a failure rate of 30 percent does seem too high, and the Bank is justified in moving resolutely on this front.

It has to be recorded that the Bank's openness makes it vulnerable to criticism that other agencies, including the Fund, avoid. The Bank is continually engaged in evaluating its activities, not only through special reports such as those discussed above, but also through the Operations Evaluation Department, which reports directly to the Board. The solution is not for the Bank to scale back these evaluations, but for other agencies, including the Fund, to be required to undertake them.

2.2 Technical Assistance

The Bank lends to countries to finance technical assistance, provides training for developing country officials through the Economic Development Institute (EDI), and makes its own experts available for technical assistance to members.

In 1992 EDI put on a total of 117 seminars and courses, attended by over 2,900 participants. The largest number of courses and participants were in Africa, a special target of EDI. EDI runs two major scholarship programs for students from developing countries. It has also been seeking to build up research institutions in developing countries, in part by creating networks of institutions within each region.

In 1992 a Bank task force examined technical assistance (TA), charged with the goal of improving its effectiveness and the specific tasks of recommending how to organize the Bank's TA activities, and to improve coordination with other agencies, especially the UNDP. The task force recommended, among other things, the establishment of an Institutional Development Fund to provide grant support for TA. The Fund was set up, and given a budget of $25 million for its first year of operation.

This amount pales against the total of technical assistance provisions in Bank loans and credits, which in fiscal year 1992 amounted to more than $1.8 billion. Technical assistance is big business. Given its potential for good, the TA industry needs an overall evaluation of the type undertaken by the Bank in studying its own TA activities.

2.3 Analysis and Research

The Bank budget shows total spending of $90 million on research, policy, and dissemination. A vast amount of policy work on individual countries is undertaken in the course of operations. Each adjustment loan is accompanied by an analysis of the macroeconomy. In addition, the Bank prepares a "Country Economic Memorandum" for each country, generally every two years. The Bank has recently changed its public disclosure policy, and now makes most of its analytic work, much project information, and project reports available to the public.[24]

Bank research has many outlets, including working paper series and journals. The World Development Report receives worldwide attention, and also helps set the Bank's internal policy agenda. Other publications that come out of the Bank's research departments, such as the World Debt Tables, provide an outlet for staff opinions as well as valuable data for researchers and policymakers.

How influential is all this research and publication? I know of no systematic study, but have the impression that it is quite influential in many developing countries, and that it has had an increasing impact on the academic community in the United States in recent years.

2.4 Aid Coordination

The World Bank chairs the consultative groups for many countries, at which the donors meet to discuss a country's economic program and financing needs, and to pledge their contributions to meeting those needs. The Bank thereby helps coordinate aid. It coordinates aid also through IDA, taking the contributions of donor countries, and lending them in a coherent fashion dictated by Bank policy.

Cofinancing with the Bank by donors is another form of aid coordination. Some countries, especially Japan, will piggyback on a Bank loan to a country, thereby increasing the amount of aid provided through the loan, and increasing the leverage of the Bank in its loan negotiations. In fiscal year 1992, there was cofinancing on 115 loans (out of a total of 222), and the cofinancing on average almost doubled the amount of lending.

The aid coordination function is a highly valuable one, which increases the effectiveness of national aid programs at the same time as it in effect increases the Bank's financial resources.

2.5 International Finance Corporation

Since the World Bank demands government guarantees on its loans to member countries, it has great difficulty in financing the private sector directly. This does not of course mean that its activities do not contribute to the development of the private sector, because many of the structural changes supported by the Bank - for example in the financial sector, or in trade reform - are crucial to the efficient operation of the private sector.

The IFC was set up to lend directly to the private sector. It is an affiliate of the World Bank, and shares the Bank's president, but it is effectively run by an Executive Vice-President. The anomaly of the IFC's status as a public institution devoted to promoting the private sector has not kept it from being very active. While its own operations amount to less than $1 billion per year, it is typically involved as a co-financier or in a syndicate, and can therefore claim to be having a larger effect than the volume of its own operations indicates. It appears that many private sector lenders and investors want the comfort that is offered by the participation of a member of the World Bank group. The IFC's presence must be seen by others investors as a signal that their rights will be vigorously protected.

The IFC has recently had a major capital increase. Some of the shareholders see a much larger future role for the IFC, as World Bank borrowers graduate, and move into the commercial markets for their financing. We return to these issues below.

2.6 Summary

The Bank engages in a very wide range of activities. Its adjustment lending appears on the whole to have been successful, but there is a perception that the quality of projects has declined. It is a major provider of technical assistance, and has recently examined its record and recommended changes in the provision of TA. Its analytic work is on average good, and its aid coordination provides a valuable service to donor countries. While the Bank is a very large organization, so are the activities that it undertakes.

3 Reforms and a Possible Merger

Both agencies undertake similar functions: lending, almost entirely to governments; analysis of systemic and national economic issues; and the provision of technical assistance. In addition, the World Bank plays an important role in coordinating aid.

Each of these services except aid coordination is also provided by the private sector. The question is whether there is any case for continuing public sector provision. We start with lending, where there is a difference between the IMF and the IBRD. IMF stabilization loans are frequently very large, and come with policy conditionality; further, they are by definition made to governments in trouble. Could the private sector make stabilization loans? Certainly some large stabilization loans were made to major governments in trouble by the House of Morgan before World War I. But given the decline of gunboat diplomacy, it is doubtful that the private sector would make stabilization loans to governments on which no effective conditionality could be imposed. To be sure, the private sector participated in financing packages during the debt crisis, but that was always under official leadership. And it is hard to see the official sector leading if it was not itself lending.

Thus it is likely that lending for stabilization with conditionality will continue through official channels. Of course, the Fund has not lent to any member of the G-7 since 1977. That is largely because exchange rates have been flexible during that period (except within the EC), and governments have been willing to let the exchange rate take the strain.[25] Developing member countries are likely to continue to maintain an exchange rate peg. This implies a need for stabilization loans, and therefore for a Fund role.[26]

Successful countries such as Spain, Japan, and Korea, graduate from IBRD borrowing and go into the capital markets on their own. Even successful countries that have not yet graduated, such as Thailand, may decide to borrow directly from the capital markets. Many of the remaining countries must be borrowing from the IBRD because it is cheaper to do that than to go to the market; and in some cases they could probably not borrow in the markets at all.

If so, we have to ask whether the IBRD is mispricing its loans to the latter classes of borrowers, or whether there is some externality in the international capital markets which justifies such pricing. The externality may be the difficulties private sector lenders have in imposing conditionality on their borrowers. It is clear that private sector lenders prefer the comfort of a governmental (IMF or IBRD) presence when they lend to developing countries that have not yet achieved easy market access. There would then be a case for IBRD lending to weaker borrowers, as a catalyst for private sector lending.

Note though that this argument implies a diminishing future role for direct IBRD lending, and possibly a declining average quality of IBRD loans. Whether that is so depends on whether certain economies are doomed never to grow, something which we do not know, but which the convergence literature suggests is unlikely.

The argument that IBRD lending catalyses private lending returns us to the view of the Bank's founders that it should serve mainly as a guarantor rather than a lending agency. The IBRD itself is exploring the possibility of expanding its guarantee role. The major issue is whether a public sector agency should provide this function. Private lenders often express a wish for such guarantees from the public sector, for example in lending to the former Soviet Union, but it would have to be seen whether they are prepared to pay the unsubsidized price. Once again, the case for a public agency's involvement would be its greater ability to collect on loans, and to impose conditionality.[27] Since these advantages of the IBRD relate to lending to governments rather than the private sector, the case is mainly one for its guaranteeing loans to the public sector. Nonetheless, public sector involvement in guaranteeing private lending at an early stage is likely to speed the development of international capital flows. I would thus argue that the IBRD or IFC should develop the capacity to provide some form of guarantee, for example against political risk, of private sector lending, for a limited period, say five to ten years.

Both agencies have also served an important emergency lending role, in the debt crisis, and there is an argument for retaining that capacity for future unforeseen events - though it is hard to see that the emergency lending role alone would justify the existence of both agencies.

To sum up on lending: there is a case for the Fund to continue to make stabilization loans, and for the Bank to continue lending to countries that do not have market access. However Bank lending is likely to decline in relative importance in coming years, particularly since there are so few countries that are not now members. There is also a case for the Bank to expand its guarantee activities.

The arguments made here do not, strictly speaking, lead directly to a role for the Bank and the Fund. Perhaps some existing or new agency would do the job better. That is a theoretical possibility, but the costs of setting up a new organization or reorganizing functions argue for the continued use of the nineteenth street twins.

The analytic and systemic analysis functions carried out by the agencies could be done by the private sector if it had the same access to information and feedback. It is doubtful that it does, for much of what is most useful in Fund and Bank research is the unique combination of theory and worldwide experience on which it draws. There are real advantages to doing research and analysis in organizations where the data and experience are generated as part of the lending activities of the agencies. The Fund's lead role in analyzing the international monetary system is also unique, and would be hard to duplicate in another type of organization.

For all their advantages in carrying out research, the international agencies still need to adopt a far more open policy on information. It is encouraging that the World Bank has been moving in this direction.

Technical assistance can be and is provided by the private sector - often by people with experience in the international agencies. It is not certain that the agencies have a natural advantage in this area, except in bringing the fruits of their experience to member countries through EDI and the IMF Institute. In particular, IFI staff does not provide resident technical assistance for long periods, for example a year. It will not be possible to judge whether the IFIs should continue providing technical assistance until they start charging for their services. I would guess that there would still be a demand for their services, at least because of their brand name (or reputation).

Finally, the World Bank's aid coordination function is important, also an offshoot of its lending activities. We should identify IDA as part of the aid coordination function. To the extent that industrialized countries provide aid to foster economic growth, it is probably better done through the World Bank than bilaterally, because of the economies of information that reside in the Bank's deep involvement in many countries.

Should these agencies exist at all? The answer is yes. Without the Fund, the poorer countries would have a much more difficult and costly adjustment process to shocks. The private capital markets have not yet done a good job of lending to countries. Even when they do lend, they typically want the comfort of an official presence. This the Fund provides. It is also singularly well-placed to take the lead in analyzing and suggesting solutions to the problems of the international financial system.

The Bank plays a valuable role in lending to member countries that are not commercially credit-worthy, in coordinating aid, in technical assistance, and in its research and policy analysis. Absent the Bank, we would invent another institution like it.

But doesn't the existence of these agencies prolong adjustment, and create aid dependence. That is true, but that is why conditionality and clear analysis are needed. I believe that the debt crisis would have been over sooner if the official agencies had not been involved. But I also believe that the adjustment crisis - which was very deep - would have been much worse without these agencies.

I conclude that the activities of the Bank and Fund would be needed even if they did not exist, and that there is a case for continued public sector involvement in providing these activities. Combined with the transaction costs of setting up new agencies, that leads to the view that there is a continuing role for both agencies, with the possibility that Bank lending will decline over time, and that its guarantee function should expand.

Assuming that both agencies will continue in existence, what reforms should be made in each? There is a strong case for the Fund to stick to two main subjects: the international monetary system; and for member countries, short-term macroeconomic policy. The Fund is relatively small, feels that it is elite, and should become elite. This means it should stop trying to compete with the World Bank in fighting poverty, improving the environment, and similar good causes not inherently related to the Fund's purposes.

The reason to focus is that both topics are inherently important, and need to be done well. The more the Fund dissipates its efforts, the less it will have influence in the key areas. No doubt the Fund wishes the G-7 would give it more of a role in their own interactions, but that role will have to be earned by the creation and publication of evidence that the Fund has something to offer them. In Africa, the Fund seems to be retreating from its longer-term activities, and that is as well. It should make sure that it concentrates on short-run macroeconomic policy in Eastern Europe and the FSU as well. That is a crucial job, which needs all the Fund's attention. It can contribute through its lending, its surveillance, and its technical assistance.

The Bank engages in more self-examination than the Fund, and reorganizes itself more frequently. Nonetheless, it has a clear idea of what its basic activities should be, and until recently appears to have carried them out well. In some areas, such as Africa, it is less sure of what to do, but so is everyone else.

The Bank should not give up adjustment lending, and should of course continue to try to improve the quality of its projects. It may do that by providing longer-term technical assistance to the technically less well-equipped borrowers. The Bank should pay more attention to the environment, to poverty, and to the role of women in development than it did a few years ago and it is. In general, the Bank should be looking ahead to new issues - to the next popular wave, whatever it may be, rather than reacting defensively when criticized for neglecting a newly popular issue.

Looking ahead would mean greater involvement for the Bank with domestic interest groups in member countries. As such orgnizations become more important, not only in the United States but also elsewhere, the Bank will have to continue to expand its non-governmental interactions, talking directly to the public in member countries rather than only through the governments.[28]

There is no compelling case for downsizing the Bank. It takes on an immense range of tasks that would have to be done anyway. There is an argument for some decentralization, for building up resident missions, for better coordination with the regional banks, and for providing more longer-term technical assistance to poorer members. There is a good case for encouraging Bank (and Fund) staffers to spend a year or two in a developing country as part of their career development within the agencies. Certainly it would give them a better idea of the difficulties confronting developing countries than they are likely to get from Washington.

It is often argued that the Bank and Fund should more truly represent the interests of all their members. The idea sounds appealing. In its research and analysis, the staff has an obligation to be fair to the truth and therefore to all members; that is part of the leadership role of the institutions. But to ask the Boards to more truly represent the interests of all raises complicated questions: industrialized country Board members are quite likely to assert that their view are in the long-run real interests of all members, and that much of the criticism is pure rhetoric. If the appeal is directed to anyone, it must be to management, and if management is to be effective, it cannot afford to engage in unproductive rhetoric. To a considerable extent, the Boards of both institutions in practice recognize that.

Finally, should the agencies be merged? That is a superficially attractive suggestion, which should be rejected. Already the Bank stretches the capacity of management's control. The merged institution would be larger and more difficult to control. It would also be extremely costly to make the change.

However, the most important reason to reject a merger is that it would make the successor institution too powerful. Both the Bank and the Fund are now extraordinarily powerful in the smaller member countries. What they say goes. Staff in both institutions is quite self-confident that it has the right answers, even when they disagree with outsiders. The main check on each agency is the presence of the other, across the street, working on a similar issue. That check should remain in place. And it should be strengthened, by subjecting the analyses and arguments of the agencies, even with regard to proposed policies in individual countries, to far wider public scrutiny.

Table 1. Purposes of the IMF, Article I of the Articles of Agreement

(i) To promote international monetary cooperation through a permanent institution which provides the machinery for consultation and collaboration on international monetary problems.

(ii) To facilitate the expansion and balanced growth of international trade ...

(iii) To promote exchange stability, to maintain orderly exchange arrangements among members, and to avoid competitive exchange depreciation.

(iv) To assist in the establishment of a multilateral system of payments in respect of current transactions between members and in the elimination of foreign exchange restrictions which hamper the growth of world trade.

(v) To give confidence to members by making the general resources of the Fund temporarily available to them under adequate safeguards, thus providing them with the opportunity to correct maladjustments in their balance of payments without resorting to measures destructive of national or international prosperity.

(vi) In accordance with the above, to shorten the duration and lessen the degree of disequilibrium in the international balances of payments of members.

Table 2. Fund Balance Sheet, April 30 1992. ($billion)*

Assets		Liabilities	
Currencies and securities	129.8	Quotas	127.7
SDR holdings	1.0	Borrowing	5.2
Gold⁺	5.1	Special disbursement a/c	3.6
SAF loans	2.6	Other	5.3
Other	3.3		
Total	141.8	Total	141.8

Source: International Monetary Fund Annual Report, 1992, p145.
* Original data in SDR's; calculated at an exchange rate of $1.40/SDR.
⁺ Gold valued at 35 SDR/oz ($49/oz)
SAF ≡ Structural Adjustment Facility; Special Disbursement Account contains funds available for SAF lending.
The Fund also has potential access to SDR18.5 billion ($26 billion) of borrowing under the GAB (General Arrangements to Borrow), which have been in existence since 1962. The GAB are currently set to expire in December 1993, but are expected to be renewed.

Table 3. Fund Administrative Budget, year ending April 30 1992. ($million)

Expenses	
Personnel expenses	236.0
Travel expenses	54.4
Data processing	18.3
Communications	7.5
Other	38.9
Total	355.1
Income	
Net operating income	451.0

Source: International Monetary Fund Annual Report, 1992, pp. 143, 146.
* Net operating income data specified in SDR's; calculated at an exchange rate of $1.40/SDR.

Table 4. Fund Lending, year ending April 30 1992. ($billion)

Total disbursements			8.3
Purchases from General Resources Account		7.4	
Standby and first credit tranche	3.3		
Compensatory financing facility	1.9		
Extended Fund Facility	2.2		
Loans		0.9	
Special disbursement account	0.2		
ESAF Trust resources	0.7		
Repurchases and repayments			6.7
Repurchases		6.7	
Loan repayments		0.0	
Outstanding Fund credit			37.4
Standby arrangements		13.3	
Extended Fund Facility arrangements		12.1	
CCFF		7.5	
SAF		2.1	
ESAF		2.3	
Trust fund		0.2	
Number of indebted countries	82		

Source: International Monetary Fund Annual Report, 1992, pp. 74,102.
* Data in source specified in SDR's; calculated at an exchange rate of $1.40/SDR.

Table 5. Fund Lending Facilities, Policies, and Terminology

General Resources Account: Fund account that holds member country currencies, the Fund's SDR holdings, and gold.

Purchases: Borrowing.

Tranche policies: Access to the Fund's regular credit comes in four tranches of 25 percent of the country's quota in the Fund. First credit tranche purchases are provided if the country demonstrates a reasonable effort to solve its balance of payments problem, and without performance criteria. Upper credit tranche purchases are usually associated with a standby, a negotiated loan from the Fund to the member, based on the country's economic program, with specified performance criteria. Purchases are made in installments. Repayments are made over 3.5 - 5 years.

Extended arrangements: These provide financing for medium term economic programs, generally for 3 years. The program spells out objectives for the entire period, and policy actions for the first year, with subsequent policy changes to be agreed on in annual reviews. Repayments are made over 4.5 - 10 years.

Compensatory and contingency financing facility (CCFF): Lends to members to cover temporary balance of payments needs arising from factors beyond the control of the member.

Structural adjustment facility (SAF): Concessional loans (at an interest rate of 0.5 percent) to support medium-term adjustment programs in low-income countries facing sustained balance of payments problems. Repayments are made over 5.5 - 10 years.

Enhanced structural adjustment facility (ESAF): This facility was created in 1987, and has similar conditions to those of the SAF.

Source: International Monetary Fund Annual Report, 1992, pp. 50-51, Appendix IX.

Table 6. Details of Fund Lending, year ending April 30 1992.

Shares of total disbursements (%)	
To industrialized countries	0.0
By region:	
Africa	12.5
Asia	25.0
Europe	25.7
Middle East	5.6
Western Hemisphere	31.1

Number of arrangements	Made in 1991/92	Total outstanding
Standby arrangements	21	22
Extended arrangements	2	7
CCFF	7	na
SAF	1	8
ESAF	5	16

Source: International Monetary Fund Annual Report, 1992, pp.72-74.

Table 7. Purposes of the IBRD, Article I of the Articles of Agreement (as amended, December 1965)

(i) To assist in the reconstruction and development of territories of members by facilitating the investment of capital for productive purposes, including ... the encouragement of the development of productive facilities and resources in less developed countries.

(ii) To promote private foreign investment by means of guarantees or participations in loans and other investments made by private investors; and when private capital is not available on reasonable terms, to supplement private investment by providing, on suitable conditions, finance for productive purposes out of its own capital, funds raised by it and its other resources.

(iii) To promote the long-range balanced growth of international trade and the maintenance of equilibrium in balances of payments by encouraging international investment for the development of the productive resources of members ...

(iv) ...

(v) ...

Source: Mason and Ahser (1973), pp.759-760.

Table 8. IBRD Balance Sheet, June 30 1992. ($billion)

Assets		Liabilities	
Investments and cash collateral	29.5	Short-term borrowing	5.4
		Long-term borrowing	91.7
Loans outstanding*	100.8	Loan-loss provisions	2.5
		Other liabilities	17.1
Other	10.1	Equity	
		Subscribed capital	10.1
		Retained earnings	13.2
		Other	0.4
Total	140.4	Total	140.4

Source: World Bank Annual Report, 1992, pp198-199.
* Total loans approved ($154.9 b) minus loans approved but not yet effective ($11.2 b) minus undisbursed balance of effective loans ($42.9 b).

Table 9. IDA Resources, June 30 1992. ($billion)

Development Resources			Funding	
Available net assets		29.5	Member subscriptions & contributions	73.1
Credits outstanding	75.6			
less undisbursed balances	23.3		Other contributions*	3.4
Net outstanding credits		52.3	Other	53
Total		81.8	Total	81.8

Source: World Bank Annual Report, 1992, p. 220.
* From Switzerland and IBRD.

Table 10. World Bank Administrative Budget, year ending June 30 1992. ($million)

Expenses		
Personnel		791.2
Travel		113.5
Other		269.8
Reimbursements		(100.5)
	Total	1074.0
Income		
Net operating income		1645.0

Source: World Bank Annual Report, 1992, pp.104, 200.

Table 11. Bank Lending, year ending June 30 1992. ($billion)

Total loans		21.7
IBRD	15.2	
IDA	6.5	
Project loans	18.3	
Adjustment loans	3.4	
Gross disbursements		16.4
Net disbursements		6.3
Net transfers		-1.9

Loans by region		Number of loans
Africa		
IBRD	0.7	10
IDA	3.2	67
East Asia		
IBRD	4.4	33
IDA	1.1	13
South Asia		
IBRD	1.3	6
IDA	1.6	17
Europe and Central Asia		
IBRD	2.1	13
IDA	0.0	1
Latin America & Caribbean		
IBRD	5.3	37
IDA	0.4	8
Middle East & North Africa		
IBRD	1.3	13
IDA	0.2	4
Total	21.7	222

Source: World Bank Annual Report, 1992.

NOTES

*. The author is grateful to the discussants, Max Schieler and Jürgen von Hagen, and to other conference participants, particularly Jacques Polak and Alfred Steinherr, for their thought-provoking comments. I have also benefitted greatly from suggestions by Johannes Linn of the World Bank.

1. ICSID, the International Center for the Settlement of Investment Disputes, was set up in 1966, but has not been very active.
2. Several of these issues and related proposals are discussed in The Economist's 1991 survey of the IMF and the World Bank; see also Dell (1990), de Vries (1987), Feinberg, *et. al.* (1986), Finch (1989), Neu (1993) and Polak (1993).
3. As of April 30 1992, 71 countries, including 43 developing countries, had accepted the Fund's Article VIII obligations for current account convertibility. Nine, including Indonesia, Korea, Portugal, Thailand and Turkey, had joined the list since 1987. Several countries on the list clearly violated Article VIII at times after joining; for example Nicaragua accepted the obligation in 1964.
4. The declining cost of communications and travel have increased the centralization of power, tending to reduce the power of representatives such as ambassadors and executive directors.
5. An SDR issue is often suggested to meet a special need for aid funds, for example for the heavily indebted African countries, or for the reforming formerly socialist economies.
6. This is not to say that others do.
7. To quote from a letter from Jacques Polak, "The balance sheet of the Fund is a curious tabulation ... It mixes its outstanding credits with its ability to give new credits - both being called currencies, which is technically correct but economically meaningless."
8. See also the discussion above of a potential SDR issue.
9. In 1975, the Fund sold one-sixth (25 million ounces) of its gold holdings to finance a Trust Fund for the benefit of developing country members (the resources from that fund are recorded in Table 2 in the special disbursement account); another one-sixth was returned to member countries at the price they had received when subscribing the gold.
10. By August 1993 the Fund staff had grown to more than 2100, to deal with the expansion of membership from the reforming centrally planned economies.
11. Further, the Fund's data requirements may constitute the main incentive for these countries to collect data.
12. The first quoted phrase is from Jacques Polak, the second from Morris Goldstein.
13. Data from the Development Assistance Committee's 1992 Report, Development Co-Operation, (OECD, Paris, 1992) Chapter IV.
14. This description is due to a Bank staffer.
15. Khan's results show an improvement in the balance of payments, but this becomes statistically significant only when the period of evaluation is extended beyond the program year.
16. The information provided here is from the Fund's 1992 Annual Report, pp.114-117.
17. The Fiscal Affairs Department has prepared a useful review of its technical assistance work, which summarizes the types of assistance the Fund provides, and attempts to assess its impact by discussing the extent to which the advice is embodied in legislation. See "Technical Assistance on Tax Policy: A Review", IMF Working Paper, WP/93/65, August 1993.

18. However there is likely to be a bulge in Fund lending as the reforming formerly centrally planned economies begin to stabilize.
19. Note that IDA is careful not to describe its balance sheet as such.
20. Another interpretation would be that the industrialized countries fear the costs of a generalized default to the IFIs, and therefore provide incentives for the defaulters to return to the fold.
21. Polak (1993) provides a more detailed account of the dispute, largely as seen from the viewpoint of the Fund, but which does not differ in its essentials.
22. These studies were published in 1988, 1990, and 1992 respectively.
23. The Bank reconciles these results by arguing that adjustment policies must have made investment more efficient.
24. Project reports become public after the Board has approved the project.
25. Stabilization loans have been made within the European system (e.g. to Italy).
26. To support this view, one has also to argue that an adjustable peg rather than floating exchange rate system is preferable for some countries. I would make the argument by referring to the need for a nominal anchor to provide self-discipline for the monetary and fiscal authorities.
27. The argument thus ends up turning on the inability of private lenders to impose penalties on defaulting governments, or equivalently on the absence of a bankruptcy mechanism for governments. These issues were discussed in the international debt crisis.
28. I owe this point to Johannes Linn.

REFERENCES

Dell, Sidney (1990). "Reforming the World Bank for the Tasks of the 1990s", Exim Bank Annual Lecture, Bombay.

de Vries, Barend A. (1987). Remaking the World Bank. Washington, DC: Seven Locks Press.

de Vries, Margaret G. (1986). The IMF in a Changing World. Washington, DC: International Monetary Fund.

Economist, The (1991). "Sisters in the Wood", survey, October 12.

Feinberg, Richard E. (1986). Between Two Worlds: The World Bank's Next Decade. Washington, DC: Overseas Development Council.

Finch, C. David (1989). "The IMF: The Record and the Prospect", Essays in International Finance, no. 175, International Finance Section, Princeton University,

Khan, Mohsin S. (1990). "The Macroeconomic Effects of Fund-Supported Adjustment Programs", IMF Staff Papers, 37, 2 (June), 195-231.

Mason, Edward S. and Robert E. Asher (1973). The World Bank Since Bretton Woods. Washington, DC: Brookings Institution.

Neu, C.R. (1993). A New Bretton Woods. Santa Monica, CA: Rand .

Polak, Jacques J. (1993). "The World Bank and the IMF: The Future of their Coexistence", mimeo, IMF.

World Bank (1988). Adjustment Lending: An Evaluation of Ten Years of Experience. Policy and Research Series Paper 1.

--- (1990). Adjustment Lending Policies for Sustainable Growth. Policy and Research Series Paper 14.

--- (1992). Adjustment Lending and Mobilization of Private and Public Resources for Growth, Policy and Research Series Paper 22.

Discussion

MAX SCHIELER

1 Introduction

After almost fifty years of existence, it is a fine time to review the role of the IMF and the World Bank in today's world economy and to question their continuing raison d'être. At first glance, this might not appear to be the right moment to ask for a fundamental reform of the Bretton Woods institutions, considering their newly acquired starring role in Central and Eastern Europe. But this should not prevent us from recognizing that the reappraisal of the aims and methods of the two agencies has been a very topical issue for some time.

2 Stanley Fischer's paper - a call for adherence to the status quo

Reading the paper by Stanley Fischer - a very profound analysis indeed of the role and performance of the Bretton Woods institutions - I got the impression that he wants to "lock in" their traditional functions as well as their inherited general design. In the process, he does not neglect to point out certain deficiencies that could be improved, but firmly rejects the suggestion for the two agencies to be merged. This, for two major reasons: first, a merged institution would be larger and more difficult to control, and secondly - and more important - it would make the successor institution too powerful.

On the first point, we could refer to the existing overlaps of activities that would allow a certain downsizing of the IMF as well as the World Bank in the event of a merger. But we should also take into account the possibility of a hiving off of the Fund's functions onto other (already existing) agencies or even partially to the (capital) markets, as I will discuss in more detail later. Hence, a successor agency would not necessarily attain the dimensions of a joint IMF/World Bank body. While the management task might nevertheless become more formidable, we may also point out that (far) larger bodies already exist and they do work - at least in the private sector. Indeed there has not been a lack of mergers & acquisitions of a similar or even much larger dimension in recent years. I just want to recall the acquisition of Swiss Volksbank by CS Holding (which combined total assets of 33bn and 123bn, and staffs of 6,400 and 18,500, respectively), or the merger of Asea & Brown Boveri into ABB (which today boasts a turnover of some $ 30bn and a total staff of about 213,000) as two of the most striking examples in Switzerland.

With regard to the second argument, I would agree with Stanley Fischer that we should not underestimate the existing checks and balances the two institutions exercise on each other. However, this would certainly be different if both institutions strictly adhered to the division of labour they have already agreed upon, which would mean they would stop doing each other's job as well as their own. Such a development would imply a much smaller "checks & balances" effect. It might also be true that a merged successor institution would become more powerful. This, however, could only be within the limits set by its owners. In addition, increased authority could also be beneficial with regard to functions, where the necessary clout is lacking today, e.g. policy coordination (and to some extent implementation of economic reforms).

3 Why is there a need for reform today?

It is hard for me, however, to imagine us gathering together for another conference 25 years from now to celebrate the 75th anniversary of the Bretton Woods "sisters" in their current form. True, during their almost fifty years of existence, the IMF and the World Bank proved to be remarkable survivors. The world economy has changed fundamentally in the past five decades; unsurprisingly, the two institutions have been evolving and reforming too, while their basic responsibilities have remained much the same, raising the question whether they are still up to today's challenges. That they never ceased to exist may partly be due to the fact that they have been extremely adaptable, and may also be explained by simply quoting the already proverbial statement that "international institutions may change their names or lose their functions but they never die".

In spite of their uncontested merits, there has been no lack of criticism down through the years, either. Since the World Bank has remained closer to its original and principal function - development lending - its existence has never really been put into question. Thus, most of the criticism went to the IMF, so the following explanations will focus on the Fund too.

4 The IMF's lending activities - a job for the international capital markets?

When the Bretton Woods System of fixed exchange rates broke down in 1973, much of the original raison d'être of the IMF disappeared. Though the IMF was also monitoring economic policies, promoting the Special Drawing

Rights (SDRs) as a new reserve currency, and - in the second half of the 1970s - trying to facilitate the "recycling" of the so-called petrodollars, it spent much of the rest of the decade seeking a new role in a world of floating exchange rates. That role did not become fully clear until the outbreak of the international debt crisis in 1982, when the Fund moved into the forefront of the crisis and became a sort of traffic cop for efforts to cope with international debt.

But in the absence of industrial country borrowers the Fund has increasingly also become some sort of a "lender of last resort" for developing countries. This is role for which it is ill-suited, given its monetary character which implies lending of an essentially temporary nature. The problems of most Third World countries are more long-term and structural in nature than those caused by temporary macroeconomic instability. What the former require is long-term finance such as that supplied by the World Bank and its affiliate, the International Development Association (IDA) - a fact, that puts a big question mark on the Fund's controversial role as a specialized development agency.

As the Fund's lending activities vis-à-vis the Third World countries intensified, overlaps with the World Bank became increasingly unavoidable. The two institutions became more controversial than ever and tensions reached a climax in the famous case of Argentina in September 1988. A subsequent accord in March 1989 on cooperation between the IMF and the World Bank was hardly a breakthrough and more or less reaffirmed the traditional division of labour: the pact gave the IMF primary responsibility over short-term stabilization and exchange rates, while the World Bank was to take the lead in medium- and longer-term structural reform. The agreement also contained a procedure for dealing with conflicts, was confirmed at the G-10 meeting 1989 in Berne, and was put on record in their so-called "Dini report". (Group of Deputies (1989)) However, the pact provided little assurance of a definitive settlement of the disagreements of the past and still left areas of possible conflict - for instance, the inherent tension between tight fiscal management and trade reform. If there has been no major conflict since then, that is probably a result of their new commitments in Eastern Europe which have kept them both very busy to date.

For the Fund, unlike the World Bank, retention of a leading role in managing the "debt crisis" was almost a matter of life and death. And today it appears as if history has again come to its aid, this time through the events in Eastern Europe. This is thus the right time to question the Fund's new financial commitments in Eastern Europe, which could well oblige it to become more of a development lender than it has ever been before - even in sub-Saharan Africa.

With regard to its lending activities, we might ask whether the Fund ought not to cede this function to the international capital markets, as the markets could probably satisfy those needs more efficiently. True, with regard to development country lending, the international capital markets and the commercial banks in particular may not have done a good job in the past decade. But neither have the IMF and the World Bank, as is shown by the poor record of multilateral finance in Africa - or in the recently released Wapenhans Report which highlighted the generally poor impact of the bank's lending strategies. It is presumably too one-sided to blame the banks for their lending mistakes and their herd instincts during the debt crisis. Nobody was able to anticipate such a development, which was partly the result of the defective macroeconomic policies during the 1970s on which the Fund failed to exert its influence, which then provoked a sharp turnabout at the beginning of the 1980s.

Furthermore, the experience of the past few years also reflects a new phenomenon in global finance: the move away from traditional banking intermediation towards tradeable securities. Globalisation and liberalisation have led to a rapid growth of the world's capital markets which now provide other types of voluntary financing to LDCs, namely portfolio investment and again foreign direct investment. For many years, the international capital markets have expanded their capability to provide finance for the highly industrialised countries, which obviated the need for the latter to turn to the IMF for financial assistance. A similar development can now be observed with regard to the so-called "Emerging Markets", which tend to attract more and more private capital flows once they have committed themselves to convincing economic reforms. Examples are the NIC's and the ASEAN countries in South East Asia, or countries such as Argentina, Chile, Mexico and even Brazil, as well as the more reform-minded economies in Eastern Europe, with the Czech Republic and Hungary in the forefront.

Of course capital markets may fail to provide sufficient funds to developing countries. According to Roland Vaubel, this can only be explained by two reasons: imperfect capital markets and humanitarian motives. (Vaubel (1990)) As to the first point, with imperfect information, the capital markets also operate imperfectly. If the IMF gets better information about the true creditworthiness of its member governments than do potential private creditors, this does not mean that the IMF has to provide financing, but it does suggest that the Fund ought to publish its information - a demand that is espoused very strongly in Fischer's paper too.

As to the second reason - humanitarian motives - IMF conditionality is not a good indicator of destitution. In order to get an IMF loan, a country must be able to cite balance of payments needs, which, however, are not necessarily an indication of financial distress. A balance-of-payments constraint can even be produced intentionally. Many empirical studies show that overly expansive demand policies were indeed the main cause for the balance of payments difficulties of many IMF members. Some authors even believe that the prospect of a favourable IMF loan has in fact contributed to the emergence of such "crises"; the Fund itself has provoked the "moral hazard".

5 IMF conditionality - still an appropriate form of economic "discipline" in today's world?

Still on the subject of IMF conditionality, Roland Vaubel (op. cit.) points to another fundamental problem, namely that an IMF adjustment program is only imposed after the economic troubles have already emerged. IMF conditionality is supposed to prevent borrowers from tying up IMF funds any longer than they are needed. This, however, could be achieved far more efficiently if conditionality were also related to the reasons for a crisis. Those countries which have provoked their difficulties in a grossly negligent manner or even on purpose should be excluded right from the beginning (*ex ante*) from IMF loans. Such an *ex ante* conditionality could for example limit the admissible budget deficit as a percentage of GDP. This *ex ante* conditionality would probably significantly reduce the circle of members entitled to an IMF loan and/or encourage members to adopt what we call "good governance".

In the case of pure *ex post* conditionality, moral hazard could be reduced if the IMF announced strict rules for its conditionality and also made strict use of them. What is practised by the Fund, however, is a sort of *ad hoc* conditionality, the so-called "case-by-case approach", which impedes transparency (in which neither the governments of the borrower countries nor the IMF seem to be very interested).

6 Surveillance - a job better left to a merged OECD/IMF policy analysis institution ?

What is most disquieting, however, is that international macro-policy, which should have been the IMF's special preserve, has moved forward without the IMF having a say. With the end of the fixed exchange rate regime, the IMF has lost its exchange-rate empire, which has greatly reduced the Fund's authority over its more powerful members. So fiscal and monetary indiscipline involving key economies gave rise to high inflation in the 1970s and huge trade imbalances in the 1980s. The US mix of tight monetary and slack budgetary policy at the beginning of the last decade sent interest rates soaring and commodity prices tumbling, with devastating effects on the rest of the world. The IMF again was rendered impotent as the dollar soared by over 50% in the first half of the 1980s and then fell by a similar large amount after 1985.

The Fund's recurring failure to exercise its authority over its leading members, and to preserve an orderly monetary system, is a clear indication of the Fund's considerably weakened surveillance role. Indeed, the policy co-ordination process, as pointed out by Stanley Fischer, has become the exclusive domain of the Group of Seven and has effectively gone beyond the influence of the IMF. Referring to the fact that the Fund is already firmly embedded in the policy-coordination process by virtue of its providing "the most professional policy advice" cannot satisfy the critics. In this case, we must argue that the bulk of the IMF's members have no direct input in the process, even though the level of interest rates and the stability of key currencies, for instance, are of vital concern to all of them. The differential treatment of industrial and developing countries has also undermined the Fund's credibility as a global institution whose rules apply equally to all members.

As in the case of the European Community, the national governments of the G7 would therefore have to cede some authority to the Fund. However, this would mean the G7 countries giving up more sovereignty than they have shown a willingness to part with so far, indicating that the "marginalisation" of the IMF is likely to continue in that area. So why not pass the surveillance function to a merged OECD/IMF body? The latter would more easily become the world's unchallenged macroeconomic policy analysis institution which Stanley Fischer is looking for and would probably play a more significant role in the policy coordination process than can be done by the two separate agencies today. The same purpose could of course also be attained in another way. We could just as well envisage a disbandment of the OECD and a transfer of the vacant functions to the IMF, which would thus enlarge its scope of activities. The efficacy of both reform proposals, however, would also imply that the G7 would have to cede some authority to such an agency - of which there is no sign as yet.

7 Merger with the World Bank - a reasonable proposal for the Fund's development activities?

As for the IMF's developing country responsibilities, a merger with the World Bank would seem the most obvious solution: a proposal that has already been under discussion within the banking community, including Aloys Schwietert, SBC's chief economist. (Schwietert (1989)) Nobody can seriously deny that there is a real need to reduce the large overlaps between the two agencies. While some degree of duplication may be a good thing as it provides for a certain competition among the two organisations, there is clearly too much of it now. This issue has grown more topical again because of new and overlapping commitments in Eastern Europe. Given that close collaboration between the two institutions will be indispensable in the future, why not merge them?

Such a move could simplify negotiations on adjustment policies - easing the existing frictions with regard to conditionality - and could probably also improve their implementation. A uniform appearance in the form of a single organisation would not only eliminate the inherent problem of duplication of effort, thus making expensive coordination unnecessary in one fell swoop, but would also avoid having the two institutions played off against each other as they have been from time to time in the past (the aforementioned "Argentina case" is the most striking example).

And last but not least, such a move would probably put the Bank in a stronger position of full and effective leadership in the area of international development finance and cooperation. As the lead international development institution, the World Bank needs to improve the effectiveness of its own operations as well as its interactions with other development agencies. Although one might again point to the benefits of healthy competition, it remains rather questionable whether the existing rivalry is much of a help in that respect. Tightening up the organisation of a potentially merged IMF/World Bank body and shrinking it by devolving any overlapping work to the regional development banks would prevent a merged organisation from becoming overloaded, unmanageable or autocratic.

8 Should the IMF take over the BIS's monetary role ?

Percy Mistry, an international finance specialist at Oxford University, has even envisaged the IMF functioning as a "super agency": monitoring deregulated financial markets and the huge cross-border flows of banking and investment capital. (Euromoney (1990)) Such a "super-Fund" would establish a multilateral framework covering all aspects of international economic relations - banking, currency and capital markets, as well as trade in financial services and the financial elements of trade in goods. He therefore suggested that the Fund be merged with the Basle-based Bank for International Settlements, whose "half-hearted" monitoring of the banking and capital markets falls short of what Mistry thinks is needed. I would agree that a strong and competent international agency could do a useful job in monitoring and supervising the rapidly developing banking, currency and capital markets, especially in view of the systemic and other risk implications of the explosively growing derivatives business. Whether this should be realised in the way proposed by Percy Mistry, or by explicitly charging the IMF with such a duty is thereby not of a primary significance.

The second reform proposal, which would imply a strengthening of the IMF at the expense of the BIS, should thus also be subject to such reflection.

9 Conclusion

A parcelling-out of the IMF's functions to other organisations (or an extension of the Fund's duties) and an IMF/World Bank merger with regard to development activities looks like the most practicable and sensible alternative.

So, whatever you think about those proposals, one thing seems to be quite obvious. As was also remarked in the Economist's 1991 survey of the IMF and World Bank, the Fund in its original form will (probably) never be needed again. (Economist (1991)) Since the world will continue to change rapidly and become more interdependent, and not only in the economic sphere, we should really be thinking about the future role of the different international organisations and groupings in order to redistribute and expand the support functions for improved (optimal) decision-making. As has become more evident from this discussion, particularly in respect of the recent developments in the international capital markets, there is no mistaking the need for some kind of reform.

According to Stanley Fischer, in conclusion, the Fund should stick to the international monetary system and short-term macroeconomic policy for its member countries, while the World Bank should focus on a number of development issues. In contrast my suggestion is to let the market deal with the lending function for industrial and advanced developing countries. The market does it more efficiently. For the less developed countries the World Bank is well equipped to balance adjustment lending with long-term development issues. A merger of the IMF with the World Bank would thus seem the most obvious solution for this field of activities.

As for the IMF's other functions, a splitting up between the OECD (surveillance of macroeconomic policy) and the BIS monitoring of the international capital markets) would appear as the most reasonable proposal. An alternative reform approach would be to charge the IMF with these functions and to disband the OECD and BIS. This would have the advantage that both functions - which depend on each other to some extent - could be exercised by the same institution, i.e. a "renewed" IMF, but would also imply some specific organisational presuppositions in order to ensure the workability of such an agency.

Whatever your point of view, the Bretton Woods institutions (or a potential successor organisation) will always be accountable to their owners. This means they can only act as well and as effectively as the political will of their owners allows. This is a simple fact that we can never afford to leave out of our considerations!

REFERENCES

The Economist: "Sisters in the wood - A survey of the IMF and the World Bank", The Economist, October 12, 1991

Euromoney : " IMF/World Bank - Back it or scrap it", Euromoney, September 1990

Fischer, S.: "The IMF and World Bank at fifty". This volume.

Group of Deputies, 1989. "The role of the IMF and the World Bank in the context of the debt strategy". A report submitted to the Ministers and Governors of the Group of Ten by the Group of Deputies, Washington.

OECD: "The changing nature of IMF conditionality", Technical Papers No. 41, Paris 1991; cit. in. "Revisionsbedürftiges Statut des Währungsfonds", Neue Zürcher Zeitung, No. 300, December 27, 1991

Schieler, M.. "Die Rolle von Weltbank und Währungsfonds bei der Lösung der Schuldenkrise", Schweizer Journal 1/1988

Schwietert, A : "Merge the IMF and the World Bank? ", in Swiss Bank Corporation, Economic and Financial Prospects, 6/1989.

Vaubel, R.: "Fehlentwicklungen beim Internationalen Währungsfonds - Eine Analyse aus der Sicht der Neuen Politischen Oekonomie", Neue Zürcher Zeitung, No. 274, November 24/25, 1990.

Discussion

JÜRGEN VON HAGEN

A variation on Voltaire's famous phrase summarizes Stanley Fischer's paper most succinctly:

"Si the Fond Monétaire International et la Banque Mondiale n'existaient pas, il faudrait les inventer".

The paper seeks to provide an answer to an institutional puzzle posed by the post-Bretton Woods era: Why did the owners of the IMF and the World Bank not close these institutions down when the international monetary system for which they had been originally designed came to an end? After all, both the Fund and the Bank command sizeable resources, for which the owners might well find better uses, including other forms of development aid.

Both institutions found new fields of activity after the collapse of the Bretton Woods system. The IMF engaged in special development tasks, became an important player in international debt markets, and is now specializing in the economics of transforming post-socialist economies to market economies. The Bank added adjustment loans to its products and continued to finance development projects. Even before, the specificity of the Bank to the Bretton Woods system seems to be much smaller than that of the IMF. The usefulness of an international development bank is readily understood independently of the monetary order. In contrast, the IMF's original tasks were very specific to a system of fixed but adjustable exchange rates and to the post-War era; hence the Fund poses the greater puzzle. I will focus my comments it.

Following Niskanen's (1971) analysis of bureaucrats and bureaucracies, one might argue that it is simply impossible to abolish a large Organization once it exists, even if it loses its purpose, because those extracting rents from the organization will protect it politically. This argument would suggest that the Fund's and the Bank's management look around and find new fields of activity after the end of the Bretton Woods system to keep the organizations alive and provide them with a *raison d'être*. The post-1973 history of the Fund and the Bank shows that is exactly what happened. (See e.g. Garritsen deVries, forthcoming.) However, this answer is unsatisfactory, because it does not consider the possibility that the owners of these institutions wanted them to engage in new activities. Looking only at the fact that they continue to exist with new activities, it is impossible to discriminate between these possibilities empirically.

Fischer proposes a different answer: some scope for improvement notwithstanding, both institutions are just too good to be given away lightly. But this is too simple, too. It does not consider the possibility that there may be even better alternatives, including better institutional approaches to development lending and macroeconomic consulting.

To explain and justify properly the activities of the Fund, it is necessary to identify what the demand for its product is and explain why this demand should be served by a large, international institution rather than private suppliers. The first question, then, is, what is the product offered by the Fund?

The paper's answer is that the Fund produces a joint product of three main dimensions: short-term lending, macro-economic consulting, and technical assistance. An additional one, the provision of a forum for international consultations is less important in practice, apparently much to the chagrin of the Fund's leadership. In principle, short-term lending, macro-economic consulting and technical assistance could all be offered by private suppliers. Yet, arguments can be made why the Fund should deliver them as co-products to short-term lending, and why the specific form of the latter provided by the Fund should be supplied by a public institution.

IMF short-term lending comes with conditionalities for macro-economic stabilization or reform. For the government obtaining it, the IMF loan serves as a commitment and a signalling device. The commitment device is mainly directed inward, i.e. to the domestic public. IMF conditionalities may help governments defend unpopular policies at home and, at the same time, provide a cushion against the immediate social cost of reform. Pointing to the need to fulfil IMF conditions may be an important help to stick to a reform program over time, when the first successes raise the temptation to renege on the stabilization program. By enabling governments to commit credibly to reform programs or stabilization, IMF short-term lending increases their choice set by more than the resources provided by the credit itself.

The signalling function, in contrast, is directed outward to potential private lenders in the international credit markets. Private lenders cannot distinguish properly between liquidity and insolvency problems of countries that find themselves unable to serve their foreign debt. With asymmetric information between borrowers and lenders, moral hazard makes it impossible for the former credibly to convey their quality to the latter. This type of information problem leads to well-known inefficiencies. It bars countries from credit support to overcome temporary shortages of foreign exchange revenues and forces them into default even if their net worth is positive. The shift from bond markets to bank loans as the main instrument for international lending since the mid-1970s suggests that such information asymmetries are, indeed, important in practice (Chow, forthcoming). The IMF's stamp of approval on rescheduling programs, combined with a financial commitment making the approval credible, is helpful for such countries to get out of the credit-rationing equilibrium, and improves the efficiency of the international credit market.

There are three possible arguments why such lending should be left to a large international institution rather than private suppliers. One is that the pay-off from stabilization and reform to a large extent is non-pecuniary; this is why Fischer measures 'success' of IMF lending in terms of reduced inflation and current account equilibrium. Still, the borrowers should be able to define a monetary value of this success and pay for it, opening this business to private suppliers.

The second is that the efficient risk pooling across countries leaves room only for a small number of lenders, so that a private market might not be competitive. The third, most convincing reason is that the provision of commitment and signalling devices has the character of a public good that would not be supplied sufficiently through the market system. In the absence of a public institution providing these goods, international financial markets would be less efficient. Small and developing countries in particular would find themselves less able to engage in macro-economic stabilization. The resulting, larger degree of economic instability of these countries would aggravate the credit rationing problem and further reduce the performance of international financial markets.

A related question is, why should the supply of these services be paid for primarily by the owners of the IMF instead of the consumers of the services? If the countries obtaining IMF loans find these services useful, they should be ready to pay their full price for them. In fact, the examples of the African countries noted in the paper hint at the possibility that there is over-consumption of these services, i.e., that the price at which they are supplied is too low. Perhaps the only convincing answer is that the owners of the IMF are consumers of these services themselves, because, as commercial lenders and trade partners, they have an interest in successful stabilization and reform as well as credit market efficiency.

The next question then is, why does the IMF supply macroeconomic consulting and technical assistance in addition to supplying a public good to the financial community? The partial answer in the paper, that the Fund's analysis is often the only and usually the best one available is not convincing. It may simply reflect that Fund services are priced so low that all private competition is driven out of the market.

A better answer starts from the lending activities. Macroeconomic surveillance by the Fund can be attributed to two important functions in connection with the Fund's short-term lending. First, the latter can only serve as a commitment device if the Fund can credibly exert the threat that financial support will be withdrawn if the borrower reneges on the reform program. Effectiveness of this threat requires monitoring the borrower. Second, surveillance is information-gathering. Without sufficient information about its borrowers, the Fund cannot solve the credit rationing problem. While the Fund might restrict itself to pure watching and data-collection, many of the data sources and concepts and many observed events in the borrowing countries will be properly understood only through regular interaction with domestic officials and business communities, which makes consulting a natural by-product. Thus, macro-economic consulting improves the Fund's ability to provide short-term lending and alleviate the credit-rationing problem.

A similar point can be made with regard to the Fund's specific technical assistance. By implanting standardized data collection procedures, standardized accounting procedures, standardized methods of macro-economic analysis etc. in all borrowing countries, the Fund raises the transparency and comparability of national economic data. This facilitates monitoring the borrowers and, hence, contributes to the effectiveness of the short-term lending function. Furthermore, such technical assistance also has a public-good character to some extent. It improves access to information about a country for other interested parties such as private lenders or trade partners who are difficult to charge for their use of it.

Yet, again, the question arises of why the Fund does not rely on private markets supplying surveillance and technical assistance for it. For example, the Fund might hire international consultants or academics to produce country analyses or technical assistance on the basis of Fund guidelines assuring comparability and transparency. There is no compelling reason not to do so, as indeed the example of the Bank, where outside contracting is very common, suggests. Even if one grants the point that the Fund needs its own expertise to judge the quality of external contractors, why would this require an organization as large as the Fund ?

Instead of an answer, one may come back with a question: What is the problem with the Fund engaging in consulting and technical assistance? Fischer asserts that there is none. The Fund staff wants to be an elite consulting agency, so let them be that. However, he recommends, they should establish their reputation by making their analyses public and by disseminating their information.

I find this answer unsatisfactory for several reasons. First, current IMF practices make it unlikely that resources be allocated efficiently. For example, Fund statutes imply that Article-IV-consultations be held with countries where no current problems exist or where Fund recommendations find little echo. This locks in resources which could be used with higher marginal product for cases with pressing problems. The vast expansion of staff after the breakdown of the Soviet Union suggests that this practice leads to over-staffing in the country departments.

Second, the combination of under-pricing of services and the unique quality of the Fund as a lender likely crowds out private, high-quality suppliers of macro-economic consulting services. The paper points out that the Fund's customer relations in consulting show all signs of a monopolistic position, namely considerable power and disregard for opposing views. Yet, it is quite conceivable that even an elite supplier of consulting services lacks good solutions. The problem is that this monopoly works against the production of creative solutions to new problems. The debt crisis and the problems of transition economics show how important innovative thinking can be in international macro economics. Competition is the main provider of innovative solutions. It requires market access for new, creative suppliers.

The paper suggests that competition between the Fund and the Bank might do the job. In practice, however, there is a high degree of collusion between these two institutions. For example, qualification for the Bank's main lending programs requires Fund membership.

Third, there is an inherent contradiction between being a top consultant and bringing one's case-specific analysis to the public. All consulting relations have elements of strict confidentiality, after all, this is why doctors, psychiatrists and lawyers are bound by professional discretion. Politicians do not like to be criticized, much less so in public. It is not hard to guess what would happen if the Fund came out regularly with controversial statements about its own members. The Board would sack the critics and replace them with more diligent and less competent staff. Breaking confidentiality is a losing strategy.

Apart from that, good consultants need information that the customer has a rightful interest to keep unpublished. Reputation of being a good consultant comes from presenting successful clients, not the analysis that leads to success. This need for confidentiality obviously compounds the monopoly of information problem. The Fund could certainly publish more basic data, but not all information relevant to policy decisions. Rather than publishing information, market access should be made possible for private consultants who would use the same information with similar confidentiality.

Fourth, the Fund finds itself in an awkward position marketing its services. To justify its existence, it must identify 'big' problems. This implies that there is a risk for the Fund to take on tasks it is not properly qualified for. Can we rely on the future providing us always with the right emergencies? Furthermore, since it does not adequately price its services, those who pay for the Fund will ask that the solutions offered by the Fund match their own preferences. There is, therefore, a danger to produce remedies that serve those who pay rather than those who suffer the problem. Again, proper pricing of services and market access for potential competitors could help, because it would give the consumer of the consulting services more voice and lead to more efficient guidance of Fund activities.

To conclude, the Fund today serves important functions. It produces valuable public goods for the international economy and the financial community. As such it has a future and should remain. But there is room for improvement to solve the efficiency and competitiveness problems arising from the joint production of public and private goods. Reforms of the IMF should push in two directions. One is more efficient pricing of Fund services. If the Fund's owners fear that the developing countries would consume too little of its services when market prices are charged for them, they may wish to subsidize these countries' purchases of such services, but leave them a choice between the Fund and other providers. The other is to contract out more of its consulting services to create market access for potential competitors. Both approaches would help to make Fund services more independent from Board politics and, in doing so, would help the Fund to be the elite consulting agency it aspires to be.

REFERENCES

Garritsen de Vries, Margaret (forthcoming), "The International Monetary Fund and the International Monetary System". in: Dominick Salvatore, Michele Fratianni and Jürgen von Hagen (eds.), Handbook of Macroeconomic Policy, Westport, London: Greenwood.

Niskanen, William A. Jr. (1971), Bureau Government. Chicago: Aldine-Atherton.

Chow, Edward (forthcoming), "Debt Rescheduling and the Choice Between Bonds and Loans for LDCs' Foreign Debt". Open economies review.